This is a must read for every pastor. *Pastoring Men* addresses the number one crisis in the church today, and that is a lack of men and the lack of opportunities for them to be in ministry for Jesus Christ. I endorse this book enthusiastically and believe in its transformational possibilities for men.

REV. DAVID ADAMS
General Secretary, General Commission on United Methodist Men

The church of the Lord Jesus is in desperate need for men of God; men who know God, love God and serve God with lives surrendered to his lordship. *Pastoring Men* helps us understand why we must and how we can effectively disciple men in our churches who will become radically devoted followers of our great Savior and King. Biblical and practical, this is a much needed resource for those who long to effectively pastor and raise up an army of godly men.

DANIEL L. AKIN
President, Southeastern Baptist Theological Seminary

I sensed the kindness of God while reading *Pastoring Men,* and it refreshed my soul. Pat Morley hits a home run with this, especially for leaders who want to have an effective ministry and desire to do something more than what has been going on concerning men.

GUS BESS
Senior Pastor, First Evangelical Free Church, Tucson

Pastoring Men is a realistic, encouraging, and insightful examination of how to develop—and sustain—a first-rate, field-tested method to disciple men. Put this book at the top of your reading list.

JAMES S. BOWMAN
Professor, Florida State University (and chair of Patrick's dissertation committee)
Editor, Public Integrity

I know of no one in America who knows more about men—what they think, want, feel, and believe—than Pat Morley. Not only that, I know of no one who cares more for men and has more passion for discipling them than Pat Morley. If you care about the "men problem" in our culture and the church, this is your book. It is profoundly biblical and incredibly practical. It could change the face of the church and, through the church, the nation.

STEVE BROWN
Professor, Reformed Theological Seminary, Orlando
Teacher on the nationally syndicated radio program Key Life

Pastoring Men directly confronts a critical need in our churches today: developing godly men! The need is great, but so is the opportunity. Our churches must disciple all the men and equip them to succeed at home and in the culture. Pat Morley asks and answers the significant questions that enable pastors to effectively minister to all of their men.

KIRBYJON H. CALDWELL
Windsor Village Methodist Church, Houston

"This is a battle worth fighting." What true words! It is a battle that takes diligent, persistent, effort along with even more diligence in prayer and trust in the Lord. It is also a battle worth fighting, especially by pastors. We need more men who are faithful followers of Christ in their homes, churches, jobs, and communities and who can lead and disciple other men, as well as women and children. The Lord has given Pat many insights into the effective discipleship of men. Come join the battle to disciple ongoing generations of godly men.

ROBERT C. (RIC) CANNADA JR.
Chancellor and CEO, Reformed Theological Seminary

Patrick Morley's long-standing concern to see the light of Christ in the life of men has always been inspiring. Now this exceedingly practical book helping pastors implement discipleship programs specifically directed toward men will do much to shape the future of home, church, and the next generation. Morley writes in terms that reach men—and change them.

BRYAN CHAPELL
President, Covenant Theological Seminary

This is an excellent book! One formula for excellence is: Passion + Precision = Excellence. Patrick Morley exudes a heart aflame for effective men's discipleship while providing what pastors and lay leaders hunger for—precise, usable approaches and answers to the real needs of men today. If you have a heart to disciple men, this is your book. If you mark useable quotes as you read, plan to wear out your highlighter on this one!

TOM CLYMER
Ocean Drive Presbyterian Church

This is more than a book. It is a prophetic word that comes at a pivotal time in our contemporary history. *Pastoring Men* salutes the priority that God designed to be the leading edge of good, new beginnings of reformation and harbingers of hope. It's a clarion call that not only beckons us back to His mandate, but gives us practical ways to follow. This book can renew our churches. It restores the priority of calling men to lead, to be the first to serve, and to be the examples that will direct us back to God's best.

WAYNE CORDEIRO
New Hope Christian Fellowship Foursquare Church, Honolulu

Pastoring Men is written by a man who understands men—their needs, desires, and aspirations. Pat Morley offers a useful plan for any pastor who wants to focus on building a ministry of discipleship for every man in his church. Engaging, inspiring, and practical, *Pastoring Men* has vast potential in the process of discipling men in the local church.

ROD CULBERTSON JR.
Associate professor of practical theology, dean of student development
Reformed Theological Seminary, Charlotte

The information contained in this book is fundamental, biblical, and critical for this day and age. *Pastoring Men* articulates the needs of men both within the church and in representing the church in a secularized society. The church has, in many ways, failed at pastoring men. This book equips leaders to understand the challenge and have a clear vision for the call.

MAURY DAVIS
Senior Pastor, Cornerstone Church of the Assemblies of God
Madison, Tennessee

Every pastor knows that if you reach the man for Christ, you will also more than likely reach the entire family. Consequently, discipling the men in your church is strategic to fulfilling Christ's Great Commission. Patrick Morley's strategy is to disciple men who can impact every arena of life and ministry. This book combines the best of *Man In the Mirror* and *No Man Left Behind* to provide every pastor with the inspiration, strategy, and practical tools to disciple every man in the church. This excellent tool can create a continual flow of called, equipped, and committed lay leaders. It is a resource I and my leadership team will refer to time and time again.

MARK FULLER
Pastor, Grove City Church of the Nazarene

As a pastor to pastors, I believe you need to read this book. You'll discover how important you are in developing a vibrant men's ministry in your church. It won't happen as it should without your direct leadership. You'll discover that the results will permeate every aspect of your ministry.

GENE A. GETZ
Pastor Emeritus, Chase Oaks Church
President, Center for Church Renewal, Plano, Texas

Pat Morley knows men. He's been in the foxholes discipling hundreds for more than twenty years—weeping , teaching, counseling, and challenging them to be all that God wants them to be as husbands, fathers, employees/employers, and effective laymen in the church. As his pastor, I've watched him closely for all these years. He's the real deal. This book is a guide from Scripture to shoe leather to help all of us who are serious about change in our own lives as well as desperate to disciple others.

CHUCK GREEN
Pastor Emeritus, Orangewood Presbyterian Church

I don't think I have encountered a better apologetic for calling men to discipleship than Pat's new book. It gets inside the heart of both pastor and layman and introduces them to each other. Often much is lost in translation between pastor and the average guy; Pat becomes the mediator and translator. Real understanding is the result.

BILL HULL
Author, Jesus Christ, Disciplemaker, The Disciple-Making Church, The Disciple-Making Pastor

Men are indeed the untapped reservoir of useful energy for the kingdom of God. Patrick Morley has been used by the Lord to help men become a vital part of His work in the church and Kingdom. No one has more passion for men's ministry than this author. Read *Pastoring Men* and learn from one who knows how!

JOHNNY M. HUNT
Pastor, First Baptist Woodstock
President of Southern Baptist Convention

Pastor, this book will help you to better understand the men in your congregation . . . and to better understand yourself. It will sharpen your church's ministry to men . . . and it will sharpen you. Men are practical. And Patrick Morley is totally practical, but not predictable. Thank you, Patrick, for this invaluable tool!

JOEL C. HUNTER
Senior Pastor of Northland Church

If it were possible, I would give this book to every pastor in America. It's that good and right on target! It powerfully states what every pastor urgently needs to hear, namely, *your men desperately need you to disciple them.* Few men can explain why or how to do this better than Patrick Morley. Let him help you win with your men.

ROBERT LEWIS
Pastor-at-large, Fellowship Bible Church
Founder of Men's Fraternity

Statistics show the decline of participation of men in church. Pat Morley has confronted this situation with candor and compassion. He offers positive perspectives on how the church can reclaim men both in participation and leadership. His approach is extremely practical and very applicable for the local church. Those of us serving in the professional ministry genuinely appreciate this helpful and insightful book.

JOHN ED MATHISON
Senior Pastor, Frazier Memorial United Methodist Church

Leadership is influence. *Pastoring Men* is an insightful and practical tool to increase your influence with your men. This book will help you create, capture, and sustain the momentum you need to more effectively disciple all the men in your church. Read this book! You won't be disappointed!

JOHN C. MAXWELL
Author, speaker, and founder of ISS and EQUIP
Duluth, Georgia

Pat once again shows us that there is no task more important or urgent than discipling men. *Pastoring Men* shares with us the need, the burden, and the practical steps to "leave no man behind." Chapter 11, "Seventy Things Every Man Needs to Know" alone will prove to be an invaluable resource. I urge every pastor to read and apply this book to your life and ministry.

DWAYNE MERCER
Pastor, First Baptist Church, Oviedo, Florida

Patrick Morley has done it again. Just like *Man in the Mirror*, he has written a must read for men and pastors alike. Read it with your eyes, plant it in your heart, and you will be more of God's man than you ever dreamed you could be.

JAMES MERRITT
Cross Pointe Southern Baptist Church, Duluth, Georgia

Patrick Morley knows men. He knows their hopes, their hurts, and their dreams. Now The-Man-in-the-Mirror man provides pastors and other church leaders a tool that may become indispensable in our hurting churches that love hurting men. I commend *Pastoring Men* to you with enthusiasm. I just wish the book had been available when I was a pastor.

THOM S. RAINER
President and CEO, LifeWay Christian Resources, Nashville

The Bible repeatedly uses the phrase "act like men." So clearly there is something about Christian manhood and biblical masculinity that is desired when the gospel takes hold of a man's heart. Patrick Morley has again addressed this issue biblically and profoundly in a way that not only clarifies but also assists pastors and leaders in knowing how to shepherd and disciple men for Christ.

HARRY L. REEDER, III
Senior Pastor, Briarwood Presbyterian Church

Patrick is addressing one of the most critical issues for the church of the twenty-first century. Children will follow in the faith, values, and lifestyles of their fathers. We must engage men in the heroic places of their hearts to lead the next generation as role models of faith and integrity.

MIKE SLAUGHTER
Pastor, Ginghamsburg Church

Drawing from his vast experience, Pat has taken the mystery out of how to connect with, shepherd, and motivate men to be disciples of Jesus Christ. An incredibly insightful and practical work, *Pastoring Men* should be on every pastor's shelf as both blueprint for beginning a compelling men's ministry and as fresh wind to invigorate a stale one. This is a very important book for the kingdom.

JAY SIMMONS
Pastor, South City Presbyterian Church, St. Louis

As a pastor for fifty-plus years, I had a great desire to help men become the spiritual leaders God intends them to be. The work of Patrick Morley was very helpful to me. This newest book will be invaluable to pastors in that responsibility today. His chapters "What Do Men Want?" and "What Do Men Need?" are worth the price of the book.

JERRY VINES
President, Jerry Vines Ministries
Pastor Emeritus, First Baptist Church, Jacksonville, Florida
Past President, Southern Baptist Convention

Let's be honest: The worst kept secret in our churches is how poorly we're *really* doing at activating and equipping men for the most thrilling, fulfilling, and demanding purpose on the planet: following Jesus. With his new book, *Pastoring Men,* Patrick Morley squarely targets leaders and pastors with that challenge. Jammed with years of insight, "reality-check" statistics, and practical tips on the essential factors for discipling men, *Pastoring Men* gives us enough fire and resources to get it done. The "Seventy Things Every Man Needs to Know" topical index in part three is worth the price of the book alone.

DAVE WORKMAN
Senior Pastor, Vineyard Community Church
Author of The Outward-Focused Life

PASTORING MEN

WHAT WORKS, WHAT DOESN'T, AND WHY IT MATTERS NOW MORE THAN EVER

PATRICK MORLEY

MOODY PUBLISHERS
CHICAGO

Editor: Jim Vincent
Cover and Interior Design: Smartt Guys design
Cover Image: © David Madison / Getty Images

Library of Congress Cataloging-in-Publication Data

Morley, Patrick M.
 Pastoring men : what works, what doesn't, and why it matters now more than ever / Patrick Morley.
   p. cm.
Includes bibliographical references.
ISBN 978-0-8024-7553-4
1. Church work with men. I. Title.
BV4440.M68 2008
259.081--dc22
                        2008035062

In memory of ROBERT S. MORLEY
1923–2003

Husband of Alleen
Father of Pat, Robert, Pete, and Bill
A good man, humble, with integrity, and a hard worker

CONTENTS

ACKNOWLEDGMENTS

What comes out of a book must first go into its author. I am so grateful to the many pastors who have built into my life—Hugh Lake, John Christiansen, Chuck Green, Bob Cargo, Jeff Jakes, and Joel Hunter.

Thank you, Robert, Eric, and Andrew Wolgemuth, my literary agents and friends, for always knowing "the next right step"—a rare and valuable bit of wisdom.

Gratitude must be offered to Moody Publishers for accepting me as a men's author. Everyone on the Moody team has inspired me by their belief in the importance of this book, especially Paul Santhouse, Dave DeWit, Tracey Shannon, Greg Thornton, Steve Lyon, John Hinkley, Holly Kisly, Janis Backing, and my editor, Jim Vincent.

A special word of thanks to our dedicated headquarters staff at Man in the Mirror. They've heard everything in this book, and sharpened the concepts over the years: Pam Adkins, Jim Angelakos, Mia Angelakos, Ruth Cameron, Sharon Carey, Bernie Clark, Brett Clemmer, David Delk, Joanne Hunt, Vanessa Jones, Donna Keiderling, Kelly Laughridge, Michael Lenahan, Al Lenio, Stephanie Lopez, Liz Luke, Michael Maine, Scott Russell, Tracie Searles, Jim Seibert, Jamie Smith, Antonio Stevens, Svana Tolf, Greg Wilkinson, and Rise Wilson. Thank you for executing so well that I was free to pursue this book. And no one I've ever known is more helpful or productive than Daphne Mayer, my executive assistant. Thank you.

As always, my wife, Patsy, acted as my sounding board, offering both encouragement and wisdom.

PROLOGUE

The following letter is one I'm sure you'd love to send as a pastor—but, of course, you'd never send it. I'm writing it because I want you to know that I understand what you're going through with men.

Though it's fictitious, the letter is based on conversations I have had with hundreds of pastors during the past twenty years. I believe it represents their desire—and yours—to help men become disciples, as well as the frustration in pursuing that goal. It also reflects my passion that this book will equip you with the concepts and strategies you need to more effectively disciple every man in your church.

Dear Laymen,

I would like to get some things off my chest. Since I could never say these things to my own men (and survive), I will say them to you. I offer these thoughts humbly.

Frankly, I get nervous when some of my men get all excited and start talking men's movement lingo like *father wound, masculinity*, etc.

What usually happens is that the least respected men in the church—the ones who talk about Jesus all the time but struggle to keep a job—"take over" the men's ministry. No one would follow them on a bet—I know I wouldn't want to be in a small group they led.

So, honestly, it's just easier for me to let them do what they want. I want to help them, but in my heart I don't really think they have what it takes, and they will eventually peter out and I'll be back to zero—or worse. Don't get me wrong. I love them. And I have faith that God has good plans for them. But, at least at this point, they need to be the ministerees, not the ministers.

WHAT I CAN GET BEHIND

I'll tell you what I can get behind. I can get behind a disciple-making plan that men I respect are personally involved with.

Let me tell you a secret. If you really want to get me involved, here's what you would do. You would find between six and twelve of the most respected men in the church—normal guys. Invite them to a meeting to explore and pray about reaching more men for Christ. Give me a heads up *before* this exploratory meeting, so I'm not feeling blindsided. Don't try to take it too fast. Pray a lot. Don't be afraid to ask men for a big commitment.

Once you have some men willing to make a go of it, then come see me. Please. When you do come see me, don't act like you're the first ones who ever thought of reaching the men in our church. I've beaten my head against that wall for years trying to get men more involved.

HOW TO WIN ME OVER

Give me space—and time—to process how it would work. Don't try to "close" me right away. Everyone thinks if they just lean on me hard enough then their program can go. Show me some stats, build the case, why should I add to, change, or tweak my existing focus?

Ask me how ministry to men can help me. Find out what I think are the problems our men face as husbands, fathers, workers, churchmen, and men in general. I pick up quite a lot, you know, in the course of a day.

And come see me before you have the whole concept designed—I will need to make sure the plans mesh with our vision and other church ministries. Besides, I probably can make a unique contribution as the pastor.

We can meet and discuss why we need to reach men, how men in our church are doing, what kind of men we want to produce, what will constitute success for us, and how we will measure progress.

Make it easy for me to support a ministry to our men. Talk about getting men into small groups to study the Bible. Talk about helping men understand the gospel. Talk about how we can build men up as godly men for the home, church, workplace, and community. Talk about integrating men into the existing ministries of the church. And not just some of our men, but all of them!

Don't talk about adding a bunch of new programming like retreats, seminars, etc. First things first. Let's see how you can help make the ministries we're already committed to work.

JUST SO YOU KNOW WHAT I'M UP AGAINST

Like you, I want to serve God and have a successful ministry. I got into this field because I sensed a calling from God to make a difference for the gospel of Jesus.

The other day someone asked, "Why don't you care about the men in our church?" Why would they think that? It hurts when people question my motives.

I work hard to be an effective leader. The demands are unbelievably diverse—and they excite me. I love the variety of public communication, private counseling, leading a staff, inspiring volunteers, administrating an organization, marriages, baptisms, funerals, committee meetings, and more.

Here's what I see happening when it comes to men's ministries: A man brings me an idea, but often acts like I had nothing else to do but drop everything and embrace his idea . . . an idea he did not do a very good job researching, explaining, or finding others to support. He has no plan. In fact, what he really wants is to dump the whole idea in my lap and be done with it. He thinks I'm the professional so it's my job. Are you surprised that a pastor would speak so bluntly? Don't be. We're human too, and we all feel this way sometimes.

You have no idea how many people let me down. Hey, I'm not feeling sorry for myself, and I'm certainly not angry. Indeed, I thank God for those people who, when they tell me they will get something done, I can bank it. But often I have not found people to be very dependable. It's as though their word to the church is the first thing that gets cut. Even that wouldn't bother me so much if they would just tell me. As it is, most of the nonperformers don't tell me until the day they were supposed to be finished.

NEVERTHELESS, I WANT TO BUILD
A GROWING CHURCH

So please keep me in your prayers. Think the best of my motives. Help me see that you are really serious about reaching our men. Show me that you don't merely want to start something, and then dump it in my lap.

And by the way, you will have more clout with me if I see that you have a track record of actually ministering to men yourself.

So I'm excited about what we could do together that we could never do alone. I am eager to partner with you to grow Christ's church. When can we get together?

Warmly in Christ,
Your Pastor

1

IS PASTORING MEN
WORTH THE EFFORT?

Much has been made about the "men problem." You can hear about it on Oprah. You can read about it in *Time*. You can watch the destruction it creates with Dr. Phil.

School teachers can barely educate on the heels of it. Social services are overwhelmed because of it. Employers are stumped by it. Law enforcement feels the brunt of it. Many jails and prisons are full because of it. Politicians don't know what to do with it. Candidates avoid it.

Authors and academics have assembled alarming statistics to prove it. Health care professionals publish convincing reports to document the human cost of it. Cable shows rant at it. Talk radio personalities have all the answers for it. Movies glamorize it. Television commercials mock it.

The "men problem." Divorce courts are at capacity because of it. Families are ripped apart by it. Wives soak their pillows with tears as a result of it. Children grow up in poverty as a consequence of it. Teenagers experiment with drugs and sex to cope with it.

A lot of money gets spent to treat the symptoms of it. We open teenage pregnancy centers, establish substance abuse centers, increase budgets for social services, build homes for battered women, authorize more jail space, put extra beds in our homeless shelters, increase the number of law enforcement officers, and fit our schools with metal detectors to deal with it.

Everyone is concerned about it. Many address the consequences of it. Yet very few people are doing anything that will change the root of it.

"It" is among the most pervasive social, economic, political, and spiritual problems of all time.

Men have become one of our largest neglected people groups. As a result, they are prone to get caught up in the rat race, lead unexamined lives, and become cultural (rather than biblical) Christians.

CHECK OUT THE COLLATERAL DAMAGE

The collateral damage on marriages and families is staggering:

- Of men who married between 1970 and 1974, just 46.2 percent were still married after thirty years.[1]
- Of the seventy-two million children in America under the age of eighteen, 33 percent will go to bed tonight in a home without a biological father.[2]
- Children in female-headed families are five times more likely to live in poverty, repeat a grade, and have emotional problems compared to families where a father is present.[3]

We have become a nation of spiritual widows and practical orphans (James 1:27). These are real people—real casualties. As one police officer said, "Statistics are tragedies with the tears wiped away."

Today's average man is like a deer caught in the headlights of a Hummer. He doesn't fully understand—and so can't apply—what God has to say about a man's identity, purpose, relationships, marriage, sex, fathering, work, money, ministry, time, emotions, integrity, and dozens of other subjects.

As a result, most men are tired. They often have a lingering feeling something isn't quite right about their lives. Often their lives are coming unglued. And it is common for them to feel like nobody really cares. Even in the church, men are being left behind. The situation is so significant that the next chapter will explore this in depth.

Yet men routinely "bluff" when asked, "How are you doing?" Pastors observe this all the time. For that reason, I think we should be just as concerned about the men who have not become statistics as those who have.

It's not as though these men want to struggle or fail. But their *capabilities* are not equal to their *intentions*. As Denzel Washington, playing a recovering alcoholic ex-military bodyguard in a Latin American country, said in *Man on Fire*, "You're either trained or you're not trained." Spiritually, most men are not.

THE OPPORTUNITY

Reaching these men is one of the great strategic opportunities—and needs—of our time. Instead of the "men problem," some quarters need to start seeing the "men opportunity." Pastors are the logical choice. Pastors bring grace to the equation. They see men not so much for what they are, but for what they can become in Christ. Pastors are the ones whom God has called to instruct, encourage, correct, challenge, inspire, and call men to "act like a man." This is a significant yet solvable problem. There is no human or spiritual reason why we can't get this done. Of course, "it" will take time and dedication.

The purpose of this book is to equip you to more effectively pastor *all* of your men. God's vision is that *every* man in your church becomes a disciple of Jesus. Men's ministry needs to be redefined so that it is "all-inclusive." *This is a book about why and how to disciple every man in your church.*

Most pastors also desperately need more lay leaders. Another opportunity in discipling men is that some will grow into leadership. For example, a friend of mine started a small group with seven men in his Birmingham, Alabama, church. During the next seven years, his ministry grew to seven groups totaling 128 men. At that time his church needed about 150 leaders to function properly. One hundred of those leaders came through his small groups. But what's especially intriguing is that approximately seventy-five of those men—fully half of the church's leadership!—started in his groups as cultural Christians who would (probably) not have otherwise stepped up to become church leaders.

You would not be holding this book in your hands unless pastoring men was important to you. But if I were to ask you, "Are you effective in pastoring your men?" like most pastors you would probably say, "No." I have discovered that even pastors who rank among the most successful at pastoring their men are hesitant to say, "Yes, I'm effective."

When asked why he was so tentative, one successful pastor said, "I know too much. I know that even though we've made progress with a man by taking him through our basic discipleship course, then officer training, and now he's a leader—I still see areas in his life that need work—as in my own, or I hear about someone who had a negative experience with him and I say to myself, 'Hmmm, he's not quite there.'"

Most church leaders we talk to are profoundly dissatisfied with the number of men in their churches who are effective disciples. But the majority of churches that have tried to implement men's discipleship initiatives have not been able to sustain them. They need better information, models, methods, and processes grounded in research, field testing, and biblical authority. That's why I wrote this book.

This is not a book about how to get a men's group going in your church. This is not a book about changing the décor of your sanctuary. This is not a book about starting a "separate" men's ministry that reaches a fraction of your men. Those are secondary concerns.

Since 1973 I have been "pastoring men," and here are three promises I want to make. By the end of this book you will know:

- *The state of your men*—how they are doing, what they want, what keeps them from getting what they want, and what they need (chapters 2–5)
- *The essential factors* to successfully disciple men (chapters 7 and 8)
- *A concrete, sustainable strategy* to help you organize your passion for men's discipleship without a lot of new programming. As you will see, you are probably already doing most of what needs to be done (chapter 9)

Also, I've included an *alphabetized reference section* of (mostly) one-page summaries on seventy subjects that every man needs to know, giving you a masculine perspective that you can work into your sermons, teachings, counseling, and writing (Chapter 11).

THE STAKES

Helping pastors disciple their men is my passion for personal reasons. In 1926, when my dad was two, the youngest of four children, his father deserted his family.

The stress got the best of my grandmother. She had a stroke, so she and her four young children moved in with two of her unmarried sisters (my great-aunts). Together, those three women raised my dad and his siblings. They did a great job, but they were dirt poor.

In those days, long before government programs, the community closed ranks when some of "their people" were in need. The one sister who worked was an elevator operator at the local bank; knowing the situation, the employer paid her a generous salary of $50 a week (roughly $15 an hour in today's dollars). She bought groceries each day on her way home. The grocer told her, "Nina, you take whatever you need, and pay whatever you can."

When my dad turned six he went to work with his older brother, Harry. They had two jobs. They rose every morning at 3:00 a.m. to deliver milk and then worked a paper route. The school gave them a permanent tardy slip.

My dad never knew the warmth of a father's embrace. He never felt the scratch of a dad's whiskers. He never overheard his dad whistling or singing while he worked, never smelled his work clothes, never heard him joke around or read a bedtime story, never tossed a ball, never felt a dad tussle his hair, never heard him say, "I love you, son" or "I'm proud of you, son," and never had a father's approval or guidance.

When Dad became a man he had to decide if he would repeat or break the cycle. As the oldest of four boys, I'm grateful my dad wanted to break the cycle. But fathering was unexampled to him. So our family joined a church because Dad and Mom wanted to get some moral and religious instruction for their four sons.

Our church had a vision to put my dad to work and, because of his strong work ethic, he responded to the challenge. By age forty, my dad was the top layman in the church. I suppose that's what he thought it must mean to be a "good Christian."

Of course, there is a lot of work to do in the church, but our church did not also have a vision to disciple my dad to be a godly man, father, and husband—the real reason he joined. He did the best he could, but he was left to "guess" at how to father my brothers and me.

Something happened in the church that hurt my mother's feelings, and my dad was burned out, so we quit church when I was in the tenth grade and my youngest brother was in the third grade.

Our family was soon hit by a force from which we have still not fully recovered. I quit high school in the middle of my senior year. My brother Robert followed in my footsteps. He eventually died of a heroin overdose. My other two brothers have had a variety of employment, substance, and marriage issues.

My dad just never saw it coming. If he could have seen around the bend, I'm sure he would have done things differently. If he was still alive I know he would say, "I take full responsibility. That was my decision." And I respect that. Every man does need to take responsibility for his own life.

But I would like to suggest that the church is culpable. The church knew (or should have known) what was around the bend. The church should have had a vision to disciple my Dad. But it didn't.

Fortunately, God is the Redeemer, and this story took another turn—I fell in love with Patsy. She went forward at a Billy Graham Crusade to publicly profess her faith at the age of eleven, and has never wavered. God graciously grafted the gospel back into my family line through Patsy's family line—Patsy led me to Christ.

Then God allowed me the joy of leading my brother Robert to Christ before he died. Another brother has also professed Christ, and so has my only niece on this side of the family. Dad and Mom also both came to Christ (or came back—I'm not sure). Neither one of them ever got over their bitterness toward the church, but they both affirmed their faith in Jesus on their deathbeds.

Both of my children can never remember a time when they didn't love Christ. They are now both married to fantastic Christian spouses and serving the Lord. I wish my father was still alive so I could tell him, "Dad, we did break the cycle. It should have only taken one generation and it took two, but we did break the cycle."

My Dad and I have the same DNA, so what was the difference? Why did I succeed where he failed? The difference was that I belonged to a church that had a vision to disciple me to be a godly man, husband, and father, while my Dad did not. Church is where I learned how to study the Bible for myself, how to study together with others, and how to share my faith and lead someone to Christ.

The reason I am so passionate about equipping pastors and churches to disciple men is this: I know that in every church there are men just like my Dad. These are men with good hearts and good intentions who have come to church for all the right reasons. How tragic when they fall away.

I also believe that in most churches there are men like my grandfather—men who are not only going to pull the plug on church, but on their families too. And they have no idea of the forces of destruction they're about to set in motion—that more than eighty years later, like me, their children's children may still be trying to recover from that fateful decision.

At the Man in the Mirror ministry, we see it every day in the broken homes and shattered lives of families who have lost a husband, father, and provider.

Obviously I will never know what it might have been like to grow up in a family with a dad who was discipled to be a godly man, husband, and father. My hope and prayer is that by learning and applying the skills in this book, you will feel equipped to more effectively pastor men like my dad and the grandfather I never knew. And men like me who sincerely want to break the cycle but can't do it without your help. May the young boys growing up in your church today never have to one day repeat a story like mine.

THE ANSWER: THE DISCIPLE-MAKING CHURCH

Scientists keep looking for a holy grail that unifies the cosmos—a "theory of everything." Pastors don't have to keep looking. We have a unifying theory. Jesus taught us the holy grail for unifying His church. It's making disciples. Discipleship is the core mission Jesus gave His bride. Making disciples is the irrefutable biblical mission of your church.

Discipleship is the process by which men become civilized. The institutional church is God's appointed means—the "first responders"—to help men become disciples. However, the church (in general) has not been making disciples at a proper pace. According to one survey, only 16 percent of church-attending adults are involved in organized discipleship classes, and twice as many women as men. (Discipleship, of course, is a lot more than attending classes; we will examine discipleship closely in Chapters 5 and 6.)

One day a highly placed executive in one of America's largest evangelical denominations told me, "In our denomination, we are not making disciples. And that's because our pastors have never been discipled."

Later, my wife and I went to dinner with the chancellor of a seminary and his wife. I told him what the denominational leader (from a different denomination) had said. He lamented, "Well, I'm not surprised. We find that when our students arrive, they have never been discipled. And we have no plans to disciple them while they're here." (Since that time he has initiated a pilot program with full-time staffing to disciple their students.)

So people who have never been discipled go to seminary where they are not discipled, and then they are sent to churches where their main responsibility is to—what? Make disciples.

Talk about an elephant in the living room! As a result, many pastors feel ill-equipped to disciple their men. They don't feel like they understand what their men are going through or how to help them. The unhappy result is that men don't get what they need from their church, and the church doesn't get what it needs from their men. That's why I wrote this book—to give you the confidence and tools you need to disciple your men. This is not an approach to make the world more comfortable, but different.

If you project out twenty or fifty years, can you visualize any way of ever getting the world right if men are wrong? The "men problem" is the root cause behind virtually every problem that ails us. It's an untreated cancer that keeps producing more and worse tumors.

One day a major donor said, "Pat, I can't support your ministry anymore."

I said, "That's fine, but tell me why."

He said, "My heart is really in prison ministry and teenage crisis pregnancy centers."

I laughed out loud. I said, "By all means please support that important work. But why do you think so many young men end up in prison? And why do you think a young teenaged girl would hop into bed with a boy?" (We dialogued more and he did continue his support.)

Let's treat the symptoms, of course, but let those who can—pastors—also treat the disease. A disciple-making church offers the only *systemic* solution to what ails us. As someone has said, "The church has many critics, but no rivals."

We need a fresh, research-based, pastor-led, biblical, field-tested approach that results in lasting change—one that is "actionable."

WE NEED A FRESH APPROACH

There have always been men's movements. The contemporary secular and Christian men's movements both started circa 1990. The secular men's movement went "blip" and promptly disappeared.

The problem with the secular men's movement was that it had no answer for "Tuesday." Men were lured into the woods on Saturday where they painted themselves up like Indians, beat on tom-toms, talked to trees, and cried out in existential pain. By Sunday they felt relief. But on Monday they had to return to civilization, and by Tuesday the futility and pain had returned.

The contemporary Christian men's movement has survived because Jesus Christ prevails on Tuesday. Instead of war paint, whoops, and grunts, men are being discipled into the gospel of Jesus. By the late 1990s, the nexus of the movement had shifted from loud stadiums into the quiet corridors of the local church.

Yet by the early part of this century, the Christian men's movement could be characterized as "a lot of men with really good hearts doing the best they could." There had been a lot of false starts.

Many pastors and laymen had devoted as many as ten years to untested strategies that really were doomed to fail from the start. And I didn't see any reason to think things would be different in another ten or twenty years—unless we came up with a fresh approach.

WE NEED A RESEARCH-BASED APPROACH

At the same time, I have also sensed the need for a more research-based approach to men's discipleship. So in 2002, to augment my master's in theological studies, I embarked on doctoral research which led to earning a PhD in management in 2006. For my dissertation I studied the question, "Why do some churches succeed at men's discipleship while others languish or fail?"

My research revolved around two major issues. First, I wanted to learn, "How do church-based men's discipleship ministries that succeed differ from those that languish or fail?" Second, I wanted to discover, "What are successful pastors doing differently than the pastors of ineffective or failed ministries to men?"

I wanted to know from a management perspective, "What are the factors that lead to success or failure when implementing a men's discipleship program?" To get at the answers, I decided on multiple-case-study research. I compared and contrasted churches that had effective men's discipleship programs to churches that had ineffective or failed programs.

We will dive into the deep end of the pool and cover my research findings in chapters 7 and 8, "Success Factors in Discipling Men," but here is the indisputable bottom line: *The senior pastor is the key to everything.* These are the three main factors in the highly effective churches:

1. A senior pastor with the *vision* to disciple every man in the church.
2. A senior pastor with the *determination* to succeed.
3. A senior pastor who found a *sustainable strategy* to make disciples.

Of course, Jesus is the perfect example of these three factors. In fact, His sustainable strategy has outlasted every institution, organization, kingdom, and government ever established.

When it comes to men's ministry, I am aware of how brutally many overzealous laymen have treated their pastors. Yet, without you, the pastor, men's discipleship in your church will never be more than a fringe activity. And, as we will see, you can be successful at this without adding a lot of new programming.

WE NEED A PASTOR-LED APPROACH

I cannot overstate this: *No one has more influence with your men than you do.* While writing this book I was invited to speak to a special men's class at a local church during the Sunday School hour. My speaking was well publicized—both the senior pastor and the executive pastor announced it. About thirty-five men attended and we had a wonderful time. Simultaneously, the senior pastor was teaching a three-week series for men on Sunday evenings. He had five hundred men attend his men's classes. It was a priority to this pastor, and the men sensed it.

As the pastor, you can accomplish what laymen can only dream about—and so much more quickly. With the support of his senior pastor, John started a small-group ministry in his very busy 1,000 member church in Atlanta. Over the span of seven years, his ministry grew to ten groups with a combined total of about 120 people.

Then a new senior pastor came on board. He shared John's vision for small groups. He convinced the leadership that the congregation should stop coming to the church building on Wednesday nights. Instead, he wanted to break people into small groups that would meet in homes.

In the spring he announced that they would start the new small-group ministry in the fall. Over the summer he preached on the importance and value of small groups. On the first night, 817 people met in small groups.

It took seven *years* for a talented, committed layman (he's in top management with a Fortune 500 company) to recruit 120 people into small groups—even with his pastor's full *support*. With the pastor's *personal involvement*, it took only seven *months* to recruit 817 people into small groups—an increase of nearly 700 percent.

There's no getting around it—the senior pastor is the key to everything.

Everything points to this overarching conclusion: For a critical mass of men to become disciples in a church, pastors will need to take the lead. To succeed you will need biblically sound, research-based, field-tested strategies and models. It would not be fair to ask you to develop these tools on your own.

WE NEED A BIBLICAL APPROACH

Suppose you wanted to start a company to make computers. You put together a business plan to manufacture 100,000 computers over the next five years. You raise $100 million from an investor.

Five years later your investor returns and asks for a report. You say, "We're doing great! We did it! We produced 100,000 units! We made 15,000 refrigerators, 10,000 toasters, 21,000 microwave ovens, 50,000 lava lamps, and we're up to 4,000 computers!"

Your investor replies, "Wow, 4,000 computers. But that's only 4 percent of what you projected."

"Oh yes," you say, "but look at all the other useful things we've produced!"

"That's wonderful," he says, "but I was planning to use those computers to change the world. Now it cannot happen. You've made the world more comfortable. I wanted to make it different."

For 2,000 years we (the church) have only had one business plan: "Go and make disciples" (Matthew 28:18–20). The final marching orders from Jesus are "Go and make disciples." Those orders still stand. They have not been amended, altered, or rescinded. More millions of people and more billions of dollars have been mobilized by this brief message than any other speech in recorded history.

Our "investor," Jesus, could have directed us to make anything he wanted. He could have said, "Go and make *worshipers*." But he didn't. He said, "Go and make disciples." He could have said, "Go and make *workers*." But he didn't. He said, "Go and make disciples." He could have said, "Go and make *tithers*." But he didn't. He said, "Go and make disciples."

Does that mean Jesus isn't interested in worshipers, workers, and tithers? Of course He is. But Jesus knew we don't get worshipers by trying to make worshipers. We get worshipers by making disciples. Jesus knew we don't get workers by trying to make workers. We get workers by making disciples. And so on. Everything falls into place when we make disciples. True disciples can't wait to work (and worship, tithe, serve, perform social justice, evangelize, love one another, and so on).

The central mission of the church—the overarching goal—is to "make disciples."

Discipleship is the "portal" priority through which all the other desired outcomes of the *ecclesia* are achieved. (The "portal" priority concept is explained graphically in chapter 9, "A Strategy to Reach Every Man.") The key to success at every point is, "Go and make disciples." The pastor's chief role is to make disciples.

There is one, and only one, way in which a man can win the battle for his soul. It is simple and concrete. His single greatest need is to become a disciple of our Lord and Savior, Jesus Christ. The goal of pastoring men, then, is to disciple men into the gospel.

WE NEED A FIELD-TESTED APPROACH

A large part of my purpose and calling—and also for Man in the Mirror, ministry—is to help bring vision, strategic thinking, and organization to the Christian men's discipleship movement.

I am a men's specialist—a "one trick" pony—a consultant on men's issues, and an advocate for men. (I hesitate to say "expert" since I think of an expert as someone who knows more and more about less and less until finally he knows everything there is to know about nothing!)

From the time I became a Christian in 1973, my overarching passion has been to challenge men to stop, examine their lives, be reconciled to Christ, and make needed changes based on God's greater purposes for their lives.

Since 1986 I have taught a new Bible message (almost) every week at The Man in the Mirror Bible Study—150 men of all ages and stations in life who meet every Friday morning at a local civic center. I figure I've prepared and delivered over 1,000 different messages tailored specifically to men.

When I wrote the book *The Man in the Mirror* in 1989, no one, and least of all me, ever imagined the millions of men God would touch through that book! After all, I was an anonymous commercial real estate developer plying my trade here in Central Florida.

In fact, if it weren't for pastors, I wouldn't be in ministry today! In 1989 we had a warehouse full of unsold copies of *The Man in the Mirror*. So we offered them for free to pastors. Seven thousand pastors took up the offer, and that's how the book took off.

And the rest, as they say, is history. I have written fourteen books for men and several hundred articles for and about men. In 2000, we started a program to offer books by the case for just over $1 each. At this writing, about eight million books have been distributed to men through churches. Our faculty members have conducted over one thousand men's seminars in churches throughout the United States and the world. The Man in the Mirror Bible Study went online in 2001 and is now downloaded thousands of times each week—many for men's groups that meet in churches, conference rooms, and cubicles around the world.

Annually we work with over thirty thousand leaders who disciple men. Our Leadership Training Center has equipped thousands of leaders in conferences that teach a model that I will unpack for you in chapter 9, "A Strategy to Reach Every Man."

I tell you these things because I want you to know that I am not writing from an announcer's booth; I am actively in the game, as are you. In this book I consider it my privilege and duty to share with you what we have learned through these field-tested experiences.

Research-based, field-tested concepts are important so you don't waste your time—often measured in years—on second- or even third-level priorities. For example, a lot of thinkers have tried to turn the church's failures with men into a gender issue. They offer solutions that address making the church more male friendly. I'm certainly not against this, but it falls in the category of "second things." It's just a theory, and one that may prove costly. As my dissertation committee often asked me, "Sez who?"

If you're not careful, you can end up with a committee talking incessantly about decorating themes instead of how to lead men into a vital communion with the living Christ. I'm almost embarrassed to write those two concepts in the same sentence.

I don't think Jesus minds if your church wants to park a Harley in the narthex—it's not the main thing, but neither is it prohibited (and it's probably a culturally relevant idea). But I do think Jesus desperately cares if your church wants to disciple men into His gospel and help them become friends of God.

It takes a long time to make a disciple, the process is often messy, and it rarely proceeds in a "step-by-step" sequence. To illustrate, I've included a case study of how I became a disciple in Chapter 6.

In chapter 10, "Why the Man in the Mirror Men's Bible Study Works—A Case Study," I will break down for you what I think makes this long-running, field-tested Bible study an effective model for men's discipleship.

WHAT HAPPENS WHEN A MAN
BECOMES A DISCIPLE?

As the pastor, you hear a loud knock on your door. It's Jason Steele—a "Sunday only" Christian for seventeen years. But three years ago you decided that discipling men needed to be one of your top priorities. Two years ago, your church sponsored a seminar to create momentum among men on the fringe, and Jason attended. Though it wasn't anything you hadn't said all along, the speaker came at things from a fresh angle, and the message rang Jason's bell. (Actually, the only reason an outside speaker can harvest is that you have faithfully prepared the soil. See John 4:36–38.)

Jason surrendered his life to Christ at that point—whether for the first time or as a recommitment, it's hard to say.

When offered a six-week, follow-up discussion group, Jason leaped at the chance to sign up. At the end of the six weeks, the leader asked him for "six more weeks" to go a little deeper. Eventually, the group gelled into a long-term Bible study and prayer group.

Jason, like many men in your church, has come to know and love Christ with a passion. And now here he is, standing in your doorway. He says, "Pastor, you have to give me something to do—a work or service or ministry of some kind. As I have grown to understand more about the unfathomable work of the cross, I can no longer sit idle. I can no longer be happy unless I do something to serve this great God. What can I do to help you?"

This is a great day in your life. Even though the results seemed small at first, you persevered with "discipling men" as a top priority. The long hours of building into the lives of your men, the countless prayers for God to send workers, your determination—at this moment all of it seems worth the effort.

Soon after Jason, other men begin to trickle, then flood, into your office. At the five-year mark, you actually run out of ministries for men inside the church! Now you start "sending" workers into community-based ministries.

One day the financial secretary brings you a report that the church has a surplus. As the men have grasped their roles as stewards, they have been much more generous. Gone is the need to plead for finances. You have been able to respond to additional requests from missionaries for support that you once had to turn away.

One afternoon your secretary announces at 3:00 p.m. that all your marriage counseling appointments for the day are finished.

"What?" you say, in a mild state of shock. As your men have come to understand their duty to love and nurture their wives, marriages have been healed and the counseling load has dwindled. On that happy day, you arrive home early and have a meaningful conversation with your own wife!

Then one day, your youth minister brings you a report that the youth facilities are out of space. Apparently, as the young people have watched their fathers transformed before their very eyes, they want in on what's happening. They have flocked to the youth meetings to learn more about this Jesus, this radical person who changed their fathers' lives.

Growing men. More workers. Better leaders. Bigger budgets. Restored marriages. Curious youth. A balanced workload. A strong reputation in the community. An increase in first-time visitors. Spiritual satisfaction. A calling come true.

Sound too good to be true? There are churches all over America experiencing these results because the pastor has focused on discipling men.

IS PASTORING MEN WORTH THE EFFORT?

There is raging in the cosmos and all around us a titanic battle between the forces of good and evil for men's souls. This battle is raging out of control in neighborhoods across America—your neighborhood. Sound overstated?

Think for a moment about the casualties taking place on your street, where your men work, even in your church. Men leave homes, women weep, a little twelve-year-old girl prays, "God, why is my daddy always so angry?"

This is a real battle. These are real men with real families.

The single greatest hope for these men and the world is Christ and His church. I love the church, but the church on the whole has not been able to muster an ongoing will or comprehensive strategy to disciple men. Pastoring men is not a top priority in *any* denomination based upon their actual allocations of financial and intellectual resources.

Nevertheless, we should be optimistic. Together, we can create a national dialogue about the importance of reaching men—men like my dad, my grandfather, and me. I thank God all the time for inserting me into a disciple-making church. In fact, I shudder at the thought of what might have been.

This is a battle worth fighting. Woodrow Wilson said, "I would rather fail in a cause that will ultimately succeed than succeed in a cause that will ultimately fail."

This is also a battle we can win. The challenge before us is daunting, but not impossible. In fact, Jesus Christ will win. We cannot, we must not, and, by God's grace, we will not fail. Pastoring men is worth the effort.

Ultimately, though, we need to pastor men because it's the right thing to do. Pastoring men may not be easy or glamorous, and it's often thankless work. Yet when a man conquers "it," that will likely change the entire course of his family for many generations to come.

And what if you're behind? A Chinese proverb says, "The best time to plant a tree was twenty years ago. The second best time is now."

PART 1

UNDERSTAND YOUR MEN

HOW ARE YOUR MEN DOING?

When historians write the "cultural autopsy" for our generation, what will they say? A lot will depend on how well the church responds to the needs of men today. To give men what they need, we must first understand how they are doing.

Demographically, men are quite different. They are black, white, Hispanic, rich, poor, rural, suburban, urban, trade workers, professionals, conservative, liberal, short, tall, skinny, fat, bald, gray, young, old, bright, and not so bright. For every man who sits on a board at a company, another lays on a bunk in jail. Some like to ponder their next chess move; others prefer screaming over a touchdown with 70,000 of their closest friends.

In another sense all men are quite similar. Each man's wiring diagram is not so different from any other of the male "species." Whether I am speaking with men from Alabama or Alaska, at the Pentagon or in prison, executives in New York City or Mennonite farmers in Pennsylvania, cowboys in Texas or Chinese businessmen in Malaysia, I have found that, as men, our similarities dwarf our differences.

You've heard the numbing statistics about men and the havoc they've created. Instead of recounting those stats, in chapters 2 through 4 I want to give you a psychographic profile of men. This profile fits almost all men, especially men in the workforce. Also, it makes no difference whether you have a small church or a big church, a rural church or an urban church, a charismatic church or a mainline church, or whether your congregation includes upper-income executives or farmers—these similarities among men transcend demographic profiling.

For example, a pastor wrote me and said, "Over 70 percent of my men are in farming and ranching. If I say something to them about my view of debt, their response is, 'Yeah, but you were never in farming. You can't make it in this business without large loans and taking on debt.'

"Some of my men are under almost unbelievable financial stress. Hail, drought, and harsh weather have made this year especially disappointing. One of my best men was advised by his lawyer a year ago to declare bankruptcy, which he didn't do. 'I'm looking to lose $50,000 this year,' he told me last Sunday. He is really under pressure and is working his 'tail' off! Scarce is time for his precious wife and two teenaged children."

You could easily substitute "manufacturing" or "software" for "farming" and "ranching," and nothing else would change. So, yes, these are generalizations, but the pattern is pretty close.

A MAN'S INTENTIONS

A man is a noble creature. After all, it's men who insist, "Women and children in the lifeboats first." Men are famous for making heroic sacrifices. By nature, men lead, protect, and provide for their families and fight for justice.

The doctrine of total depravity notwithstanding, most men have it in their hearts to do the right thing. Most men are trying to earn an honest living, be loving husbands, good dads, contributing citizens, and, if religious, solid churchmen.

No man fails on purpose. None of your men woke up this morning and thought to himself, *Well, I wonder what I can do today to tick off my wife, neglect my kids, let my boss down, and ruin my life?* Of course, men often fail, but I don't think anyone would suggest they fail on purpose. This conflict between "the man I want to be" and "the man I am" is why men show up on Sunday morning. Men come to church because they are looking for some help. Many of your men could easily write the following letter on a Sunday morning and slip it in your hand after the service. It's what they are going through.

Dear Pastor,

As I was sitting in church on Sunday, I decided to write you this letter. When the service began, this is what I found myself thinking . . .

I'm here, pastor, I'm here. I worked 55 hours this week (that's five days from 8 to 6 and two hours every night after the kids went to bed), slept 48 hours (I'm short one whole night), spent Saturday morning shuttling between soccer games, worked Saturday afternoon on the yard, took my wife to dinner Saturday night, and now here I am on Sunday morning.

All week long the world has told me to buy everything from computers to cars, and to want everything from more sex to more fun. My boss is not happy with me, nor I with him. My spouse appreciates my problems, but she has problems of her own. She's frustrated that I don't spend enough time with the family, but doesn't complain about the money. Besides, I can't share many of my struggles with her—like sexual temptations, work overload, and how to cover all these bills. The kids need more of me, but it's not like they can really tell the difference—I've always shorted them.

Meanwhile, I read my Bible and prayed four mornings this week—a total of one hour. I don't wake up in the morning wanting to fail. My intentions are good, but I still fall short. I've come here to receive some encouragement and direction from God. Now, what do you want me to do? What can you say to me?

With great appreciation for all you do as our pastor,
Jim

It's hard to solve a problem we don't really understand. We already know that a lot of men are not right, right? But before we try to "fix" the problem, let's slow down and try to understand what is really going on. How are men doing—really? The following profile applies to all men who have not been equipped as disciples, and sometimes even if they have.

HOW ARE MEN DOING?

Men Are Tired

First, most men are tired. Since I work with men as a vocation, sometimes I'm asked, "If you could only make one observation about how men are doing, what would it be?" This is it: If there is one thing you can know for sure about your men, it's that they're tired. And not just physically tired—although that too—but mentally, emotionally, relationally, morally, and financially tired. They are exhausted from the fast pace of our demanding, me, now, instant, online, real-time culture. You know the words that get tossed around: *stressed, slammed, weary, in need of relief, wasted, fragile, short-fused.* They are all synonyms that add up to "tired."

The average Christian male is up to his neck in debts and duties. He has a "picture" in his mind of what it means to be a "good Christian." He believes in this picture—it's what he thinks he "needs" to do to be a "good boy"—to be happy. He often measures his spirituality by whether or not he can live up to these standards. They are, after all, good ideas. But they are not the gospel.

- I need to spend quality time with my wife.
- I need to be a super dad to my kids and attend (maybe coach) all their activities. My dad did (or didn't) do this for me, and I'm going to be there for them.
- I need to make lots of money so my family can live in a beautiful home in a "better" neighborhood, my kids can wear the right labels, there is less pressure on my wife to work, and I can become financially independent.
- I need to join a men's small group where I can grow with some brothers.
- I need to attend a weekly home growth and fellowship group.
- I need to have a daily quiet time for fellowship with God.
- I need to keep the Sabbath and have my family in church to worship God.
- I need to serve God through a personal ministry—probably through the church.
- I need to be a good citizen and neighbor.
- I need to be a star at work if all this is going to happen.
- I need a successful and satisfying career.
- I need some time for myself.

And now *I'm* tired! Just reading the list is a bit overwhelming. Of course, this is a crooked, performance-based view of faith.

Your men are tired. As a result, most of them are in a "structural hurry." Hurry is structured into a man's schedule. For some men, the car that was once a sanctuary has become a mobile office. They're constantly on the cell phone trying to wrap up a sale as they navigate to the Little League fields to prove to themselves that they are "okay" as Christian men. One man told me he speeds to work to "save time."

The price of pace is peace. The forced, steady application of the will to make things happen leads to weariness.

Of course, it's not just your men. I suspect that you are probably a little tired too.

No wonder men wince when you ask them to do something. No wonder men plop down in front of the television to vegetate instead of read a book or have a conversation with their wives. No wonder, no wonder, no wonder. We have created a culture which requires more energy than men have to give. Sometimes we call this the rat race.

They Feel Something Isn't Right

As noted in chapter 1, *men often have a lingering feeling that something isn't quite right about their lives.* This is the second element of our psychographic profile, and it's the inevitable result of running the rat race. A woman told me she was having difficulty figuring out how to offer support to her husband. He loves his work. Occasionally, for stretches of months at a time, he will work 12-hour days. Then suddenly his mood will swing, and he will mope around for months. When she asks him what it is he wants, he cannot articulate an answer. Something isn't right about his life, but he's not sure what it is.

"I can chart these cycles on paper," she told me. "They're completely predictable. I just don't know what to do for him anymore. He is extremely successful. He has the job he always wanted. We have a beautiful home and two lovely children. What's his problem?"

It does beg the question: How can a man get exactly what he wants and still not be happy?

Their Plans Aren't Working

Third, men's lives are not turning out like they had planned. Each week, on average, four to eight new men visit the Man in the Mirror Bible study I teach here in Orlando. Our average visitor is typically friendless, overextended in most areas, has at least seen his Bathsheba, is up to his eardrums in debt, lacks meaning and purpose, feels under a lot of pressure, and is generally miserable. All of this is carefully masked behind a game face because the man knows that if the sharks smell blood, it's over.

Many of these men have made a profession of faith in Christ, but they have not been trained (discipled) to integrate their faith into their daily lives. As a result, they get caught up in the rat race—the conflict between who they are created to be and who they are tempted to be. When they lead unexamined lives, men tend to be Christian in spirit, but secular in practice. Many become cultural Christians who love this life more than the next. Let's give them some credit, though; they come to the study because they sense they need a spiritual solution.

They Feel "Unglued"

Fourth, a lot of men feel like their lives are coming unglued. The problem is not that men are failing to meet their goals. In most cases they are. The problem, it turns out—they're the wrong goals. A man in his thirties explained, "When I got out of school I made out a list of everything I thought I would need to be happy. Fifteen years later I have everything on my list. Now I realize . . . it's the wrong list."

How does a man give his best years to a system that never had any possibility of satisfying the hunger of his soul?

They Feel Nobody Cares

Fifth, most men feel like nobody, with the possible exception of family, really cares about them personally. A pastor invited one of his businessmen—a prominent one—to lunch one day. The man took the pastor to his private club. After forty-five minutes of eating and exchanging social pleasantries, they finished their meal. The man set down his napkin and said, "So tell me. What's on your mind? What can I do for you today?"

The pastor said, "Nothing, really. I just wanted to spend some time with you and get to know you better as a person."

"Well, there must be something I can do for you."

"No, not really."

"Are you sure? How are our finances?"

"No, really. I just wanted to get to know you better—man to man."

Two or three more similar exchanges took place.

The man sat there incredulous. Belief slowly crept across his face, and tears welled up in the man's eyes. He struggled to maintain control of himself. A minute went by. The man regained his composure and said, "In my entire career, no one has ever asked me to lunch unless they wanted something from me."

They're Committed to Values, Not Christ

Sixth, many men are committed to a set of Christian values but not to Christ. At lunch one day, I asked Ron to tell me about his Christian experience. He waxed eloquent about chairing a pastor relations committee and teaching Sunday school. But after ten minutes, he had still made no mention of Christ. It was clear that Ron was not giving a clear testimony of faith and repentance. I asked a follow up. No progress. Another question. Same conclusion.

Suddenly it dawned on me, *He doesn't know the Lord!* Ron was a pillar in the community and in the church—but not a believer! Then I shared my story. I told him how I had been committed to *a set of Christian values*, but not to *faith in Jesus.* When I told him that Christianity is not about having the *correct information* or even the *correct behavior* but a *correct relationship* with God through Jesus, he became visibly shaken. Through an exchange of e-mails over the next several hours he surrendered his life to Christ in faith and repentance.

They're Disappointed with God

Seventh, most men only know enough about God to be disappointed with Him. Bill made a profession of faith at an early age, but thought Christianity was just a bunch of rules that he soon concluded he could not keep. He never really took *possession* of his *profession.*

He started bluffing his way through life as though he really had it all together. Actually, he did have his own morality well within his grasp. By his late thirties "life" wasn't working, but he was trapped by the pretensions of his own bluff. One day he said, "I feel like I'm a 1,000 piece puzzle with ten pieces missing. I don't know what they are, or where to find them."

They listen to your sermons, they try to do the right things, they have it in their hearts to be faithful Christians, but they don't have much joy, and certainly lack victory over sinful habits. They feel a sense of shame. That's because—whether offered to them or not—they have not become disciples.

It's really not your fault. Men are responsible for their own actions. You do, however, hold the key to helping them get on, or back on, course.

THE GRACE OF FUTILITY

The situation is far from depressing, however. That's because the God of creation is firmly and sovereignly in control. In fact, God is sovereignly and graciously orchestrating all of the seemingly random circumstances of your men.

The feeling of futility is the chief tool by which God sovereignly draws men to Himself of their own free will. The apostle Paul explains:

> For the creation was subjected to frustration [futility], not by its own choice, but by the will of the one who subjected it, in hope that the creation itself will be liberated from its bondage to decay and brought into the glorious freedom of the children of God. (Romans 8:20–21)

In other words, God sovereignly introduces futility into the world so that men might come to their senses and be liberated and redeemed.[1] Essentially, He makes life so miserable that your men turn to Him of their own free will.

Why are many Christian men so frustrated? It is exactly because God has set eternity in men's hearts (see Ecclesiastes 3:11). They have a built-in sense that life does have meaning, and their frustration is that they have not yet found it. They don't have enough religion to make them happy when they look in the mirror, but they have enough to remind them how unhappy they have become.

Their careers aren't turning out the way they planned or, what's sometimes worse, they are. Their marriages are not working the way they're supposed to, many times their kids don't seem appreciative, and they're up to their receding hairlines in financial problems.

The result? A pervasive lack of contentment stalks them. As Thoreau wrote, "The mass of men lead lives of quiet desperation." They often find themselves frustrated, discouraged, disillusioned, confused, afraid of the future, lonely, and riddled with guilt over poor decisions. They are restless.

They are wondering, "Is this all there is? There must be more to life; there's gotta be." They find their lives are futile—not because they didn't get what they wanted, but because they did. They have met their goals and wonder, "So what?"

Perfect. Don't you wish all your men would be so humble and curious?

AN IRONIC REALITY

Of course, there are other types of men in your church. Some are doing great—they're full-fledged disciples and leaders. Others are trapped in destructive cycles. But if you focus on loving and discipling your men as described in this chapter, you will always have more than enough to do.

When a man fails, he sets powerful forces of bondage and brokenness in motion. It can take several generations to break the cycle. As America staggers beneath the load of dozens of major problems—like divorce, fatherlessness, poverty, pornography, adultery, abortion, abuse, disrespect for authority, ethical failures, and truancy to name a few—where have the men gone? What has happened to our men? At the root of virtually every problem is the failure of a man, ironically a man who got up this morning wishing that his life would make a difference.

These are not bad men. They are, for the most part, men with good intentions. Sinful, yes, but men for whom Christ died. He takes no delight in the death of the wicked. Yet they lack spiritual power. In the next chapter, we will develop a summary of what men want from life.

POINTS TO REMEMBER

- The similarities of men dwarf their differences.
- No man fails on purpose.
- Men are tired.
- Men often have a lingering feeling something isn't quite right about their lives.
- Men's lives are not turning out like they had planned.
- A lot of men feel like their lives are coming unglued.
- Most men feel like nobody, with the possible exception of family, really cares about them personally.
- Many men are committed to a set of Christian values, but not to the person of Christ.
- Most men only know enough about God to be disappointed with Him.
- As a result, their lives feel futile.
- The feeling of futility is the chief tool by which God sovereignly draws men to Himself of their own free will.
- God is sovereignly and graciously orchestrating all of the seemingly random circumstances of your men.

WHAT DO MEN WANT?

We have a saying around our office: "Give men what they *need* in the context of what they *want*." Men do what they want. Our task is to figure out what that is, then show them how the gospel meets their desire.

In this chapter we'll look at what men want, and in the next chapter, what keeps them from getting what they want.

So what do men want? When I was younger, I had a long list. Over the years I've whittled my list down to three things. I realize that all taxonomies are imperfect summaries, yet when men find *their cause, their companion,* and *their God,* everything else generally falls into line. What men want can be summarized into three categories:

1. *A cause* we can give our lives to that will make a difference—a mission, significance, meaning, purpose
2. *A companion* to share it with—relationships, love, wife, family, friends, acceptance
3. *A conviction* that gives a reasonable explanation for why numbers 1 and 2 are so difficult—a belief system, worldview, philosophy, religion

This is the essence of manhood—finding *something* we can give ourselves to, *someone* to share it with, and a *system* that explains how to make sense of our lives. These three form the contours of a man's identity and purpose.

Of course, when men find the wrong cause, the wrong woman, or the wrong god, everything falls apart, though slowly and rarely detected until the damage has been done.

Notice that we are not yet talking about what men *need*, just what they *want*. Nevertheless, these are God-given desires. That makes them holy, though many men, of course, corrupt them along the way, which is why you and I have a vocation in ministry. An important part of your "pastoring men" skill set is to have a good handle on what men want. Let's delve deeper.

1. A *CAUSE*—SOMETHING WE CAN GIVE OUR LIVES TO

First, men want *something* they can give themselves to that will make a difference. Pounding in the breast of every man is an intense desire to lead a significant life. A man's greatest felt need is his need to be significant—to find meaning and purpose in life, to make a contribution, to discover what he was created by God to do.

Bill, an executive in a major company, was hired because of his accomplishments and extraordinary gifts. Yet, rather than helping him celebrate his gifts, his employer increasingly assigns him projects far outside his interests and competencies. This creates deep frustration and confusion.

Ron, on the other hand, hasn't held a position that fits his gifting for several years. After spending twelve satisfying years with the same company, he has held four different positions in the last six years. He earns less today than he did ten years ago. Understandably, his self-worth and dignity are at a low point. He feels like a failure.

These men are not alone. Many men today are groping for a deeper sense of worth and contribution. They long for a calling that can satisfy their deep desire for value and meaning.

Besides the obvious differences in anatomy, a man has different instincts than a woman. By nature men are drawn to gather, hunt, explore, adventure, and conquer—we want to give ourselves to a mission. Why do young men dream about becoming explorers, discoverers, adventurers, warriors, and knights? It is because we each have been created by God to spend ourselves in a worthy cause.

A man even told me once, "Under certain circumstances I would be willing to die for you." Where does that come from? There is a noble impulse to manhood inside each of us.

Men are made for the task. It is our starting place, our most innate need, and the underlying motivator of our behavior. A man on an important mission is a happy man. It is what brings us joy, pleasure, peace, and contentment. How many times have you said, felt, or heard a man say:

- "I want my life to count—to make a difference!"
- "I need to feel like my life is going somewhere—that I have a direction."
- "I believe that I was created for a purpose."
- "I want to do something worthwhile with my life."
- "I want my life to matter. I need a mission. I need a cause into which I can invest myself."
- "I want to invest in the lives of people around me."
- "I want it to mean something that I have walked the face of the planet."
- "I don't want to be a shooting star that streaks across the sky one night— then disappears."

This compelling desire animates not just great explorers, missionaries, and top managers but all men. And not just the "great" men. Michael Novak, in *Business As a Calling*, says,

> Being a middle manager is not primarily a way station on the way to the top. ... Middle management, many know early, is their calling. They want to be super good at it. They want to make a contribution. Most of all, they need to know in their own minds that they have done so.[1]

Whether he is a middle manager or a heating and cooling technician, every man has an inbred, intuitive sense that he is created to make a difference. As men, we are not frustrated because we think significance cannot be found. Rather, we are sure it can be found, and our frustration is that we have not yet taken hold of it.

Viktor Frankl, survivor of four Nazi concentration camps, tells the story of a diplomat who began psychiatric therapy because he was unhappy in his work. The psychiatrist repeatedly urged the diplomat to reconcile his relationship with his father. Yet after five years he was more unhappy than ever. He went to see Frankl.

After a few meetings, it was clear that this man's desire for meaning was frustrated by his vocation. He yearned to engage in some other line of work. At Frankl's urging he changed jobs and became quite content.[2]

Frankl's point: In most cases of unhappiness we need only assist a man (or woman) to find meaning in his life. As Frankl says, "Man's search for meaning is the primary motivation in his life."[3]

A man will feel most alive, most useful, and most significant when he is doing what he was created to do. How happy would a lion be if he couldn't roar? How happy would an eagle be if he couldn't fly? How happy would a porpoise be if he couldn't swim?

WHAT YOU CAN DO | *Help Men Find Their Cause*

Pastors, this is a lay-up. If we simply and concretely show men how they can find purpose and meaning in the gospel, most will respond. Men love a challenge. Use these ideas to incite your men:

- Tell them, "Until you find a cause worth dying for, you will not have a cause worth living for."

- Tell them, "I would rather die for a worthy cause than live for no reason."

- Quote President Woodrow Wilson, who said, "I would rather fail in a cause that will ultimately succeed than succeed in a cause that will ultimately fail."

- Quote Dwight L. Moody, who one day heard, "The world has yet to see what God will do with, and for, and through, and in, and by the man who is fully and wholly consecrated to him." Moody thought to himself, "He said a man. He did not say a great man, nor a learned man, nor a rich man, nor a wise man, nor an eloquent man, nor a smart man, but simply 'a man.' I am a man, and it lies with the man himself whether he will, or will not, make that entire and full consecration. I will try my utmost to be that man."[4]

- You don't have to say it will be easy. Writer Bruce Barton noted that Jesus called forth men's greatest efforts not by a promise of great rewards, but great obstacles.

- Read more under the related topics "Purpose and Meaning," "Cultural Mandate," and "Work" in chapter 11.

A man doing what he was created to do will be a happy man. The apostle Paul tells us that we were created in Christ to do good works (Ephesians 2:10). Jesus says, "This is to my father's glory, that you bear much fruit" (John 15:8).

2. A *COMPANION*—SOMEONE TO SHARE LIFE WITH

Second, men want *someone* to share this with. This is the need for relationships, love, family, community, and acceptance.

Most men mainly look for this in a woman with whom they can share their lives. "The Lord God said, 'It is not good for the man to be alone. I will make a helper suitable for him'" (Genesis 2:18). Marriage is the mysterious, mystical fusion of two separate lives headed in two separate directions into what the Bible intriguingly calls "one flesh." Marriage is the highest order of human relationship, and there isn't a close second. Even children phase in and out of our lives.

It's no secret that men are more task-oriented and women are more relationship-oriented. Anyone who ever attended a Labor Day picnic knows this. The men huddle up to exaggerate about football and cars, while the women gather to swap stories about their children.

I realize these are stereotypes, but stereotypes work because they are generally true. For example, in the following pairings, which would you most likely assign to a man and which to a woman?

- Head and heart
- Logic and feeling
- Task and relationship
- Provider and nurturer

You probably picked *head, logic, task,* and *provider* as the "man" words. Even so, men are also relationship-oriented, if not mainly. And some men thrive on relationships. Even the most hardened taskmaster will be a lonely fool if he has nobody with whom to share his joys and sorrows.

That's why in the great movies, the hero always repairs to his love interest so she can share in his victory or console his defeat. A man goes out and hunts his bear, but then brings it home to get approval from his wife. Oswald Chambers put it like this: "The last sign of intimacy is to share secret joys."

On a scuba diving trip with my son and friends, we all felt that our grouchy divemaster was at the least disinterested in us and probably despised us for reasons unknown. Later, I struck up a conversation with him. He told me that three days earlier the woman he lived with for six years had found out he was cheating on her and thrown him out. They had essentially lived as a married couple, and this was tantamount to a divorce. At six feet two with bulging biceps he looked mean as a snake, yet he was reduced to putty over the woman he had betrayed.

We talked about the pain of hurting someone we love. Then he said, "Basically, I'm an [expletive for a centrally located bodily orifice]." He was in as much pain as any man I can remember. He had lost his "someone." However, since he had no faith foundation, he was stymied about what to do next.

Then he said something that is enough to drive a man to Christ. He said, "My life doesn't make any sense right now." By losing his "someone to share it with," he had lost part of his reason for living. We talked about grace, forgiveness, and God.

WHAT YOU CAN DO | *Help Men Value a Companion*

• Tell your men: The party will be over soon. There will only be two rocking chairs sitting side by side. Doesn't it make sense to invest today in the woman who will be sitting next to you then?

• Teach your men: No amount of success at work will ever be adequate to compensate for failure at home.

• Disciple your men to prove their love by the way they spend their time. Relationships create responsibilities, and the chief responsibility of relationships is time. Challenge your men to give time to whom time is due.

• Find additional concepts under "Marriage," "Friendships," and "Love People" in the topical summaries in Chapter 11.

3. A *CONVICTION*—A SYSTEM THAT EXPLAINS WHY LIFE IS SO DIFFICULT

Third, men want a *conviction*—a belief in a system that gives a reasonable explanation for why numbers 1 and 2 are so difficult.

A man visited our Bible study and told me, "I have achieved everything I wanted—a luxury home, a beautiful wife, perfect kids, a high-powered job, and lots of money. Not long ago I deposited a $100,000 check into my account. That evening, my wife and I had a drink to celebrate, but I was downcast. She said, 'What do you want?' I had to tell her, 'I don't know.'"

Another man seemed to have it all together: professing Christian, great career, and a lovely wife who was three months pregnant. He chucked the whole thing and left her.

Even if we have a crystal-clear calling and the world's most perfect mate, it's hard. We must do our work while feeling the prick of thorns. This raises questions like the following:

- Why is life so hard?
- Will my life make a difference?
- How can I find peace in my relationships?
- If there is a God, does he know what I'm going through? (the issue of His omniscience)
- If he knows, does he care? (the issue of His omni-benevolence)
- If He cares, can he do anything about? (the issue of His omnipotence)
- What happens when I die?

These are the kinds of questions addressed by all belief systems, philosophies, worldviews, and religions. Christianity and secularism are not trying to solve different problems. They are trying to solve the same problems in different ways.

Christianity is a system (a belief system) that perfectly explains why life is so hard, and what to do about it. The problem, however, is that every other system (philosophy, worldview, religion) also promises the same thing. And the good ones actually work—sometimes for as long as forty years. But all systems other than Christianity eventually fail, frequently at the worst possible moment, and often after you have given that system the best years of your life.

All belief systems other than Christianity are counterfeits. All systems other than Christianity rest on foundations that are not true. Then how do these false systems remain in existence? That's because all systems have traces of truth—or they would never make it into circulation in the first place. As a philosophy professor of mine is fond of saying, "It takes a lot of truth to float an error."

Christianity is the only system that is all true all the time. Fortunately, the Bible doesn't describe a utopian world free of pain. That would make Christianity a wishful farce. Instead, the Bible describes the world exactly as we see it—a fallen world, but not without what Francis Schaeffer called "leftover beauty." The Bible describes a world groaning in pain that needs a Redeemer, Sanctifier, and Sustainer.

More importantly, the Bible describes how a man can rise above futility, sin, and despair and find peace, hope, and victory by surrendering his life to the lordship of Jesus Christ. The irony of surrender is that it leads not to defeat but victory.

WHAT YOU CAN DO | *Help Men Embrace Their Christian Conviction*

• Exhort your men not to give the best years of their lives to a lie. And accept that advice yourself by living a surrendered life.

• Find and reflect on the following additional concepts in the alphabetized topical summaries (chapter 11): "Worldview, Christian," "The Fall," "Cultural Christianity," "Success Sickness," and "Unexamined Life."

SO WHAT DO THESE THREE WANTS
LOOK LIKE FROM DAY TO DAY?

Every man seeks the same ultimate thing. He may call it by many names: *happiness, success, contentment, fulfillment, pleasure, delight, love, peace, significance, purpose,* or *meaning.* Those words are all "placeholders" to describe a single overarching concept. He wants to experience joy in his life.

The question is: How does this pleasure, this fulfillment, this joy come to a man? What does he measure? How does he keep score? For most men and all non-Christians, I believe this list of priorities captures most of what men want day to day:

1. To have a successful and satisfying *career*
2. To make enough *money* to be financially independent
3. To own a beautiful *home*
4. To have a good *wife*
5. To raise a happy *family*
6. To have an absorbing *sport* or *hobby*
7. To worship a *God* who gives them what they want

So he arrives home and asks her, "How was your day?"

She responds, "Good. How was your day?"

If today's progress equaled or exceeded what he wanted from these priorities, he answers, "Good."

Is it sinful to want career success, more money, to live in a nicer home, to drive a nice car, have a diversion you love, or to be able to take a nice vacation?

No, of course not—at least not necessarily—and these are good things to have. I know that I want them! But they are "second things." Unless a man is discipled to want what he needs (as discussed in chapter 5), he will settle for lesser things—mere *wants*, futilities that God has ordained to disappoint. As C. S. Lewis put it, "You can't get second things by putting them first; you can get second things only by putting first things first."[5]

When he finally gets sick of answering, "Not so good"—that's when he will "want" to reexamine his conviction. That's when he will be interested in what he needs.

WHAT DO MEN WANT WHEN THEY COME TO CHURCH?

When a man finally comes to church, why does he come? Of course, there are many reasons (e.g., moral and religious instruction for children, spiritual vacuum, desire to find God). Whatever his reasons, it is good that he wants to come!

One thing we can be pretty sure about: when a man comes to church, he wants to find rest for his soul. Running after those priorities would wear any of us down! If I was pastoring a church, I would hoist a sign over the entrance to our sanctuary that said:

To all who are weary and burdened, come and find rest.

I would keep the sanctuary a sanctuary.

Unfortunately, because there is so much to do, a lot of our churches emit the impression to men that Jesus said, "Come to me, all you who are weary and burdened, *and I will give you more work to do.*"

Of course, what Jesus actually said was, "Come to me, all you who are weary and burdened, *and I will give you rest.* Take my yoke upon you and learn from me, for I am gentle and humble in heart, and you will find rest for your souls" (Matthew 11:28–29). Work is part of discipleship, but it is the last part. To have a man succeed in the work of the church but fail in his family is tragic. Let's be careful not to "send" men to work before we have "equipped" them to be godly men, husbands, and fathers.

THE PASTOR'S TASK

In the movie *Black Hawk Down* a soldier said to his superior, "You really believe in this mission down to your very bones, don't you Sergeant?"

The sergeant replied, "These people have no jobs, no food, no education, no future. I figure we have two things we can do: We can help, or we can sit back and watch the country destroy itself on CNN. I was trained to fight, how about you? I was trained to make a difference."

Training is a big deal. Twenty-five percent of Secret Service duty is training—their credo: "Repetitive training to overcome the negatives of self-sacrifice." For lack of training, a lot of men have not been able to make a difference—and they have settled for second things.

You are the key to training (discipling) men.

WHAT YOU CAN DO | *Help Men Become Disciples*

• Train/disciple your men to understand how what they want fits into the larger picture of what God is doing in the world. Tell them: It is true that the Christian life is a broad road of happiness, joy, peace, blessing, success, significance, and contentment. Ironically, however, it is gained by choosing the narrow road of surrender, obedience, self-denial, self-sacrifice, truth, worship, and service.

• Give men what they need in the context of what they want.

Knowing what men want is a key component of the pastoring-men skill set. In the next chapter, let's explore what keeps men from getting what they want.

POINTS TO REMEMBER

• All men want to be happy. They find happiness by finding three things:
   1. A *cause* we can give our lives to that will make a difference—a mission, significance, meaning, purpose

2. A *companion* to share it with—relationships, love, family, acceptance

3. A *conviction* that gives a reasonable explanation for why numbers 1 and 2 are so difficult—a belief system, worldview, philosophy, religion

- On a day-to-day basis, these are the priorities for most men and all non-Christians:

    1. To have a successful and satisfying *career*

    2. To make enough *money* to be financially independent

    3. To own a beautiful *home*

    4. To have a good *wife*

    5. To raise a happy *family*

    6. To have an absorbing *sport* or *hobby*

    7. To worship a *God* who gives them what they want

- When men come to church, we need to give them what they need, but in the context of what they want

WHAT KEEPS MEN FROM GETTING WHAT THEY WANT?

No man fails on purpose. Yet many men find it difficult to be a husband and father, find job contentment, keep themselves morally straight, and lead balanced lives. This chapter will give you a greater understanding of the challenges and opportunities that keep your men from getting what they want—their cause, companion, and conviction.

So what keeps men from getting what they want?

LIES: OUR NATIVE TONGUE

It begins with a lie—many lies, actually. There are two languages in the world: *truth* and *lies.* The first language—the native tongue of every man—is the language of lies. When the father of lies ruled our lives, "lies" was the only language we knew (John 8:43–44). Before I became a Christian, I would often lie even if the truth could have served me better. It was my native tongue—a language that flowed freely from my lower nature.

When you and I received Christ, we became bilingual. We learned a second language—the language of truth.

But what happens to anyone who doesn't regularly practice speaking their second language? They revert to their native tongue.

If we do not abide in Christ day by day, if we do not regularly practice our second language, we will revert to our native tongue. You know this is true because you know self-deceived Christians who regularly lie to you—and not about little things.

How do men fall back into their native language? Every morning your men go into a world where all day long they are tempted to exchange the truth of God for a lie (Romans 1:25).

All men either live by the truth or a good lie. This is another way of discussing the belief systems mentioned in the last chapter.

No individual, Christian or otherwise, will choose to live by an obvious lie. Which counterfeit dollar bill is most likely to make it into circulation? Isn't it the one that looks the most like the real thing? In the same way, the only lies that make it into circulation are ones that appear to be true. A good lie is probably only one or two degrees off course. Otherwise it would be rejected. The popular prosperity gospel is one example.

What does a good lie look like? A good lie can take many forms. For example, good lies about happiness might tell a man that to be happy he needs to . . .

- Make this much money
- Get that promotion
- Drive a certain car
- Have an hour a day for myself
- Achieve a certain desire or goal
- Lust after that woman
- Have my wife act differently
- Have my children behave better
- Have investments do well
- Be able to eat what I want
- Have a ministry that gives me strokes

THE BIG LIE

Do men really "need" these things to be happy? Each of these statements boils down to this core lie: "Jesus is not enough to make me happy." Using all the media at his disposal—thousands of cell towers, TV antennae and satellites, newspapers, and even friends—the great deceiver Satan wants men to believe that God isn't capable of giving men true joy and contentment. This is the Big Lie.

As a pastor, it's good to remember that for every truth you tell your men, they are hearing hundreds of lies—many of them good lies—throughout the week.

WHAT YOU CAN DO | *About the Big Lie*

• Explain to your men that there are two languages in the world: truth and lies.

• Explain that all men either live by the truth or a good lie.

• Explain that it's not that easy to discern the difference between the truth and a really good lie. Expose or correct the prevailing "good" lies that sound very close to the truth.

• Some of your men are living by a good lie. They need to see how they have believed a false gospel.

• Some of your men are monolingual. They still only speak one language—lies. Regularly present those men with the gospel of truth.

• Some of your bilingual men have reverted to their native tongue. They need to be challenged.

• For your solid Christian men, remind them how we all must renew ourselves daily and abide in the truth of the gospel of our Lord and Savior Jesus Christ through faith and repentance.

• Explain to your men that a "good" lie will work—for as many as forty years. But a lie is still a lie, and eventually it will betray them, and usually at the worst possible moment.

IDOLS AND THE BIG LIE

Idols also keep men from getting what they want. I race a vintage Porsche and have used racing as a platform to build relationships with men and share my faith. One day a man who never misses a chance to race asked me quite seriously, "When does my passion for racing become an idol?" Good question.

All idolatry is rooted in *unbelief*. This unbelief can take many forms, but at its root is the powerful lie, "Jesus Christ alone is not enough to make me happy.

I need something else." An idol is something we worship. The issue is making anything besides the Trinity the object of our worship. It is looking to anything except Jesus Christ for identity, meaning, and ultimate purpose. An idol is anything that becomes an object of inordinate affection. An idol is anything of which we say, "I *must* have this to be happy."

John Calvin said that men are "idol factories." Perhaps nothing interferes with a man's faith more than the root problem of making idols—it's the "next step" after believing the Big Lie. The average American Christian male has made an idol of something that competes with his full surrender to the lordship of Christ. Men can make idols of almost anything, but common examples today include these:

- Money
- Titles and positions (especially if the job doesn't generate a large income)
- Homes (i.e., attaching personal worth and identity to a dwelling)
- Country club memberships (i.e., being part of the "right" crowd)
- Ministry titles (e.g., elder, deacon)
- Relationships (e.g., idolizing a wife)
- Affiliations with important people
- Cars, boats, planes, motorcycles
- Their bodies (i.e., physical appearance)
- Superior intelligence
- Their own righteousness
- The praise of men (what C.S. Lewis called "to win worship"[1])

As you can readily see, all these affections are horizontal, focused on people, things, and ourselves. All such friendship with the world is spiritual adultery (James 4:4).

Idols make promises they cannot keep, which is why you can be on a winning streak and still feel empty.

WHAT YOU CAN DO | *About Idols*

- Most men don't really understand the definition of an idol. Periodically define "idols" and give appropriate examples.

• Remind your men that we are "idol factories."

• Challenge your men to consider how they can make even their own spirituality into an idol—like a church position or exceptionally righteous behavior.

SUCCESS SICKNESS

Biblically speaking, three things keep men from getting what they want: the world, the flesh, and the devil. In practice, lies and idols infect many men with a disease we will call "success sickness."

Trent (not his real name) rose rapidly to become the youngest K-Mart manager in the history of the company. They sent him to troubleshoot a store that was losing $1,000,000 per year.

Trent supervised the renovation of the store, then orchestrated a turnaround from losing $1,000,000 a year to making $1,000,000 a year. He said, "I was part of that. When it was all over, I would get to work at the usual time, about 6:00 a.m., sit in the parking lot, look at the store all lit up, and ask myself, 'Why am I so miserable?'"

To not get what you want can be painful. Perhaps more painful, though, as Trent discovered, is to get what you want and still not be happy. Of course, a lot of men don't reach their goals. Many more men, however, do achieve their goals only to find out that success—at least success the way they had defined it—doesn't satisfy. What's that all about?

All men want to be successful in what they do. That's normal and healthy. However, many men get carried away with their idols and end up contracting a bad case of "success sickness."

Success sickness is the disease of always wanting more, but never being happy when you get it. We are the nation that weeps if we only win a silver medal. Success sickness is the intangible pain of not achieving goals that should have never been set or, like Trent, achieving them only to find they didn't really matter.

The greatest problem we see in our work at Man in the Mirror is not that men are failing to achieve their goals. In most cases, they are achieving them. The problem is, they are the wrong goals. Many men get what they want only to find it doesn't matter. We all know that failure means to not get what you want. However, we could also say failure means to succeed in a way that doesn't really matter.

The unhappy result of believing the "success will make you happy" lie is that many men today are struggling with problems that success can't solve. What William James profanely called the "bitch goddess of success" does not satisfy them. As Michael Novak pointed out, "The aftertaste of affluence is boredom." [2]

Regrettably, many men don't learn this lesson until they've given it ten, twenty, or more years—often the best years of their lives. What a strategic opportunity to pastor men about success sickness and success that matters.

WHAT YOU CAN DO | *About Success Sickness*

• Explain how lies and idols lead to success sickness.

• Challenge your men to consider to what extent they have this disease.

Now let's discuss three symptoms of "success sickness."

SYMPTOMS OF SUCCESS SICKNESS

The Rat Race

The first symptom of success sickness is the rat race. Picture men, lots of men, men under pressure, zooming down the fast lanes of life, straining to keep pace. Some are oblivious to what they're doing. Some are starting to wonder about it. Others are weary. Still others have "hit the wall."

What is the rat race? The rat race is the conflict between who man is *created* to be and who he is *tempted* to be. It is the endless pursuit of an ever increasing prosperity that ends in frustration rather than contentment.

Francis Schaeffer, noted cultural commentator of the twentieth century, explained that most American adults have adopted two impoverished values: *personal peace*, not wanting to be bothered with the troubles of others, and *affluence*, a life made up of things, things, and more things.[3] A friend sheepishly told me that he has a weakness for golf clubs. He has ten expensive drivers in his closet. Ironically, it's the old beat-up one that's his favorite.

In our work with men we regularly meet men who have "prayed a prayer" for salvation, but for the last five, ten, fifteen, or more years they have been living by their own ideas. They have built on the foundation of their own best thinking. They read the Bible for comfort, but the *Wall Street Journal* for direction. They seek personal prosperity, often at the expense of family.

The result is that many men have been knocked off balance. Pursuing their career goals, they neglect their wives emotionally, and slowly, the two of them grow apart. Taking a cue from dad, their kids often run in their own mini-rat races, and dads sometimes feel left out and unappreciated. Twenty years later it slowly dawns on these men that they gave their best years to careers that promised what they couldn't deliver. In fact, a man will often feel "dumped on" and "used" in his career, a festering bitterness that only further infects the other areas of his life.

Eventually, they begin to ask the painful questions: "What's it all about? How can I be so successful and so unfulfilled at the same time? Is this all there is?" The rat race charges an expensive toll. It will take everything your men have to give.

So how do men get caught up in the rat race? Galatians 5:7 asks the question this way: "You were running a good race. Who cut in on you and kept you from obeying the truth?" Paul teaches the answer two verses later: "A little yeast works through the whole batch of dough" (verse 9). That "yeast" is the man's lie of choice.

WHAT YOU CAN DO | *About Men Running in the Rat Race*

• From time to time, draw men's attention to the difference between the rat race and God's race.

• Find additional concepts under "Rat Race" in the alphabetized reference section in chapter 11.

The Unexamined Life

The second symptom of success sickness is leading an unexamined life. Evan was the national sales manager for his company. One day he traveled to Texas to spend a day making calls with one of his salesmen. At the end of the day that salesman, Steve, walked Evan into the airport to catch his plane back to the Midwest.

As they parted, Steve said, "Evan, you're amazing the way you sell our product. You're brilliant. But as smart as you are, you baffle me. You don't have a clue about where you came from, you don't have a clue about where you're going, and you don't have a clue about your purpose in life."

With that, Steve turned and walked away. For months and months Evan kept hearing Steve's searing comments over and over.

Many people had prayed for Evan's spiritual salvation over the years. In February of the following year, Evan was invited to an evangelistic event where he gave his life to Jesus Christ. In April he had a heart attack at the age of forty-four, and faced bypass surgery.

The night before the surgery, he took his wife out to dinner. Evan told her how he had an incredible peace and calm. His wife, Tracie, on the other hand, was a basket case. Tracie held a PhD in education and worked at the local university.

Evan took her hand and said words that echoed those he had heard a year earlier. "Tracie, you're amazing when it comes to education. You're brilliant. But as smart as you are, you baffle me. You don't have a clue about where you came from, you don't have a clue about where you are going, and you don't have a clue about your purpose in life."

Tracie stared out the window.

Evan had learned from Steve and others. He realized that men face no greater temptation than the tendency to lead unexamined lives. He had learned that to lead an unexamined life means to rush from task to busy task without taking time-outs to reflect on life's larger meaning and purpose.

Such a pace robs men—and women too—of purpose. The price of pace is peace.

I love technology. Technology is a friend, but this friend also has a dark side. As a man increases his labor-saving devices, he also increases his workload and the access other people have to him. The drone of these devices often leaves a man with no place to sit and simply think.

Socrates said, "Know thyself," and Plato wrote, "The unexamined life is not worth living." When men choose to run the gauntlet of the rat race, they barter away their times of reflection and self-examination.

Most men have not carefully chiseled their worldview by a personal search for truth and obedience to God and his Word. Rather, they are drifting. They are not thinking deeply about their lives. Buffeted by the whipping winds of daily pressure and tossed about by surging waves of change, men long for the sure-footed sands of simpler days. They have scarcely a clue of how to reach such a place.

Lamentations 3:40 exhorts, "Let us examine our ways and test them, and let us return to the Lord." Only on the anvil of self-examination can God shape a man into the image of His Son. "Teach us to number our days aright, that we may gain a heart of wisdom" (Psalm 90:12).

Pastoring men is all about holding up a mirror in front of men so they can examine their lives.

WHAT YOU CAN DO | *About the Unexamined Life*

• Lead your men into self-examination through your sermons.

• Teach your men to periodically call "time-outs" for personal reflection and self-examination.

• Find additional concepts under "Unexamined Life" in the alphabetized reference section in chapter 11.

The Cultural Christian

We are discussing how success sickness keeps men from getting what they want. The third symptom of success sickness is cultural Christianity. Many men who are seeking material success have become cultural Christians. Years ago, as a businessman who wanted to be a disciple, I vacillated between two sets of heroes. On one hand, I was inspired by great businessmen who lived for God—the likes of Walt Meloon, who built Correct Craft into the world's premier brand of ski and wakeboarding boats.[4] I also wanted to emulate heroes of the faith like C. S. Lewis, Jim Dobson, Tom Skinner, and Bill Bright. On the other hand, I secretly aspired to the accomplishments and fortunes of business barons like Trammel Crow, Warren Buffet, Bill Gates, and Malcolm Forbes. I was torn between becoming a disciple of Wall Street or Church Street.

When I hit the ten-year mark in my spiritual journey I realized something was desperately wrong with my life, but I couldn't put my finger on any one problem. I was an active Christian, reading my Bible and praying regularly, immersed in church life, a vocal witness, and pursuing a moral lifestyle.

Curiously, I was sitting at the top of my career. Materially, I was taken care of wonderfully. Yet, when I would imagine another man thinking how I was blessed, I would want to grab him by the arms, shake him, and scream, "You don't understand! This isn't a blessing; it's a curse!"

Finally the intangible pain became so strong that I called a "time-out" for reflection and self-examination—which I thought would last a couple of weeks. I spent the next two and a half years staring at my navel.

At first all I could grasp were the thoughts described in chapter 2, "How Are Men Doing?"

- I was tired.
- I had a lingering feeling something wasn't quite right about my life.
- My life wasn't turning out the way I had planned.
- I felt like my life was coming unglued.
- I didn't feel like anyone really cared about me, personally.
- I was achieving my goals, but success didn't satisfy.

A couple of years later during a major business crisis, a thought went through my mind as I was sitting in the rubble of my collapsing empire: *There is a God we want and there is a God who is. They are not the same God. The turning point of our lives is when we stop seeking the God we want and start seeking the God who is.*

I realized I had become what we might call a *cultural* Christian. In *The Man in the Mirror* I defined the term *cultural Christianity*—the mind-set of every cultural Christian—this way:

Cultural Christianity means to seek the God we want instead of the God who is. It is the tendency to be shallow in our understanding of God, wanting Him to be more of a gentle grandfather type who spoils us and lets us have our own way. It is sensing a need for God, but on our own terms. It is wanting the God we have underlined in our Bibles without wanting the rest of Him, too. It is God relative instead of God absolute.[5]

When is a man a cultural Christian? Men become cultural Christians when they seek the God (or gods) they want, and not the God who is.

Men who are cultural Christians read their Bibles with an agenda, if they read them at all. They decide in advance what they want, and then read their Bibles looking for evidence to support the decisions they have already made. In short, they follow the God they are underlining in their Bibles, which is like making a "fifth" gospel.

In many ways they have merely added Jesus to their lives as another interest in an already crowded schedule. They practice a kind of "Spare Tire Christianity." They keep Jesus in the trunk just in case they have a flat.

They have made a plan for their lives. Their credo is, "Plan, then pray." Their lives are shaped more by following the herds of commerce than the footsteps of Christ.

Biblically, these men have let the worries of this life and the deceitfulness of money choke the word and make it unfruitful (Matthew 13:22), have let the yeast of culture work through the whole batch of dough (Galatians 5:9), and are high risk for a great crash because they built on sand and not on the rock (Matthew 7:24–27).

They want to have their cake and eat it, too. The technical term for this is *syncretism*, "the blending or attempt to combine differing philosophical or religious beliefs."

"Success sickness" is based upon a lie, and it is killing us. No wonder so many men feel what Søren Kierkegaard called "the sickness unto death."

I once read of a survey from the Billy Graham Evangelistic Association that 90 percent of all Christians lead defeated lives. "Defeated" is a great way to describe a man who has one or more of these three success sickness symptoms—the rat race, the unexamined life, or living as a cultural Christian. If we are not careful, it can be a terminal illness.

WHAT YOU CAN DO | *About Cultural Christians*

• Teach your men the difference between a cultural Christian and a biblical Christian. Use Matthew 13:22 to describe the cultural Christian and Matthew 13:23 to describe the biblical Christian.

• Find additional concepts under "Cultural Christianity" in the alphabetized reference section of this book.

HOW GOD DEALS WITH MEN WHO MAKE IDOLS

Earlier I said that, biblically speaking, three things—three temptations—keep men from getting what they want: the world, the flesh, and the Devil. That is completely true, but it is also true that God Himself keeps men from being satisfied with what they get from their vain pursuits. When men pursue idols, He will not let that stand. Here's the equation:

Men make idols + God hates idols = We've got a problem

God will not force us to revere Him, but He will make it impossible for us to be happy unless we do.

Here are three ways God will "deal" with us as men when we make an idol:

1. *He will withhold the thing we think we can't live without.* I spent the first fifteen years of my adult life working and praying to achieve something that would have destroyed me, then was disappointed when I was spared. It is a mercy to not receive that which will destroy you. "When you ask, you do not receive, because you ask with wrong motives, that you may spend what you get on your pleasures" (James 4:3).

2. *He will remove the thing we think we can't live without.* There is another name besides "idol" for something we think we can't live without—*addiction.* The problem with addictions is that we can't stop on our own. That's why God has to "help" us. Contractions, whether business or personal, often reflect God's loving discipline. He removes the shakable kingdom so the unshakable kingdom may remain: "The words 'once more' indicate the removing of what can be shaken—that is, created things—so that what cannot be shaken may remain" (Hebrews 12:27).

3. *He will give us so much of the thing we want that we gag on it.* Think of the Israelites who got tired of manna and asked for meat. God said, "Meat? You want meat? I'll give you meat." Numbers 11:19 (NLT) says, "You will eat it for a whole month until you gag and are sick of it. For you have rejected the Lord." Sometimes God wins our complete allegiance by showing us the emptiness of any other allegiance.

Nevertheless, God still tends to under-discipline, not over-discipline. "The Lord is compassionate and gracious, slow to anger, abounding in love. He will not always accuse, nor will he harbor his anger forever; *he does not treat us as our sins deserve* or repay us according to our iniquities" (Psalm 103:8–10, italics added).

WHAT YOU CAN DO | *With Men Who Make Idols*

• Think of a few of your men who are struggling. How can this model help you understand what God may be doing in their lives?

• How can this taxonomy help you pastor your men more effectively?

• Teach all your men the three ways God deals with us when we make idols.

IT'S ABOUT SURRENDER

Once a man told "Jack," a friend of mine, "I could never become a Christian because I could never give up beer and cigarettes."

"Oh, I drink all the beer and smoke all the cigarettes I want," Jack quickly replied.

"You do?" the man asked. That eventually led to a meaningful presentation of the gospel. Actually, Jack didn't drink any beer or smoke any cigarettes. Jack told the guy that although he could have all he wanted, he didn't want any. That's because Jack had lost his taste for them. God had changed the desires of his heart.

A man will never fully get what he wants until he fully surrenders to the lordship of Christ. Ironically, when he does surrender, God changes the desires of his heart to want what God wants.

POINTS TO REMEMBER

• There are two languages in the world: truth and lies.
• All men either live by the truth or a good lie.
• A "good" lie will work—for as many as forty years. But a lie is still a lie, and eventually it will betray a man, and usually at the worst possible moment.
• Men are "idol factories."
• All idolatry is rooted in *unbelief.*
• Success sickness is the disease of always wanting more, but never being happy when you get it.
• Failure means to succeed in a way that doesn't matter.

- Three symptoms of success sickness are that men (1) get caught up in the rat race; (2) lead unexamined lives; and (30) become cultural rather than biblical Christians.
- God deals three ways with men who make idols: (1) He *withholds* something the man thinks he cannot live without; (2) He *removes* something the man thinks he cannot live without; or (3) He *gives* the man so much of what he wants that he "gags" on it.
- A man will never fully get what he wants until he fully surrenders to the lordship of Christ.

REACH YOUR MEN

5

WHAT DO MEN NEED?

Once upon a time there was a manufacturing plant that produced an equal number of trousers and dresses. The plant prospered—three shifts ran around the clock. Nearly everyone in town worked there and, of course, wore trousers and dresses.

THE PARABLE CONTINUES . . .

It remained that way for generations. But about fifty years later, when some of the grandchildren had grown up, they became bored with factory work, especially the ones who wore trousers. They felt most of the trousers—and many of the dresses—manufactured at the plant were out of style *These clothes just aren't relevant to the times*, they thought. So they left to search for a better life.

With fewer people in town, the demand for trousers and dresses began to decline, especially for trousers; in fact the plant was producing only half as many trousers as dresses.

Few noticed the change day to day, but after a couple of decades the plant—which had the capacity to run three shifts—was down to a single shift. That left a tremendous unused productive capacity, though hardly anyone seemed to notice and even fewer made a fuss. After all, the troublemakers had left, and those who remained seemed content to leave well enough alone.

Because the demand they did have was heavily weighted toward dresses, plant management, as you might expect, increasingly catered to the dress division. When management felt they could afford to purchase new equipment, they naturally bought it for the dress division, since that's where the sales were.

Dress purchasers insisted the plant keep up with current styles, but management rarely heard from trousers at all. So the dress division received a large budget for new product design, while trousers hardly received any budget at all.

Since more people worked in dresses than trousers, most of management's time focused on dresses. Each year they spent less time thinking about trousers, and trousers became terribly out of step with the times. In fact, some of the designs had not changed in decades. The trousers they did make seemed to be of inferior quality—not able to stand up to normal wear and tear, nor the demands of everyday life. Since the plant wasn't making as many trousers, there just weren't enough good ones to go around.

It became a vicious downward spiral. In fact, conditions deteriorated so far that poor trousers sales eventually threatened to bring down dresses too.

Some of the more perceptive people began to ask, "Why can't they make trousers the way they used to?" Eventually, a few of the more innovative plant managers began to explore ways to solve the problem.

Management realized that if they were ever going to get the factory back to full capacity, they would need some fresh ideas to increase trouser production. They would have to design some new products to attract purchasers, stimulate demand for new trousers, retrain some managers, and retool the assembly lines to make quality trousers.

They knew they would need to find raw materials that could be made into trousers, get them into the plant, and start producing trousers suited for the times. The managers were excited and dreamed about adding a second shift. But they weren't quite sure where to start.

SOLVING THE RIGHT PROBLEM

In this chapter we will answer the all-important question, "What do men need?" Like the plant managers in the parable, where do you start?

It is easy to look at the data and come to the wrong conclusion. When you and I are at work, all day long we look at "the data." If we rely on our own best thinking, we will often come to the wrong conclusion. We will believe those we should not, disbelieve those we should, pick the wrong people for leadership, launch the wrong programs, and fear our friends while embracing those who oppose us. Consider just three historical examples.

The men of Israel made a treaty because the Gibeonites showed them moldy bread, cracked wineskins, old clothes, and claimed to come from a distant country. This was a clever ruse—they lived nearby. Where did the men of Israel go wrong? Joshua 9:14 (NLT) says, "So the Israelites examined their food, but they did not consult the Lord." The men of Israel came to the wrong conclusion because they looked at the data, but didn't ask God for direction.

Frankly, our men also put on a ruse. They put on their "game faces" so we will think everything is "just perfect." And then, when they crack, it's tempting to give them a social worker's or a psychologist's answer.

For forty days the troops of Israel listened to Goliath and cowered in fear. David looked the giant over once and said, "Don't worry about a thing. I can take him. The battle is the Lord's." Armed with confidence in God, he then went out and killed Israel's enemy. It is easy to look at the data and come to the wrong conclusion, as the soldiers did. The "men problem" is a Goliath, but God has called pastors to "take him."

Samuel, sent to anoint one of Jesse's sons to be the next king, on seeing Eliab thought to himself, "Surely he is the one!" But the LORD said, "Don't judge by his appearance or height. . . . The Lord doesn't see things the way you do. People judge by outward appearance, but the Lord looks at the heart" (1 Samuel 16:7 NLT). If you have been a pastor for very long, you know how easy it is to look at the data and come to the wrong conclusion. You have a growing list of failed initiatives that promised to grow your men but were not sustainable. You are tired of "clever." All along you knew in your heart, "There are no short cuts."

THE BIBLICAL SOLUTION

We can give men what they really need if, instead of looking at the data, we ask God for direction. Fortunately, in the Bible, Jesus has already given the church its direction. In this chapter we will see that, despite the complexity of men's lives, there is a single, golden solution. Jesus called his followers "disciples." And Jesus told those of us who are already disciples to go and make more disciples.

What men need is to become disciples of our Lord and Savior Jesus Christ, and all that this implies. It is a single concept that fully captures the essence of what it means to be "in Christ."

I know you will agree that people often use the same word to mean difference things, or different words to mean the same thing. So before going further, let's make sure we mean the same thing when we say "disciple."

WHAT IS A DISCIPLE?

When I ask pastors and lay leaders, "What is a disciple?" they often don't have a ready answer. In fact, one time I was part of a panel talking about discipleship and someone from the audience asked, "Exactly what do you mean when you say 'disciple'?" The other panelists started shuffling their papers. Since I am a one-trick pony and this is my trick, I fielded the question. Here's what I said: "We all know that the Greek word *mathetes* means a 'learner' or 'pupil.' However, when applied to the early Christians, the term "disciple" came to mean someone who had declared a personal allegiance to the teachings and person of Jesus."

Then I offered this working definition: "A disciple is someone *called* to live "in" Christ, *equipped* to live "like" Christ, and *sent* to live "for" Christ." And I amplified:

> First, a disciple is someone *called* to profess faith in Jesus Christ (this is the "evangelism" piece). Second, they are *equipped* in an ongoing process of spiritual growth and transformation (this is the "teaching" piece). Third, they are *sent* to love, serve, and abide in Christ (this is the "go" piece).

The reason I like this definition is that it is both biblical and actionable. You can build ministry around these three rubrics. Your men need a practical, not theoretical, understanding of what it means to be a disciple of Jesus, and how to live it out daily as regular guys.

Figure 1 lays out some of the biblical support for this definition:

TEXT	CALL	EQUIP	SEND
Matt 28:18–20	**Baptize** in name of Father, Son, Spirit	**Teach** to obey	**Go** and make disciples
Luke 6:47	**Comes** to me	**Hears** my words	Puts them into **practice**
2 Tim. 3:15–17	**Salvation** through faith in Christ Jesus	Teach, rebuke, correct, train to thoroughly **equip**	For every **good work**
Isa. 6:7–8	Guilt **taken away** and sin **atoned** for		Whom shall I **send**? Who will go for us?
Acts 26:20	**Repent** and **turn** to God		Prove repentance by **deeds**
Eph. 2:8–10	**Saved** by grace through faith		To do **good works**
Matt. 13:37–38	**Love God** with all heart, soul, mind		**Love neighbor** as yourself
John 3:3	Must be **born again**		
Matt. 7:24		**Hear** my words	Put into **practice**
2 Tim. 2:2		**Entrust teachings** to reliable people	Qualified to **teach others**
John 20:21			As the Father sent me, so I am **sending** you
John 13:34–35 (Rom. 13:7) (Luke 7:12)			All men know my disciples if you **love** one another
John 8:31			If you **hold to** my teaching, you are really my disciples
John 15:9			Bear much **fruit** showing self to be my disciples
Matt. 7:12			**Do to others** what you would want done to you. Sums up law and prophets.
Luke 14:27			Must **carry cross** and **follow Jesus** to be His disciple
Gen. 1:27–28 (Psalm 8:6–8)			Be fruitful, fill, subdue, and rule over **creation**

FIGURE 1

Biblical Support for the Definition of *Disciple* as One Called, Equipped, and Sent

I think the Bible makes a strong case that *calling, equipping, and sending are the "trinity" of making disciples.* Calling, equipping, and sending are the actionable components of discipleship—the learning process that forges men into passionate followers of Jesus. Isn't that what we all want? The rest of the chapter will explore each in more detail.

CALLING MEN TO CHRIST

First and foremost, men need to become born again. A disciple is *called* to profess faith in Jesus Christ—*evangelism.* Jesus said, "I have come . . . to call . . . sinners" (Mark 2:17).

I grew up in what we thought was a "Christian home," but we didn't know Christ. We didn't reject the gospel; we never heard it. Our church was focused on other things. In my early twenties, though, my soon-to-be wife, Patsy, explained the gospel of Jesus to me, and I soon embraced Christ as my Lord and Savior.

There are about 115 million men in America fifteen years of age and older.[1] Regrettably, about 60 percent, or 70 million,[2] of these men have made no profession of faith in Christ. That's sad, because many of them would gladly receive Christ if engaged in a credible way. What's even sadder, though, is how many men think they have tried Christianity, found it wanting, and rejected it, when in fact they have never properly understood it.

There's no other way to say it. To be truly happy a man must be born again—to surrender his life to Jesus. To be born again is the right starting point. And unless a man has the right starting point, everything else will turn out wrong.

This may be more difficult for men who already believe they are Christians than for those who know they are not. Søren Kierkegaard wondered of his countrymen, "Are all who call themselves Christian, Christian?" Today, it just does not seem possible that all the men who claim to believe in Jesus have truly and earnestly repented of their sins and embraced Jesus by faith.

C. S. Lewis once said, "Before you can make a man a Christian you must first help him understand that he is a pagan." D. L. Moody put it like this: "You've got to get people lost before you can get them saved."

This is exactly what Jesus proceeded to do with the religious Nicodemus in John 3:3: "I tell you the truth, no one can see the kingdom of God unless he is born again."

Jesus Christ has issued a divine summons to salvation. He has commanded men everywhere to repent (Acts 17:30). Once a man has professed faith, he should be baptized, as applicable, in accordance with your tradition.

Salvation should be made as simple as possible, but not oversimplified. I once heard a speaker say to eight hundred leaders in our community, "If you want to go to heaven and receive eternal life, all you have to do is pray this prayer." There was no mention of why men need a Savior. There was no mention of "sin" or "the cross." That was a gross misstatement of the gospel. Jesus did say to count the cost. For an "as simple as possible" explanation, see "The Gospel" in chapter 11.

When Are Men "Callable"?

It makes sense to fish for men when they're "biting." Your ministry to "call" men to Christ will be most effective if you connect with them when they face a turning point or crisis. Here is my list of reachable moments. You will no doubt be able to add to this list:

Searching for a purpose	Searching for an identity	A lack of meaning
Loneliness	Emptiness	Marriage
Divorce	Out of wedlock pregnancy	Birth of a child
Loss of a child	First job	Fired from job
Business failure	Financial crisis	Moral failure
Midlife crisis	Stalled career	Failed romance
Loss of physical strength	Sense of mortality	Empty nest
Health crisis	Aging parents	Loss of parents

Find a man's point of pain and you'll find an open door. Be there for men when they feel a need. Appeal to what men want, not what they don't really care about. For example, attract a man to your church service or event by offering a topic with a title like "How to Find True Success." From there you can segue to "How Jesus Gives Us Abundant Life." The more we touch on their wants (their felt needs), the more sticky our ministries will be.

Commitment Versus Surrender

Once Adrian Rogers, the famous Baptist preacher, went on a mission trip to Romania. Over the course of two weeks he bonded with his interpreter, but hadn't learned much about his thoughts. So toward the end of the trip he asked, "Tell me what you think of American Christians?"

"I don't want to talk about it," came the strange reply. This, of course, only made Dr. Rogers more curious, so he began to press him for an answer.

After several attempts he finally said, "Why won't you tell me? I really want to know."

Finally, the interpreter capitulated. "Well, okay then, but you're not going to like my answer. I don't think you Americans understand what Christianity is all about. Back in the 1960s you began to use the word 'commitment' to describe your relationship with Christ.

"However, any time a word comes into usage, another word goes into disuse. Until the 1960s you Americans talked about surrender to Christ. Surrender means giving up control, turning over all to the Master Jesus.

"By changing to the word 'commitment' your relationship with Christ has become something you do, therefore you are able to keep control. Surrender means giving up all rights to one's self. You Americans don't like to do that so, instead, you make a commitment."[3]

It is worth pondering.

Men need to become disciples of Jesus, and the first thing this implies is that they must be born again.

WHAT YOU CAN DO | *To Call Men to Christ*

• Regularly present the gospel and invite men to put their faith in Jesus. Offer opportunities "from the front" at thought-through intervals.

• "Be there" for men when they feel the need. Address their turning points and crises from the front. Enlist your strong disciples to be part of a "system" to reach out to hurting men (e.g., meet for ten minutes right after the service in Room 100 where strong disciples set coffee and breakfast appointments with men).

• Teach your men the difference between "commitment" and "surrender."

• Call your men to surrender. Tell them Dr. Rogers's story, then issue the call: "You must reach a turning point. The turning point of our lives is when we stop seeking the God (or gods) we want and start seeking the God who is. No amount of wanting to recreate Him in your imagination to be different is going to have any effect on His unchanging character and nature. Your principal task, then, is to come humbly to the foot of the cross and there surrender of your life to the lordship of Jesus Christ. If you would like to do that right now. . . ." (Then lead them in a prayer of surrender which includes repentance and expresses faith.)

• Find additional concepts under "The Gospel" and "Evangelism" in the topical summaries in Chapter 11.

EQUIPPING MEN IN CHRIST

Second, men need to grow in their faith. A disciple is *equipped* in a process of on-going spiritual growth and transformation—*teaching*. The second part of making disciples is teaching—to equip men to live like Christ. The church is a learning organization.

A man came to my home to fix my Internet service. He was a nice man with a good heart, but he wasn't trained to figure out my problem. The next man had the proper training and easily solved the problem. An untrained Christian is no better off than an unskilled laborer or a high school dropout. He simply won't enjoy as much of the abundant life as a man who has been discipled.

Have a Plan

It may do more harm than good to invite a man to become a Christian if we have no plan to train him how to truly know and follow Christ.

When we don't disciple (educate, train, equip) a man who professes Christ, he will almost always become lukewarm in faith, worldly in behavior, and hypocritical in witness.

The single most important thing we can do for a man once he believes is to help him change the core affections of his heart.

One day I was seemingly at the pinnacle of my spirituality. Then I saw a sensuous woman and was immediately tempted to lust. The world, the flesh, and the Devil were telling me, "Jesus is not enough to make you happy. You need this lust." That was the lie.

Fortunately I was reminded that I needed only Christ. I was, by God's grace, able to reject the temptation because I wanted to express my faith in Jesus, that He is sufficient for me.

Can you look at something or someone, be tempted to lust for it, and say,

"Lord Jesus, I don't really need that to be happy because I have you"? This pinpoints the difference between what it means to be "committed" to Jesus versus "surrendered" to Jesus.

Seek Heart Transformation

There is a sensitivity of spirit that can develop when your men are walking closely with Jesus, renewing themselves daily in the gospel through repentance and faith. The Holy Spirit speaks, and they hear.

Christianity is not about *behavior modification*; it is *heart transformation*. Rules and regulations to make a man a better Christian will not change his life. To change his life he must change the core affections of his heart. Jesus needs to become his highest and best thought in every situation.

What men need is to become disciples of Jesus, and the second thing this implies is that they need teaching, education, training, and equipping.

WHAT YOU CAN DO | *To Equip Men in Christ*

• *Help your men to slow down and examine their lives.* When your men first join you, they come tired. If men are tired, then they need rest. Unfortunately, many churches emphasize work, not rest, so ten years later their men are just as tired as they were when they joined! Your men won't be able to examine their lives until they slow down. They need to lower their "revs" so they can hear the "still, small" voice of God speak to them.

• *Equip your men with truth.* Keep in mind that all week long many of your men have had people tickling their ears. When a man comes to church, he wants some straight talk. He wants someone to hold him accountable. So give him the truth. Give him what Francis Schaeffer liked to call "true truth." At the same time remember that it's tough out there, so include some encouragement and support. Nothing lubricates a message to men more than a good laugh. It's also important not to take ourselves too seriously and lighten it up.

• *Equip your men to read the Bible on their own.* It's said that Spurgeon once lamented he could find ten men who would die for the Bible for every one who would actually read it. The Scriptures are key in this process of calling, equipping, and sending. Notice how this process is described in Paul's instruction to Timothy:

From infancy you have known the holy Scriptures, which are able to make you wise for salvation through faith in Christ Jesus [calling]. All Scripture is God-breathed and is useful for teaching, rebuking, correcting and training in righteousness [equipping], so that the man of God may be thoroughly equipped for every good work [sending]. (2 Timothy 3:15–17)

• Find additional concepts in the alphabetized reference section (chapter 11) of this book.

SENDING MEN FOR CHRIST

Third, men need to be sent to live for Christ. Jesus prayed, "Father, as you have sent me, so I am sending them" (John 20:21). A disciple is *sent* to abide in Christ, love others, bear much fruit, and do good works/deeds.

A disciple is sent to abide in Christ. Jesus said, "If you hold [abide] to my teaching, *you are really my disciples.* Then you will know the truth, and the truth will set you free" (John 8:31–32, italics added).

A disciple is sent to love. "A new command I give you: Love one another. As I have loved you, so you must love one another. *By this all men will know that you are my disciples,* if you love one another (John 13:34–35, italics added).

Prepare Your Men for Fruitful Lives

A disciple is sent to lead a fruitful life. Every man wants to give his life to a cause, to make a difference. Men are made for the task. When we disciple a man, he will eventually want to make that difference for the glory of God. "This is to my Father's glory, that you bear much fruit, *showing yourselves to be my disciples"* (John 15:8, italics added).

At some point, every true believer quivers a bit when he reads John 15:8. Once the grace and love of Christ sink in, a man will feel compelled to do something to serve his Lord. Here's how Brother Lawrence expressed it: "I tell you that this sweet and loving gaze of God insensibly kindles a divine fire in the soul which is set ablaze so ardently with the love of God that one is obliged to perform exterior acts to moderate it.[4]

Why do we equip men to live like Christ? So they can enjoy Christ by knowing Him better—sure, but also "so that the man of God may be thoroughly equipped for every good work" (2 Timothy 3:17). And that's what pastors do—

equip people to do those "good works":

> It was he who gave some to be apostles, some to be prophets, some to be evangelists, and some to be pastors and teachers, *to prepare God's people for works of service*, so that the body of Christ may be built up until we all reach unity in the faith and in the knowledge of the Son of God and become mature, attaining to the whole measure of the fullness of Christ. (Ephesians 4:11–13, italics added)

"Ordain" Your Men

Once a man has been with Christ and experienced the joy of His grace, the warmth of His love, the cleansing of His forgiveness, and the indwelling of His Spirit, he inevitably comes to a point when he can no longer be happy unless he is serving the Lord.

I once met a man who said, "All my life I wanted to be a high school math teacher. Finally, my dream came true. But I soon saw two problems. First, my students were coming to class with problems math can't solve. Second, the Christian teachers in my school didn't know each other. God put a vision in my mind about how to address those two issues. *I am an ordained math teacher.*"

He understood that every vocation is holy to the Lord. Some of your men are ordained truck drivers. Some are ordained computer programmers. Others are ordained farmers. Help your men understand what they have been "ordained" to do and they will forever be grateful to you.

All men want to be happy. A man will feel most happy, most alive, and most useful when he is doing what he was created to do—when he finds his cause, his woman, and his God.

Besides, if you don't give him the opportunity, he will go somewhere else. Don't let this happen to you: "I was bursting at the seams to serve, but they couldn't figure out how to mobilize me."

WHAT YOU CAN DO | *To Send Men for Christ*

Help your men understand what it means to be a disciple after they leave the church building:

• *Teach them how to abide in Christ.* Teach your men how to abide. Equip them with the spiritual disciplines to "continue" in Christ all week long.

• *Encourage them to love like Christ.* Show them concrete ways to love others in practical ways. Wouldn't most problems go away if your men simply practiced the Golden Rule?

• *Prepare, challenge, and "ordain" them for works of service.* Give your men tasks. Once a man gets turned on to serve, he will not rest until he finds an outlet for his passion. When he comes to you, I suggest you drop everything and engage him. If you do not give such a man a place to serve, he will still find a place to serve—but it will be elsewhere. When all the time and energy to bring the man to this point are considered, I think the best course of action is to suspend all other activity until you have engaged the man in a ministry of the church. Again, if you don't, someone else will. This is an "urgent" felt need of the man.

• Read more on "Disciplines, Spiritual," "Calling" and "Work" in chapter 11.

MOVING TOWARD HEART CHANGE

Our main task is to present the gospel of Jesus in such a way that it helps men change the core affections of their hearts so they want to be disciples. Discipleship is not merely presenting *the right information* through teaching and preaching—although that is important. Discipleship includes everything that moves men along toward spiritual maturity.

How do we do that? It could be a sermon, an encouraging or inspiring word in the hall, an unforgettable solo, getting a cup of coffee together, a Sunday school lesson, a home Bible study, a hug, a small-group experience. It also includes acts of service, such as teaching Sunday school, volunteering to work in the homeless shelter, leading someone to Christ, giving or getting a meal when sick, or setting up chairs for the mission conference—anything that moves a man forward in Christ.

Build around relationships, not programs. Discipleship is more relationship than task. Love them from the front, but then get them into "life on life" groups of all kinds (e.g., home groups, couples' groups, men's groups).

Jesus is our model for making disciples. From a learning theory perspective, Jesus was a genius. His methods overlapped. He gathered men together. He forged relationships with them. They did "life" together. They dialogued. They socialized. They went with Him. They listened to His teachings. They observed His life. He gave them assignments to build their confidence and build His kingdom.

Jesus pastored for "life change." Jesus wasn't so much interested in what men heard, but how they responded. The result? Two thousand years later Christianity is the world's largest movement, and Jesus is the most famous person on earth.

POINTS TO REMEMBER

- We can give men what they really need if instead of looking at the data, we ask God for direction.
- What men need is to become disciples of our Lord and Savior Jesus Christ and all that this implies.
- A disciple is someone *called* to live "in" Christ, *equipped* to live "like" Christ, and *sent* to live "for" Christ.
- To be truly happy a man must be born again—to surrender his life to Jesus.
- An untrained Christian is no better off than an unskilled laborer or a high school dropout. He simply won't enjoy as much of the abundant life as a man who has been discipled.
- The single most important thing we can do for a man once he believes is to help him change the core affections of his heart.
- Once the grace and love of Christ sink in, a man will feel compelled to do something to serve his Lord.
- Help your men understand what they have been "ordained" to do and they will forever be grateful to you.
- Jesus is our model for making disciples. From a learning theory perspective, Jesus was a genius.

HOW I BECAME A DISCIPLE —A CASE STUDY

In this chapter, I want to illustrate the calling, sending, and equipping of one man—me. You will quickly see my equipping and sending did not occur in a linear, step-by-step process. I think that's an important point to make. Like most men, my discipleship has been fluid, dynamic, and organic.

Since I was a little boy until now, I have never belonged to a church that had a "separate" men's ministry program or organization (although they encouraged men's small groups). You don't *have* to have a separate men's ministry to disciple men. I think that's another important point to make. In fact, my most important discipleship took place in a couples' group.

There is a "compounding" nature to discipleship. It is through repetitive exposures to the "same" ideas that the truth slowly but surely takes hold. For example, the first time the disciples experienced Jesus calming the storm they said, "What kind of man is this? Even the winds and waves obey Him!" (Matthew 8:27). The second time he did it they declared, "Truly you are the Son of God" and they worshiped Him (Matthew 14:33).

When the space shuttle is in orbit, it wants to veer off course about 90 percent of the time. Many small rockets and thrusters regularly fire to keep the shuttle on its correct orbital course. A lot of men are like the space shuttle. They veer off course a great deal of the time. Like those small rockets and thrusters, steady discipleship can direct a man's life to the right course.

PRAISE FOR DISCIPLE-MAKING CHURCHES

I praise God for the churches where I was discipled as a young man. In one of the churches, I recall Pastor Chuck Green. When Dr. Green preached, he preached to men. Of course, he preached to women too, but he was a man's man. He used a lot of humor and stories that I could relate to as a man. I didn't feel like Christianity was for wimps. He had a vision to make disciples—calling, equipping, and sending.

When Chuck was seventeen, he was paralyzed in a trampoline accident. He eventually regained enough use of his legs to shuffle along, scraping his feet as he walked with aid of a cane. I think his courage inspired me more than I realized at the time.

That's the church where both of our children answered the "call" to become Christians and were baptized. In concert with our parental training, that's where they were "equipped" through the youth programs and Sunday school classes. They also attended elementary through high school in our church's affiliated Christian school.

When our children were "sent" to college, they both lived out their faith and joined local churches. When they married, our church performed the weddings.

After twenty-five years at our church, my wife, Patsy, and I were called back to a former church. At the exit interview with our existing pastor, he asked if I had any advice to offer. I said, "Not really. You're doing great. Keep doing what you're doing. You're attracting lots of young families.

"But one thing I do encourage you to remember: I am the product. I am what this church produces. I am the goal. I represent success. All the programs are great, but only to the extent that they make disciples—just like you did for me."

GROWING UP IN CHURCH

I grew up in a church that baptized me as a child, taught Bible stories, had confirmation classes, allowed me to be an altar boy, and offered youth group meetings which I attended.

Growing up in the church, I assumed I was "in." Jesus was my example. I believed what I was told. However, I was not taught that I was a sinner in need of personal spiritual transformation. I have no recollection of any teaching that I needed a Savior, or that Jesus wanted to have a relationship with me to help guide my life. I'm not saying the gospel was not preached, only that I have no such recollection. My parents and three brothers had the same experience.

Religion for me was veneration of a majestic historical figure but with no present relevance or personal application. I believed in a God I did not understand and lived in a world which I had no reason to think he inhabited.

SEARCHING FOR MEANING AND PURPOSE

Like all young men, I wanted my life to count. I was searching for meaning and purpose. Once I kept reading, repeating, and studying a prayer to conjure up a "feeling" of connection to God, which never came.

As a high schooler, a voice inside my head kept screaming, "You were created for a purpose!" But everything in my life bored me—school, my part-time job, my family. I even bored myself. I was angry that life seemed so "little," so insignificant, and so pointless.

I had no idea who I was, why I existed, where I was going, or how to get there. My world didn't work, so I quit high school in the middle of my senior year.

The next thing I remember it was 5:00 a.m. at Ft. Benning, Georgia, and a ferocious drill sergeant was screaming for me to get out of bed for a three-mile run before breakfast. After several months of training, I was assigned to the 82nd Airborne Division at Ft. Bragg, North Carolina.

The structure and boundaries of the Army actually created a sense of safety for me. After passing the GED test, I enrolled in night classes at N.C. State University's Fort Bragg branch campus. I was still searching. For an English literature class, I read in *Hamlet*, "This above all: to thine own self be true and it must follow as the night the day, thou canst not then be false to any man."

I thought, *That's the most noble thought I have ever heard uttered!* I adopted it as my life credo and said, "I will always try to do the right thing by everyone I meet." Essentially, on that day I became a *moralist*. I thought I had broken the code.

However, feelings of loneliness soon overwhelmed me. I still wondered, "Can God help me?" A fellow soldier invited me to a church in nearby Fayetteville. They allowed me to be an assistant to the couple leading the high school youth group. The relationships filled a void, but only part of it.

I set an appointment with the pastor and, with tears streaming down my face, told him how lonely and sad I was. He smiled and said, "You will get over this. It's just something we all have to go through from time to time." I left his office knowing that we both were lost.

Having failed to find meaning and purpose in religion, after the Army and college I decided to try my hand at business. I became a *materialist* in addition to a moralist. Soon I was meeting all my goals, but the more I achieved the more miserable I became. Life was futile.

THE PAIN LEADING UP TO NEW BIRTH

In the meantime, I had met Patsy. She wanted to marry a Christian, so I convinced her I was one. Within weeks of our marriage, however, it was obvious that we had an ambiguity of terms about what it meant to be a Christian.

I thought being a Christian meant "living by a set of Christian values." I was surprised to learn that for Patsy being a Christian meant "a personal relationship with Jesus grounded in faith." I thought it was a *task*—something I did to make God happy (or at least avoid His wrath). But for Patsy it was a *relationship*—a love relationship in which God actively guided her daily life.

I wanted what she had. But I didn't want to give up anything to get it. So I tried to "imitate" her while living like I had always done. The harder I tried, the worse things became. One dreary day I came home from work in my new luxury car, closed the garage door, then tried to knock down the garage wall with the sole of my foot for ten minutes or so. The angst was eating a hole through me.

Sunday morning I said to Patsy, "Let's go to church." At this point, I was blaming my wife for my miseries and thought, *If we go to church maybe it will help Patsy, and I might meet some investors for my real estate deals.*

After the service, several young couples surrounded us in the most pleasant way—like they really cared. Two of the husbands took a personal interest in me. We went to lunch. We talked. We went to their homes for dinners. They invited us to a Friday night Bible study that met in the home of an optometrist and his wife.

I tried—I really did. I wanted to perform. I wanted to make them happy. I wanted to be like them. I did my best. But I couldn't. I was selfish and, worse, pretended that I was not.

Waves of frustration swept over me. One morning I was ranting and raving, trying to expel my pain by taking these frustrations out on my wife. I said things to her that a man should never say to a woman. With tears rolling down her face, she just sat there and "took it like a man."

When my rage was winding down, our eyes met and I was transfixed. I wanted to look away, but I couldn't. After she held my gaze for what seemed like a brief eternity, she asked, "Pat, is there *anything* about me that you like?"

I wandered off to my office and spent the morning staring out my window. I wondered, "What happened to you, Morley? You wanted your life to count, to make a difference. But you're just a nobody headed nowhere." And it was true.

I had taken one step forward, but then two steps back. It was time for another try at "religion."

CONVICTION OF SIN AT SUNDAY SCHOOL

We started to attend a Sunday school class for young couples led by a wonderful middle-aged couple. It was a case of "equipping" before the "calling" had taken place! The man read from Ephesians 5:25–33. I only remember the first few words: "Husbands, love your wives, just as Christ loved the church and gave himself up for her to make her holy."

At the particular moment he read, I was staring at the floor. My face flushed and I started sweating profusely. Within a minute or so my undershirt was soaked. I have never felt more embarrassed in my life. I was certain that everyone knew that I was not loving my wife as I should. I was sure they were all now staring at me. I couldn't look up—I didn't want to. A powerful force of true moral guilt swept over me. It was the first time I recall feeling what I later came to understand was conviction of sin. But I didn't know what to do with it. I soldiered on.

THE CALL TO SURRENDER

In his sermons, the pastor was telling me about Jesus in a way I had never considered—a personal God interested in me personally.

As we drove away from church one Sunday in August, 1973, I was picking on Patsy for something I cannot now remember. Something inside of me snapped. I finally came to the end of myself. I pulled out my white handkerchief and surrendered. I prayed, "God, I just can't do this anymore. I'm a sinful man, and I need you to save me. Jesus, I surrender my life to you, and ask you to come into my life and change me." I have never been the same.

Of course, every man's story is different in the details. But in another sense every man's story is the same: the feelings . . . the futility . . . the pain . . . the lashing out . . . the drawing toward Jesus . . . the witnesses . . . the "hearing" of God's Word . . . the conviction of sin . . . the preaching of God's Word . . . the coming to an end of self.

Fortunately for me (and for my wife, children, parents, and brothers), our church had a vision to disciple me to become a godly man, husband, and father. The pastor was *determined* to make this happen. And the church had adopted a *strategy* that not only got me started, but had additional steps to *sustain* my growth and service.

And best of all—at least for me—our church acted quickly once they learned I had received Christ.

A DISCIPLE EQUIPPED
Through Study, Memorization, and Reading of the Bible

I've had so many awesome opportunities to grow, but the most systematic and comprehensive one came when Patsy and I were invited to join a home Bible study led by Jim Gillean. Jim was an engineer who really made us all think about what the Scriptures meant and, more importantly, how they applied to everyday life.

During those Bible studies I learned how to read the Bible for myself, how to pray, and how to have a daily devotional.

Scripture memorization was popular at the time, and I memorized hundreds of verses—one of the best "equip" things I ever did. I still recall verses every day that I learned back then.

At a weekend seminar, the speaker noted the book of Proverbs has 31 chapters. He suggested we read one chapter a day each month. I took the challenge and for fifteen years or so, I read a chapter in Proverbs every day. With that kind of exposure, I was soon quoting "Proverbs" in my everyday language.

To Be Sent

We were invited into Jim's Bible study as part of a package to both "equip" and "send" us. We were "sent" when they asked Patsy and me to lead a six-week Sunday school class for new Christians that repeated several times a year. Part of the deal was that all the pastors and lay leaders for evangelism, new Christian training, and home Bible studies met once a week to be "equipped" in our own Bible study.

Leading the class for new Christians was definitely "learning by doing." Even though the new believers' questions were simple and basic, I still had to scramble because I was a rookie at serving Christ. Leading helped me grow like a weed.

To Evangelize

Our church hosted a Campus Crusade for Christ weekend training to teach people how to do personal evangelism. Patsy and I attended, and I just ate it up. They "equipped" us on Saturday and "sent" us on Sunday! I led my first person to Jesus on a Sunday afternoon home visit.

I started taking businessmen to lunch, sharing my testimony, and asking, "Where are you on your spiritual pilgrimage?" If they didn't understand the gospel, I would read them Campus Crusade's Four Spiritual Laws, and most of them became Christians too.

SENT INTO THE MARKETPLACE

Six of us in the business community started meeting in a weekly small group to share, learn, and pray for each other. Howard Dayton, who later founded Crown Ministries (now Crown Financial) would come each week with first drafts of the material that would eventually become the Crown course. He asked our opinions but, of course, we didn't have much to say because most of us were pretty young in our faith and knowledge. The main thing about this group was that we were "for" each other, and that "equipped" me to have adult male friendships for the first time.

One day I proposed to our small group that we fan out in the community and take positions in politics, education, and civic life. I volunteered to take the "civic life" category and joined the Winter Park Chamber of Commerce. They immediately put me on the Program Committee, and six months later I was the chairperson. I prayed, "God, why am I here?" I sensed God had "sent" me there to start a prayer breakfast, so I acted.

Just before Thanksgiving 1978, the Chamber hosted its first Prayer Breakfast with about 150 people attending. Several received Christ. The Chamber is no longer involved but the Leadership Prayer Breakfast is still going strong, and hundreds of business leaders have become Christians as a result.

A CHALLENGING TIME
OF EQUIPPING AND SENDING

About the time of the first prayer breakfast, someone invited me to attend a week-end men-only retreat hosted by The Fellowship at Windy Gap, North Carolina.

The main speaker was Tom Skinner, former gang leader and evangelist. Tom's messages focused on the kingdom of God, loving God, and loving other people—especially people who are different from us. It was the first time I can remember "hearing" that I didn't have to work myself into a stupor to earn God's approval and love (although I have no doubt the words had been spoken to me before—it was just my time). It was also the first time I remember being challenged to love people outside my comfort zone.

Tom liked to play tennis, and they had courts at Windy Gap. The next night I skipped out on the main session and walked up to the courts. Tom was there hitting balls. We struck up a conversation. He talked to me as though I was the only person on Earth still living. I felt the love of God coming through him into me. It was a supreme "equipping" time for me.

Sent to Start Leadership Conferences

Being the task-oriented man I was, I immediately asked Tom if he would come to Orlando and share his message with all my tired, worn-out Christian friends. He said yes, and soon we hosted the first of several Christian Leadership Conferences in Orlando. I remember my Christian workaholic friends coming up to Tom after his sessions with tears streaming down their faces.

One man said, "I feel such relief. I have been under such a heavy burden. I just always felt like I needed to do more and more to please God. I was afraid that I was leaving something undone. For the first time I realize that what He wants most is a relationship with me—to love me and make me a whole man."

Sent to Start a One-on-One Friendship

One thing Tom said that weekend at Windy Gap gripped me: "If you want to change your city or church, don't try to organize a big revival. Instead, find some like-minded men and become to each other what you want your city or church to become. Meet together and share your lives with each other. That will create a model so attractive that others will want to be part of it." That really grabbed hold of my insides.

As soon as I returned home, I started praying for God to send me a man. On the following Sunday, I saw Ken Moar, a friendly man thirty years my senior. He agreed to meet with me once a week. We sought to become to each other what we wanted our church and community to become. We still meet, and virtually everything I've ever done in ministry was first discussed with Ken, including The Man in the Mirror Bible Study, and the Man in the Mirror ministry.

SENT TO SERVE IN THE COMMUNITY

Talking with Merthie

In 1980, here in Orlando, we had a racially charged civil disturbance that was big enough to make the evening network news. I went home for lunch and, that day, our African-American housekeeper, Merthie, was there. It was awkward. I finally found these words coming out of my mouth, "Merthie, how long do you think it will be before we are able to be right with each other?"

She said, "Oh, I don't know."

"Well, Merthie, what keeps you going—what is your hope?"

She said, "Oh, I don't know."

I said, "Merthie, do you think we will ever get by all of this, and learn to live together as Christians?"

"Oh, I don't know," she said once again.

I went into my home office and began to sob. I thought, *I am a Christian. I need to do something to respond to this.*

Taking a First Step

Eventually, with the input of an African-American college professor that I knew fairly well and motivated by my relationship with Tom Skinner, I convened a meeting of black and white men; not to change Orlando, but to become to each other what we think Orlando should become.

I made a list of twenty white men, and the professor made a list of twenty black men. We invited them to come to a Saturday morning meeting. Half came—ten black and ten white. At the meeting, there was disagreement about the first step. As it turned out, exactly half of the black men wanted to do a task and the other half wanted to do relationships. And exactly half of the white men wanted to do a task and the other half wanted to do relationships.

It should be clear that this is not an ethnic issue. It is a human issue. Some men are wired for task and some are wired for relationship. But because I was under the influence of Tom Skinner, I exerted my will to take the "relationship precedes task" approach.

We met one Saturday morning each month for the next five years. We called ourselves "The Black/White Fellowship."

Interestingly, more tasks and "sending" came out of that group than you can imagine: men going to seminary, starting ministries, meeting financial needs, helping the poor, fixing houses, assisting with medical needs.

God "sent" me to lead The Black/White Fellowship, but He used my relationship with Merthie to inspire me to go. I'm also pretty sure this would never have happened if I hadn't met Tom. As Tom liked to say, "A relationship is the most powerful force in the world."

BEING EQUIPPED ALONG THE WAY

The equipping part of discipleship can be programmatic and linear, like through Sunday school, a small group curriculum, or a preaching series. A lot of discipleship, though, just "happens" as we intersect with people, ideas, and opportunities. Here are some of the ways I've been equipped that don't fit neatly onto a timeline.

Through Christian Books

As a visual learner, one of the most powerful ways I've been equipped is through reading. Christian literature began affecting me early. Frankly, though, some of the early books I read were too advanced for me. I just didn't have the theological vocabulary I have today. But I soldiered on, and several authors left deep imprints on my faith and worldview—men like Francis Schaeffer, J. I. Packer, Oswald Chambers, and C. S. Lewis. But all these authors were much too dense for me in the beginning.

For Parenting

Nothing could be more important for a man with children than to be equipped as a godly father. As we started our own family, a very attractive couple in our church who raised four successful boys invited us to attend a parenting class. We already knew about the class, but the clincher for us to attend was a personal invitation to me from the man. I felt honored to be asked personally by a leader in the church.

I had never been methodically "equipped" in the area of parenting. My wife, Patsy, had handed me many pages and even chapters of great parenting books to read—Dobson mostly. However, listening to our teachers and comparing notes with our peers brought everything down to street level.

A TRANSITION INTO MINISTRY

Some of your men will be called to lead. Some will even enter ministry as I did in 1991. I won't tell you all the details of my "sending" into ministry, but several preludes are worth a mention.

First, I became bi-vocational. I didn't have this category in my vocabulary at the time, but I was spending more and more of my time doing ministry and leaving the business to others.

After The Black/White Fellowship my wife and I became the host couple for Campus Crusade's Executive Ministries in Orlando. In the last half of the 1980s we hosted evangelistic dinner parties and small follow-up dinners in our home. We saw dozens of business leaders and their spouses profess faith.

I started The Man in the Mirror Bible Study in 1986. The concept was to have a place to "equip" the businessmen "called" through the outreach dinners. As it turned out, none of those men ever attended, but a whole different group of business types showed up. And our involvement with Executive Ministries led to a host of other ministries.

In 1989 Reformed Theological Seminary started a campus in Orlando, and my company did the real estate work. I was intrigued, so I started taking classes. R. C. Sproul and other great professors opened my eyes to a whole new world of theology, Christian history, and so much more.

By 1991, there just wasn't enough time to do it all, so I left business and started Man in the Mirror.

TO LIVE FOR CHRIST

Each of your men is unique and God deals with them as individuals. Nevertheless, all men need to be called to live in Christ, equipped to live like Christ, and sent to live for Christ. I hope this case study creates a sense of freedom and variety about the many ways your men can become disciples of Jesus.

POINTS TO REMEMBER

- There is a "compounding" nature to discipleship. It is through repetitive exposures to the "same" ideas that the truth slowly but surely takes hold.
- "I am the product. All the programs are great, but only to the extent that they make disciples—just like you did for me."
- When Dr. Chuck Green preached, he preached to men. He was a man's man and used stories that I could relate to as a man. I didn't feel like Christianity was for wimps. He had a vision to make disciples—calling, equipping, and sending.
- I thought Christianity was a *task*—something I did to make God happy (or at least avoid His wrath). But for Patsy it was a *relationship*—a love relationship in which God actively guided her daily life.
- I tried—I really did. I wanted to perform. I wanted to make them happy. I wanted to be like them. I did my best. But I couldn't. I was selfish and, worse, pretended that I was not.
- In his sermons, the pastor was telling me about Jesus in a way I had never considered—a personal God interested in me personally.
- I've had so many awesome opportunities to grow, but the most systematic and comprehensive one came when Patsy and I were invited to join a home Bible Study.

7

SUCCESS FACTORS
IN DISCIPLING MEN

What are the factors that lead to effective discipling of men? In chapters 7 and 8 I want to show you what research has revealed about churches that are effectively pastoring men—nine major themes and their related success factors.

As mentioned in chapter 1, several years ago I was alarmed at how many highly capable, willing, and proven pastors (and laymen) had burned out on men's discipleship. They simply did not know how to sustain their men's ministries. Yet others were flourishing.

In 2002 I decided to study this problem academically by pursuing a PhD in management. I wanted to understand, "Why do some churches succeed at men's discipleship while others languish or fail?" What were the successful pastors doing differently from the pastors of the ineffective or failed ministries to men?

I do not believe the actions of the Holy Spirit are limited by research studies, but research can clarify what's working for others. The Spirit usually does His best work when people know what they're doing—whether it's piloting an airplane, performing surgery, programming a computer, selling a car, managing a company, or pastoring men.

My first step was to understand what scholarly management literature had to say about sustaining change and the implementation factors that lead to success. I was amazed at how rich and diverse the literature is for businesses, while churches as organizations have been sorely neglected. Many well-known, proven concepts have simply not migrated to churches where new "wineskins" are needed.

THE PROBLEM WITH INTRODUCING CHANGE

I quickly discovered that the odds of *any* new initiative succeeding are quite low. Only about one-third of all organizational initiatives succeed, and that's regardless of sector—whether public, private, or nonprofit. Shockingly, 67 percent fail outright,[1] while up to 70 percent of all new products fail.[2] Only 44 percent of new business start-ups succeed beyond four years.[3]

Research shows that, all things being equal, most of your new initiatives will never get past the idea stage and, of those that do, two-thirds will fail. But things don't have to be equal! You can dramatically improve your particular results by knowing what works. By the end of this chapter, you will have a research-based snapshot of what works in churches that have effective men's discipleship ministries.

All truth is God's truth, and the truth about implementing and sustaining change has been thoroughly studied and documented in management literature over the last one hundred years. Here's an example of one such insight:

> One key reason why implementation fails is that practicing executives, managers and supervisors do not have practical, yet theoretically sound, models to guide their actions during implementation. Without adequate models, they try to implement strategies without a good understanding of the multiple factors that must be addressed, often simultaneously, to make implementation work.[4]

NINE ESSENTIAL THEMES FOR SUCCESS

Once I understood the success factors from the literature, I designed an inductive, multiple-case study to investigate the presence or absence of those factors in churches that have been successful and unsuccessful in implementing men's discipleship.

I was able to organize the success factors I found into nine essential themes:

1. Leadership
2. Vision
3. People
4. Planning
5. Resources
6. Execution
7. Communication Plan
8. Resistance
9. Sustainability

Ironically, the themes I discovered can all be found by reading the Book of Nehemiah—written nearly 2,500 years ago! I wasn't surprised. (More on Nehemiah as we go.)

I have memorized these nine themes. Whenever I have a problem, I run through the list. That helps me clarify the problem.

There is no secret knowledge. We are not doomed to repeat the mistakes of the past. However, that doesn't mean this knowledge is lying on top of the ground like nuggets of gold. It must be mined. So let's dig in. We'll cover the first five themes in this chapter, and the other four in the next.

Incidentally, I see no reason why these findings can't be generalized for other areas of your church and ministry.

OVERVIEW: THE THREE MAIN FACTORS

Many variables have to be in place to succeed, but my research clearly identified three main factors that tower over the others:

- *Vision:* a vision to disciple *every* man in the church.
- *Determination:* a personally involved pastor who is determined that men's discipleship will work "no matter what."
- *Sustainable strategy:* a "sustainable" strategy to move men forward as disciples.

The Big Three

First, success hinges on having a vision to disciple every man in your church. In the effective churches, the senior pastors had a clear vision and a passionate commitment to disciple every man in their churches. And they "sold" their visions hard yet were patient about giving people time to get on board. The research revealed it is clearly not enough for a layman or even an associate pastor to have this vision. That's not to say men won't be discipled if the senior pastor is not on board, but the results will be a fraction of what they could have been. In the ineffective churches, the senior pastors did not see men's discipleship as a top priority.

Second, you must be "determined" to make men's discipleship work. The most striking finding was the level of personal involvement by the successful senior pastors. This is not to say that the senior pastor has to do everything. In the successful churches other pastors or laymen often did the work—but the senior pastor never fully let go. They viewed themselves as the ongoing champions for men's discipleship. That stood in sharp contrast to their counterparts in the ineffective and failed programs. The word that best captures the will of the pastor to see it through is "determination."

But determination is not a strategy. *Third, successful men's discipleship depends on having a strategy to sustain your efforts.* "Sustainability" easily ranks as the number one problem in men's discipleship ministry. In the effective churches, the senior pastors had a planning model, method, or process they employed to not only create discipleship momentum, but also to sustain it. They discovered a way to sustain discipleship—their determination was not in vain. However, the ineffective and failed churches created a lot of momentum from time to time, but had no strategy to keep it going.

What Is a Strategy?

I want to be very careful about the use of the word *strategy*. For our purposes, the concept is more important than the word. By the word *strategy* we're talking about "a sustainable way to get men's discipleship done."

People often use different words to mean the same thing, and the same words to mean different things. You may prefer *strategy, system, model, method, process, program, plan,* or some other word. I don't want to get hung up on words. *Webster's Online Dictionary* defines these terms in a way that suggests they're all getting at the same thing—an organized way to achieve a desired outcome:

• Strategy: An elaborate and systematic plan of action.
• System: A procedure or process for obtaining an objective.

- Model: A simplified description of a complex entity or process.
- Method: A way of doing something, especially a systematic one; implies an orderly, logical arrangement (usually in steps).
- Process: A particular course of action intended to achieve a result.
- Program: A series of steps to be carried out or goals to be accomplished.
- Plan: A series of steps to be carried out or goals to be accomplished.

Developing a strategy is a learnable skill. By the end of this chapter and the next, you will have the essentials of a sustainable men's discipleship strategy.

Our model for this is Jesus. His *vision* was to seek and to save the lost. His *determination* ranged from clearing the temple to His submissive prayer in the garden of Gethsemane. His *sustainable strategy* was training disciples to train other disciples. All the factors are important, of course, but when these three are in place the others appear to follow in the course of time.

Vision. Determination. Sustainable strategy. Keep these three in mind as you read about the nine essential themes and related success factors. Each theme will include findings from research literature, biblical corroboration from Nehemiah, and an example of the theme in action.

THEME 1: LEADERSHIP

Bill Bright, founder of Campus Crusade for Christ, frequently said, "Everything boils down to leadership." All the research ever recorded concludes that you can't launch a broad and extended change initiative, program, or process under the leadership of middle managers. Even Jesus launched His kingdom through personal involvement.

The research is quite clear: The senior pastor is the key to men's discipleship. He doesn't have to do it all, but he does have to make "men's discipleship" into a genuine priority that the whole church understands and adopts.

Unquestionably, instability and turnover in key leadership positions always hurts momentum. Football teams and NASCAR teams come to mind.

Implementation Factors from the Literature

Research studies in the literature found the following factors necessary for effective leadership:

- Personal involvement of the senior leader in the change initiative
- Commitment to long-term results (determination)
- Transformational style
- Organization-wide support from the CEO, the senior or top management, the implementation team, the champion, and the implementing managers

Biblical Corroboration in Nehemiah

Nehemiah 1 portrays a man who weeps, mourns, fasts, prays, and repents for his people—a humble man. Jim Collins, author of the bestseller *Good to Great*, found that leaders of great companies were a mixture of personal humility and professional will—what he termed a "Level 5" leader.[5] The rest of the Book of Nehemiah presents a case study of a transformational leader with an iron will who was personally involved in making his vision become reality. And Nehemiah found support from his CEO, the king. Nehemiah said, "Let him send me to the city in Judah where my fathers are buried so that I can rebuild it" (Nehemiah 2:5), and the king granted his request.

An Example of Leadership

Dr. Pete Alwinson is the senior pastor of Willow Creek Church, a Presbyterian church in Winter Springs, Florida. Pete actually started his church with a men's Bible study that met on Tuesday mornings. The church has grown to a congregation of eight hundred on Sunday mornings.

Pete puts his money where his mouth is when it comes to men's discipleship. Every week he schedules three men for breakfast or lunch to get to know them better, understand their needs, and pray for them. And he doesn't let the men pick up the check! For Pete, the relationship is the task.

He also teaches men's Bible studies. He personally conducts the annual elder training. And he participates in an annual men's wilderness adventure—as one of the guys.

When I asked him to rate his commitment and involvement to implement his men's discipleship program, he said, "Well, I'd say it's 100 percent. I'm 100 percent committed to this. . . . Our church started from a men's ministry. . . . The main thing I do is develop men." Later he added, "I believe as it goes with the men of the church, so goes the church." That kind of passionate commitment attracts men.

WHAT YOU CAN DO | *To Promote Leadership*

- Be firmly committed to not only support but to be personally involved in both the initial implementation and the ongoing execution until sustainability is reached—let's call this "determination."

- Encourage the senior church staff, including lay leaders, to believe in the program, because they are needed to help build organization-wide commitment. Any church staff involved in implementing the program must also be committed to long-term success. A program champion who is capable and committed will need to recruit a team of like-minded individuals.

THEME 2: VISION

The second success theme, vision, was a powerful factor found in each of the case-study churches. The leaders and people developed strategies, plans, and resources that clearly followed the senior pastor's vision.

Vision is more powerful than labor. Vision sets forces in motion that, once released, can no longer be contained. Consider these visionary statements, all of which reached or are approaching fulfillment:

- "We will put a man on the moon by the end of the decade."—President John Kennedy
- "To organize the world's information and make it universally accessible and useful."—Google's mission statement
- "Imagine a world in which every single person on the planet is given free access to the sum of all human knowledge."—the founder of Wikipedia
- "A computer on every desk and in every home."—Bill Gates, retired chairman of Microsoft
- "I want to make it possible during my lifetime for anyone in the world to taste a Coke."—the CEO of Coca-Cola in the 1950s
- "If we're going to be nationwide, then we need batteries in every place in America that sells batteries."—Norm Miller, then-chairman of Interstate Batteries, in 1978

It would be difficult to overstate the power of a well-formed vision statement. For example, today you can go to any city in America with a population of one thousand or more people and buy an Interstate battery. To put a vision in "just the right words in just the right order" can enflame people's imaginations and commitment. One great idea can change the world.

Implementation Factors from the Literature

Research studies in the literature found the following factors necessary for effective vision:

- The gathering and analysis of information
- The creation of a clear and compelling vision
- The creation of a sense of urgency for change
- The introduction of an initiative that works and is perceived to work

Biblical Corroboration in Nehemiah

After Nehemiah had gathered information from his brother (1:3), he prayerfully thought about it (1:4–11). God put a vision into his mind to rebuild the city of his fathers (2:5). He first shared his vision with the king (2:4–5). Once he arrived in Jerusalem, he secretly surveyed the damage under cover of darkness (2:11–16). When he introduced his vision and plan, it captured the imaginations of the leaders in Jerusalem. They believed his plan would work! (2:17–18).

Two Examples of Vision

At Willow Creek Church, the motto of Dr. Alwinson since 1988 has been, "No man left behind." It's crystal clear, reflects a sense of urgency, and has inspired a large following.

His vision and goal is for *every* man in his church to be discipled. The results are pretty amazing: 95 percent of his men profess faith in Christ, 75 percent are engaged in spiritual growth, and 75 percent are serving the Lord in some capacity.

The vision of Tom Lipsey, senior pastor of Montgomery Community Church in Cincinnati, is "to see every man in the church become a radical follower of God, very devoted and effective in his family, doing life together in accountable relationships with other men, and sending them out in mission whether at work, home, or in the community." In others words, the vision is to make disciples of as many men as possible. That's especially significant since men's discipleship was not a priority when he arrived.

Both of these successful pastors see men's discipleship as the key to building strong men, marriages, families, churches, and communities. They are passionate about their visions, which helps them foster church-wide commitment.

Ironically, neither could articulate specific goals they had for their men's discipleship programs! But they are guided by an urgent vision to disciple every man in their churches.

In fact, they depend on their visions to "catch on" and mobilize the resources of their churches to make disciples of men. They tend to use their influence rather than positional power to build support.

However, neither of these pastors neglected their other programs. But it did mean that when resources were inadequate, the men's discipleship programs did not suffer.

WHAT YOU CAN DO | *To Bring About Vision*

- Gather and analyze information that points to the problem, need, and opportunity—information that will challenge and inspire your leaders to action. You can use statistics and points from part "1: Understand Your Men" to create a vision. Start by giving a survey found in the article "A Bulletin Insert Survey to Count Your Disciples," located at www.pastoringmen.com. This amazingly simple survey will tell you what percentage of your men are disciples in each of three categories: called, equipped, and sent.

- Create a clear, resonant, inspirational vision statement that creates a sense of urgency. The more pithy and memorable the better. The vision must seem to the leaders and people like it will work, and then it must work in practice.

- Develop an *all-inclusive mindset*. Traditionally, when asked, "How many men are in your men's ministry?" a pastor might respond, "Eighteen." The "all-inclusive" mindset would say, "If we have 100 men in our church, then the size of our men's ministry is 100. The only question is whether or not we are doing a good job to disciple them." Here are some examples of vision statements that capture the all-inclusive concept:

  "No man left behind."

  "Every man a disciple."

  "A disciple-making ministry to every man."

THEME 3: PEOPLE

The third theme is "people." *People* here means people who "make disciples"—not the men who will be discipled. Jim Collins is famous for saying, "Get the right people on the bus." It's so true. One long-ball hitter is often more productive than three average people. My father-in-law has a favorite saying: "Amateurs teach amateurs to be amateurs." It's not enough to recruit men with good hearts; you also need men who have skills. Most men are not trained to make disciples nor to sustain an ongoing men's ministry.

Implementation Factors from the Literature

Research studies in the literature found the following factors necessary for finding the right people:

- *Expertise*. Recruit capable, committed people who understand what is expected from them.
- *Training*. Train those people with the skills required to implement the change.
- *Culture*. Creating a culture that offers psychological safety for people to dialogue about their reservations.

Biblical Corroboration in Nehemiah

Nehemiah challenged his people with a compelling vision to rebuild the walls of Jerusalem (2:17). He created an atmosphere for people to speak up (2:18). He recruited the leaders of the city to do the work (2:16).

An Example about People

To say you need to be personally involved doesn't mean you have to do everything. Far from it. At Willow Creek, Pete has empowered a leadership team to plan and execute their men's discipleship program and activities.

Pete concentrates on selling his vision to disciple every man in his church. All of Pete's lay leaders have bought into his vision. That's probably because to be a leader in Pete's church, you must first complete a special men's discipleship program that he teaches and make a commitment to the church's philosophy of developing men.

An Example of How Not to Do It

Once I spoke at an incredibly well organized and heavily attended men's event. When the leadership team and I gathered in the pastor's study for prayer just before the event started, I noticed they all looked extremely tired. I made a mental note to look into it. Here's what I discovered later.

The senior pastor has recruited a highly capable businessman with a reputation for "getting it done" to be the event chair. The event chair then recruited a dozen other capable businessmen. Together, they put together an awesome plan to turn men out for the event.

However, after digging deeper, I learned that none of these men were very mature spiritually. In fact, they were a collection of baby Christians and cultural Christians. Since they did not have enough Christ for themselves, they really did not have enough to give away. In the process of filling the sanctuary "in the flesh" they had all gotten themselves worn down. I thought to myself, *It will be a long time before these men will ever say "Yes" again.*

WHAT YOU CAN DO | *To Have the Right People*

• Recruit capable men for every position.

• Have church policies that set priorities and allocate resources to train and support these capable men.

• Include the right people in the planning process to build a sense of ownership. They should understand what is expected from them but in a culture that allows them psychological safety to speak out and process their reservations.

THEME 4: PLANNING

It will come as no surprise that the churches effective in men's discipleship had a plan, and the others did not. What may surprise you, though, is that their plans were often (1) vague and (2) stored in the senior pastor's head.

Surprisingly, having an elaborate written plan is not an essential success factor. In an executive program I attended at the Harvard Business School for owners and presidents of smaller companies, I learned that operators of smaller enterprises often don't have written plans. That doesn't mean they don't have plans—just not in writing. Successful businessmen—and pastors—always have a plan, even if they keep it in their heads.[6] That certainly was the case in this research.

Implementation Factors from the Literature

Research studies in the literature found the following factors necessary for successful planning:

- Making the adoption decision
- Formulating strategy
- Developing concrete plans (who does what by when)

Biblical Corroboration in Nehemiah

Nehemiah made his decision and formulated his strategy while still in Persia (1:8–11). He developed a comprehensive plan to rebuild the wall once he arrived in Jerusalem and analyzed the situation (2:11–16).

An Example about Planning

Ironically, while the vision of his church is tightly focused, Pastor Alwinson described both planning and execution as "messy"—a condition not uncommon in nonprofit organizations, according to Collins.[7] "Because church work overall is messy, leadership is incredibly messy," Alwinson told me. "You are dealing with paid and volunteer staff in the church. Implementing change and leadership in that kind of a context can be extremely difficult. You don't have money or position to leverage anything," he continued. "It has to be based on relationship."

At first, the lack of written plans made things appear chaotic and disorganized. But that was not the case at all. Pete knows how to keep "men's discipleship" moving along. And his determination keeps them on track.

First, they create momentum by periodically hosting men's events and activities. Second, they capture momentum by inviting attendees to join follow-up groups. Third, they sustain momentum by assimilating men into the existing ministries of the church. And they keep repeating the cycle over and over again. (This foreshadows the No Man Left Behind model I will present in chapter 9.)

WHAT YOU CAN DO | *To Promote Planning*

• Select a *sustainable* men's discipleship planning strategy—a proven model. Most of the failures we observe started here—picking a model that was doomed from the start. Once all the data have been gathered and analyzed by the involved parties, the decision is made to adopt a specific model. This process proceeds slowly to give everyone time to register concerns and work out their issues.

• The strategy will suggest planning issues. Formulate a concrete plan to imple-ment the program using the model you have selected. The concrete plans should identify who will be involved, how they will be resourced, and what the schedule will look like.

• Create an atmosphere in which people can express their reservations. The planning process needs to consider how the program will be sustained from the start (e.g., the necessity of ongoing senior pastor involvement and devel-oping organization-wide commitment). These plans do not necessarily need to be elaborate or even written.

THEME 5: RESOURCES

Once you have the right strategy (model) for men's discipleship, the next crucial step is to make sure you provide enough resources to see it through. My Uncle Bud was a hero in the Korean War. He was a full-bird colonel in command of a tank battalion that got cut off behind enemy lines. They had advanced faster than their supply lines and got starved from the resources they needed to fight. The results were nearly catastrophic. By God's grace, Uncle Bud was able to ma-neuver his men back to safety. Almost every men's discipleship ministry we see is "starved" for resources.

Implementation Factors from the Literature

Research studies have found the following six resources are necessary factors to successfully implement an initiative:

• Structures: Creating organization structures (such as a committee)
• Time: Building in enough time to complete the mission
• Money: Allocating enough budget

- Expertise: Assigning staff with needed expertise
- Training: Providing training to those who need it
- Compensation: Providing rewards and incentives (monetary or non-monetary)

Biblical Corroboration in Nehemiah

Nehemiah carefully assembled the resources he would need—written authorizations (2:7), timber for construction (2:8), capable people to do the work (3:1–32), and money (7:70–72). He created an organizational structure to assign the work (3:1–32).

An Example about Resources

Harvest Community Church in Charlotte, North Carolina, started in February 1996 with five families and a vision "to develop people into followers of Jesus Christ with a passion to worship God well and communicate His love to others." In June of that year, Jeff Kisiah joined Harvest and was assigned men's discipleship as one of his responsibilities. God did some great things, but without training in a systematic approach, they experienced the typical roller coaster. In fact, after eight years only 25 percent of their men were involved in ongoing spiritual formation.

Then in 2005, Jeff sensed God's call to focus on men's discipleship. He attended our No Man Left Behind training. After learning the components of a sustainable discipleship system for men, he structured a new small-group initiative which was launched at their annual men's event on Labor Day Weekend 2005. They call their initiative "MVP" (for Men of Valor and Prayer). By the following May, 40 percent of their men had participated at some level. By January 2007, 60 percent were participating in some disciple-making venue. By June 2008, the numbers jumped again to 75 percent involvement.

Jeff continued to involve other leaders and made sure they also received training. By mid 2008 Harvest Community Church had 350 regular attendees of which 125 were men. Of the men, 95 percent professed faith, 75 percent were involved in growth groups, and 85 percent were serving the Lord in some capacity. That's an increase in male discipleship from 25 percent to 75 percent in only three years.

WHAT YOU CAN DO | *To Allocate Resources*

• Have the planning team identify the structures, time, budget, expertise, training, and any incentives that will be needed. In the beginning, it might be a planning team of one.

• Obtain the approval and endorsement of these resources by the senior leadership or other appropriate decision-making entity.

• Include training. Training may be the most overlooked resource in men's discipleship ministry.

POINTS TO REMEMBER

• Research shows that, all things being equal, most of your new initiatives will never get past the idea stage and, of those that do, two-thirds will fail.

• You can dramatically improve your particular results by knowing what works.

• Three main success factors tower over the others:
  – *Vision:* A vision to disciple *every* man in the church
  – *Determination:* A personally involved pastor who is determined that men's discipleship will work "no matter what"
  – *Sustainable Strategy:* A "sustainable" strategy to move men forward as disciples

• Possibly the most powerful idea we have been able to develop is what we call *the "all-inclusive" mind-set*: If you have 100 men in your church, then the size of your men's ministry is 100.

MORE SUCCESS FACTORS IN DISCIPLING MEN

In chapter 7 we looked at success factors revealed by research for the first five themes that lead to effective men's discipleship. To complete the picture, here are the final four themes and their related success factors. Then, in the next chapter, we will tie this together with an actionable model that can give you a sustainable strategy to more effectively disciple all of your men.

THEME 6: EXECUTION

In football, regardless how nice or talented a player is, he's going to be taken out of the game if he repeatedly fumbles the ball. Failure to execute loses more games than not having a good plan—at least if football coaches are to be believed. Nearly every losing football coach offers the same answer: "We just didn't execute."

If you have just the right mix of leadership, people, planning, and resources, you still have to execute. That's where the rubber meets the road.

When I built office buildings in my first career, I would marvel how on one jobsite every corner of the building would be occupied by workers. But on another jobsite, there would only be one or two subcontractors working. Invariably, the difference was in the construction foremen. Some just execute better than others. A lot of it's training, of course, but mostly it's a matter of discipline.

Implementation Factors from the Literature
Research studies in the literature found the following factors necessary for proper execution:

- Conducting pilot projects
- Implementing the change
- Getting feedback
- Making adjustments
- A contingency for taking too much time
- Obtaining systematic feedback to evaluate results

Biblical Corroboration in Nehemiah
Forty leaders and their crews worked side-by-side and shoulder-to-shoulder to rebuild the wall (3:1–32). (Today think Baptists, Methodists, Assemblies of God, Church of God, Evangelical Free, Presbyterians, Episcopalians, Catholics, non-denominationals, house churches, Pentecostals, and Methodists— all those men shoulder to shoulder, lifting and hauling together.) Some built large sections; others built next to where they lived. They each did according to their ability and resources.

The wall was just the pilot project Nehemiah needed for his plan to restore the nation (7:1–4). He had mechanisms in place to get feedback about progress (4:6). Nehemiah also had a contingency plan (4:16–18).

An Example of Execution
One church that has existed for thirty-six years faced serious problems when it marked its twenty-fifth anniversary. The pastor and leaders recognized the people lacked spiritual depth and commitment, and the church was not very well organized.

After concluding that classroom-style teaching had not generally produced satisfactory discipleship results, the church started an intensive one-on-one discipleship program, scheduled for sixteen weeks.

The senior pastor was the champion and involved himself every step of the way. First, he and a key layman recruited their leadership team. The team developed the implementation plan. Then they ran a pilot program parallel to the existing discipleship classes. The team gave people an opportunity to offer feedback, buy in, express reservations, and slowly get comfortable with the new program.

By taking it slowly and making adjustments along the way, they gained church-wide commitment. Then they launched the initiative for the whole congregation. They strongly encouraged every existing and new member to complete the program.

In the ten years that followed, an estimated seven hundred people completed the program. Attendance approximately doubled to eight hundred. Today, a decade later, the church is sending a number of missionaries from the congregation, it is debt free, and has 70 percent of attendees tithe—and 60 percent of those give more than a tithe.

And there's more. People have been trained to study the Bible for themselves. The burden on the pastoral staff to shepherd and train members has decreased. It has become less likely that someone can simply drop out and not be noticed or cared about.

You may be thinking, *But this program was for both men and women.* Exactly. The mind-set for men's ministry should not be *men only*, but *anything that disciples men is men's ministry.*

WHAT YOU CAN DO | *To Help Execute the Program*

• Begin with *a pilot project* that runs parallel to the existing program structures. The pilot projects give people a chance to get used to the program, debug it, attract additional support, quell resisters, and prevent major mistakes. Those tasked to implement the program are involved at all stages of planning to increase ownership and the probability of success.

• Once the pilot project demonstrates success, roll out *the discipleship program* to the entire church.

• Once the program is initially implemented, seek *feedback* through formal evaluations and maintaining a system to gather information. This will increase the likelihood of the program's success. Examples of feedback include debriefs and project audits.

• Build a contingency into the initial implementation plan. Mid-course corrections probably will be necessary to optimize the program, and several years may be required to achieve sustainability. Taking longer than expected is a typically recurring problem that should be planned for in advance.

THEME 7: COMMUNICATION PLAN

Three very different public figures all have realized the power of a good communication plan. In his autobiography, rock musician Eric Clapton revealed that during the early years of his career he shunned marketing, advertising, and publicity. He felt the purity of the music should be enough. He eventually realized his naiveté and embraced the idea that people can't acquire what they don't know about.

Billy Graham was once asked the secret of his success. He replied, "Prayer and publicity." The danger of not wanting to secularize our work is that we over-spiritualize it. We are presenting the gospel in a fallen world—a world of people who need help to hear. Mr. Graham said, "If Jesus were living on earth today, I have no doubt that His methods would be just as up-to-date as possible. Newspapers, magazines, television, the Internet, satellites—I think He would use them all to get across His message."[1]

Dwight L. Moody said, "We pray like it is all up to God. We work like it is all up to us."

To do less is to presume upon God to provide "immaculate communication."

Implementation Factors from the Literature

Research studies have found the following elements are part of an effective communication plan:

- Publicity about the benefits of change
- Publicity that highlights short-term successes

Biblical Corroboration in Nehemiah

When Nehemiah was ready to go public with his ideas, he called the leaders together and extolled the virtues of his vision and plan (2:16–18). They celebrated the short-term success of completing the wall with a great celebration (12:27–43).

An Example about Communication

At Willow Creek Church in Winter Springs, the weekly bulletin keeps a spotlight on men. Special event announcements are regularly distributed to men. The church's Web site is also an active location for information on the men's discipleship program and activities.

When the men return from their annual May Wilderness Adventure, they have a dinner for all the men in the church about two weeks later. They show a brief highlights video (great to build interest for the next year) and give men three or four summer options to consider (e.g., a service project, a men's Sunday school class, a men's Bible study, and a social activity like paintball or mountain biking). Their philosophy is "don't surrender the summer."

WHAT YOU CAN DO | *To Promote Communication*

• Begin with a pervasive, organization-wide communication plan that reinforces your plans, and especially the vision for the program, at every opportunity. This includes bulletin items and inserts, pulpit announcements, and manned table displays in the foyer.

• Include personal invitations (actually, "repetitive" personal invitations). This is the most effective method of getting men involved.

• Mention your vision during sermons to increase perceived importance.

• Be sure the communication plan includes benefits of participation, and early success stories should be publicized. However, the leadership should be cautious about declaring victory too early.

THEME 8: RESISTANCE

Because of the fall, resistance is "built in." Paul said he would stay on at Ephesus, "because a great door for effective work has opened to me, *and there are many who oppose me*" (1 Corinthians 16:9, italics added).

You can expect resistance on two levels. First, there's *behavioral* resistance from individuals: people like routines, set patterns, and predictability; some feel threatened by meeting new people or programs that require time commitments. Second, there's *systemic* resistance from the church as an organization: a church operating at full tilt will resist adding something else.

Implementation Factors from the Literature
Research studies have found the following elements are effective in dealing with resistance:

- Mechanisms to identify resistance
- Processes to deal with behavioral and systemic resistance

Biblical Corroboration in Nehemiah
Sanballat and Tobiah fiercely opposed Nehemiah and his plan, so the people "prayed to our God, and posted a guard" (4:9). But that wasn't all—there were other types of internal resistance. The workers got tired, the rubble made it difficult to work (4:10), and others ran out of money (5:1–6). But Nehemiah had mechanisms to identify resistance (4:11–14). When they faced opposition, Nehemiah had worked out a communication plan to deal with resistance (4:19–20).

Examples of Resistance
Jim Smithies, pastor of lay ministries at Bethel Bible Church in Tyler, Texas, watched as his church resisted implementing the "Church of Irresistible Influence" model for reaching the community.[1] But through patience, time, and having a forum to process reservations, the church leaders eventually caught the vision. Pastor Smithies describes the process and eventual success:

> It took us a year to get the elders to consider trying to impact our community. We got to the point that there were two or three champions on the elder board that said, "This is a no-brainer. Biblically this is a no-brainer. We have a plan; we can't come up with any reason other than sinful self-centeredness for not trying this."
>
> So there is that persuasion phase, and eventually, if we're on a biblical path, the discipleship pathway, it's going to grow to the point where there are a couple champions on the elder board that say, "This is what we're going to do." Then my responsibility, and I think the senior pastor's responsibility, is to have a plan and people that can make it work. And, our climate is changing; it's easier now than it was. God has brought some new men on the

elder board that want to become more purpose-driven and more outreach-driven, and more discipleship-driven—so all of those components matter. It's very much an organism, and it's very much a dynamic. And I like that; you just have to be willing to deal with that in a relational context without ruining the relationships in the process of the frustration. And that's where, I think, it's been a challenge, and God has been merciful.

At Willow Creek Church, individual resistance from strong women who wish the senior pastor would devote more of his time to women's issues does come up from time to time. Pastor Pete Alwinson tries to win them over by saying something like, "In my opinion many of the issues in church and culture are caused by weak and immature men. I believe I can do more for women and children by equipping men to be stronger."

At Montgomery Community Church in Cincinnati, Pastor Tom Lipsey inherited and did not replace the church's senior leadership team. Those leaders wanted to cling to the old structure and strategy—ones that had failed to produce an effective church. Tom just waited. It took ten years, but most came around and those who didn't moved on.

WHAT YOU CAN DO | *To Respond to Resistance*

• Expect resistance. Don't presume your vision will just happen. Every substantial new idea will experience resistance, what we often call "push back." And it is not just people who resist change (behavioral), but also the church as an organization (systemic) because the system will try to maintain the *status quo*. So it is important not to presume your vision will just happen, but actually to expect resistance.

• If considerable resistance is encountered, then program elements may need to be redesigned in response.

• Proactively identify resistance from both individuals and the church as a system trying to maintain equilibrium. The leaders and planners should discuss up front how they plan to process and deal with resistance. A strong communication plan, pilot programs, and allowing plenty of time for people to process the new idea may reduce or eliminate resistance.

• Keep talking about an idea until it either catches on or, through prayer, it becomes clear it is not God's will. Some of my smaller ideas catch on right away, but usually it takes many months and sometimes years for people to process the impact and implications of a substantial idea.

THEME 9: SUSTAINABILITY

Lots of really great, well-executed ideas bomb (remember the stats at the beginning of chapter 7). Sustaining the idea is the meat of the coconut.

By a wide margin, the reason pastors get so frustrated with pastoring men is the degree of difficulty they have sustaining ministries to men. After the initial flush of enthusiasm, "someone" has to keep men's discipleship ministry "center stage" until it becomes enfolded into the routines of the church.

The research reveals that "someone" is the pastor. The pastor is the key to everything—and that includes sustainability. It is your vision, your determination, your sustainable strategy that will make men's ministry last. Without your personal involvement, men's ministry probably won't happen. That's just reality.

How to sustain men's ministry needs to be part of the planning process from the beginning. In the next chapter I will show you a model that you can use to build a sustainable strategy—one that will survive once the novelty wears off.

It will come as no surprise that the churches effective in men's discipleship knew how to sustain momentum, and the others did not. The word I think best describes the attitude of the pastors successful in reaching men is "determination." They just wouldn't take "no" for an answer. They were convinced they would ultimately prevail. They considered their efforts God's will. They were not to be denied.

Implementation Factors from the Literature

Research studies have found one key element that contributes to sustainability.

• Once the program is adopted, the leadership should enfold the initiative into the routines of the organization.

Biblical Corroboration in Nehemiah

Despite fierce resistance from within and without, Nehemiah and his team rebuilt the wall in fifty-two days. But the city was large, and the people were few

(7:4). To sustain the vision and plans Nehemiah had started to implement, the city needed ongoing leadership. So Nehemiah appointed his brother to lead them (7:2). He appointed staff to maintain the city (7:3). And he repopulated Jerusalem with people (7:4-5). He repopulated the towns of Israel (7:73). He normalized Jerusalem and stabilized the land promised to his fathers.

An Example of Sustainability

Dennis McFadden, a pastor at Shoreline Community Church in Monterey, California, sustains momentum with men through their small groups. They found that a relationship-based, rather than an event-based, ministry model is more sustainable. They do events, but "events are just to give us an opening to create new relationships."

McFadden has worked men's discipleship into the routines of his church. Periodically McFadden appoints new leaders to the leadership team. Momentum is also sustained by letting men run with ministry ideas they come up with on their own. During Sunday service announcements McFadden will say something like, "Guys, did you like the last men's breakfast? What do you think?" And then the men that attended let out a roar. This builds equity in the event in the other men's eyes—a kind of tipping point. McFadden quotes Jesus, "'They'll know you're Christians by your love for one another.' We feel that's what's going to transform our church—the love our men have for one another. And we have to be in relationships for that to be manifested."

WHAT YOU CAN DO | *To Promote Sustainability*

• Help to sustain a new program by making it one of the habits, or routines, of your church. This is best accomplished if the initial planning considers how the program will be normalized in the church from the very start. "Routinization" is accomplished when people see how the church has truly benefited, staff have job descriptions that include men's discipleship support, and by insuring leadership successors are true believers in the program. Basically, sustainability is the byproduct of putting the other eight of the nine themes in place.

• Stay focused on a huge goal for the long haul. There really are no shortcuts— whether business, ministry, or relationships. A shortcut takes years to develop. Often a small band of leaders stays the course. This group of leaders will often say things like: "We will prevail no matter what" and "We can do this." And they remind one another, "This is not going to be easy—nothing good is easy."

REMEMBER THE BIG THREE

We've looked at a host of success factors organized into nine essential themes. Frankly, that could get to be a bit overwhelming. But if you apply the three main factors discussed at the beginning of chapter 7, you will find the other factors will fall into line. Again, here are the big three:

- *Vision:* A vision to disciple *every* man in the church (the "all-inclusive" mind-set).
- *Determination:* A personally involved pastor who is determined that men's discipleship will work "no matter what."
- *Sustainable Strategy:* A "sustainable" strategy to move men forward as disciples.

In the next chapter, I will offer a model you can use to build a sustainable strategy.

POINTS TO REMEMBER

Nine essential themes are present in every successful organization:
- Leadership
- Vision
- People
- Planning
- Resources
- Execution
- Communication plan
- Resistance
- Sustainability

REFERENCES FOR SUCCESS FACTORS
Books

Ansoff, Igor and E. McDonnell. *Implanting Strategic Management.* 2nd ed. New York: Prentice Hall, 1990.

Collins, Jim. *Good to Great.* New York: HarperBusiness, 2001.

Kotter, John P. *Leading Change.* Boston: Harvard Business School, 1996.

Rogers, Everett M. and Everett Rogers. *Diffusion of Innovations.* 5th ed. New York: The Free Press, 2003.

Senge Peter M., Art Kleiner, Charlotte Roberts, and George Roth. *The Dance of Change.* New York: Doubleday, 1999.

Journals

Alexander, L. "Successfully Implementing Strategic Decisions." *Long Range Planning* 18, no. 3 (1985): 91–97.

Ayas, K., and N. Zeniuk. "Project-Based Learning: Building Communities of Reflective Practitioners." *Management Learning* 32, no. 1 (2001): 61–76.

Beer, M. "Why Total Quality Management Programs Do Not Persist." *Decision Sciences* 34, no. 4 (2003): 623–42.

Freedman, M. "The Genius Is in the Implementation." *Journal of Business Strategy* 24, no. 2 (2003): 26–31.

Houston-Philips, K. "Leadership Development Partnerships at Dow Corning Corporation." *Journal of Organizational Excellence* 22, no. 1 (2002): 13–27.

Johnson, K., C. Hays, H. Center, and C. Daley. "Building Capacity and Sustainable Prevention Innovations." *Evaluation and Program Planning* 27, no. 2 (2004): 135–49.

Kotter, J. P. "Leading Change: Why Transformation Efforts Fail." *Harvard Business Review* 73, no. 2 (1996): 59–67.

Kotter, J. P. "Ten Observations." *Executive Excellence,* (August 1999): 15–16.

Kotter, J. P. "What Leaders Really Do." *Harvard Business Review* 79, no. 11 (2001): 85–96.

LeBrasseur, R., R. Whissell, and A. Ojha. "Organisational Learning, Transformational Leadership and Implementation of Continuous Quality Improvement in Canadian Hospitals." *Australian Journal of Management* 27, no. 2 (2002): 141–62.

J. D. Linton. "Implementation Research." *Technovation* 22, no. 2 (2002): 65–79.

Miller, D. "Successful Change Leaders." *Journal of Change Management* 2, no. 4 (2002): 359–68.

Maurer, R. "Sustaining Commitment to Change." *The Journal for Quality & Participation,* (Spring 2005): 30–35.

McNish, M. "Guidelines for Managing Change." *Journal of Change Management* 2, no. 3 (2002): 201–11.

Okumus, F. "A Framework to Implement Strategies in Organizations." *Management Decision* 41 (9) (2003): 871–82.

Pluye, P., L. Potvin, and J. Denis. "Making Public Health Programs Last." *Evaluation & Program Planning* 27, no. 2 (2004): 121–33.

Popper, M. and R. Lipshitz. "Installing Mechanisms and Instilling Values: The Role of Leaders in Organizational Learning." *The Learning Organization* 7, no. 3 (2000): 134–44.

Repenning, N. P. "A Simulation-Based Approach to Understanding the Dynamics of Innovation Implementation." *Organization Science: A Journal of the Institute of Management Sciences* 13, no. 2 (2002): 109–27.

Thurston, P. H. "Should Smaller Companies Make Formal Plans?" *Harvard Business Review* 61, no. 5 (1983):162–88.

A STRATEGY TO REACH EVERY MAN

In the previous two chapters we looked at the many success factors necessary to effectively implement men's discipleship. But I highlighted three "main" factors for effective men's discipleship: a *vision* to disciple every man, the *determination* to make it happen, and a *sustainable strategy* to keep it going.

If you have read this far, you no doubt have the vision and the determination to pastor your men. In this chapter let me show you a model around which you can build a sustainable strategy to disciple each and every one of your men over the long haul.

YOUR SYSTEM IS PERFECTLY DESIGNED . . .

In business we have the helpful idea, "Your system is perfectly designed to produce the results you are getting."

For example, if you manufacture cars and every third car that rolls off the assembly line is missing a front right fender, your system is perfectly designed to produce that result.

Your church has a "system" perfectly designed to produce the kind of men you have sitting in the pews. That may be scary to you—even overwhelming.

But in this chapter I am going to show you a proven strategy to systematically move your church toward the vision of discipling all of your men. It's basically the Cliffs Notes on *No Man Left Behind,* a book David Delk, Brett Clemmer, and I co-authored (Moody, 2007).

At Man in the Mirror, we have been developing and tinkering with the No Man Left Behind model since 1996. This model, depicted in figure 2, is a system perfectly designed to call, equip, and send every willing man in your church to become a passionate follower of Christ at each man's own pace.

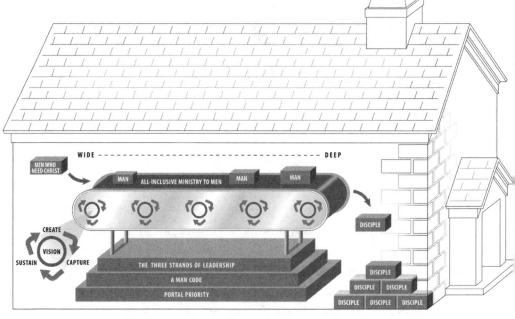

FIGURE 2
The No Man Left Behind Model

The model is simple. On the left you have men who need Christ. A conveyor belt moves "every man" along toward discipleship at his own pace. The create-capture-sustain cycle is the engine that powers the conveyor belt. Repetitions of the create-capture-sustain cycle keep the conveyor belt moving. And the conveyor belt is built on three foundations.

THE STRATEGY: MANAGING THE MOMENTUM

The key to sustainable strategy is "managing momentum." We've all watched a football game where one team seemed to have the game sewed up. But they made a couple of mistakes, the other team got excited, made a big play and, suddenly, the momentum was gone. A key concept of the No Man Left Behind model is "managing the momentum." In fact, the heart of the model is the concept of "creating, capturing, and sustaining momentum." Figure 3 illustrates the create-capture-sustain cycle.[1]

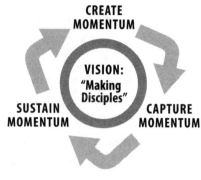

FIGURE 3
The Create-Capture-Sustain Cycle

CLARIFY YOUR VISION

First, notice that everything revolves "around" vision. Everything rises and falls on the vision. It is the focal point. Men want to be part of something bigger than themselves. Few men will attend an activity unless they feel like it's going somewhere, especially younger men.

The vision for your men's ministry is "to make disciples." You can say it more cleverly than that, and I recommend you do. Find a phrase that resonates with men—like "no man left behind." But the essence of the vision is "to disciple every man in the church." It's to call, equip, and send men to become passionate followers of Jesus Christ.

Describe every involvement that men have with your church in terms of this vision. The men who serve as deacons, the men who lead the scout troop, the men who play in the worship band, and the men who teach the fifth graders—thank them for being Kingdom Men (or Men of Valor, or Iron Men). None of those men would be included in the old definition of "men's ministry" (a separate men's organization), but all of them are vital to the vision God has for your church. Churches that are growing men have learned to communicate their vision in resonant ways.

How should you present this vision to your men? Since the term "disciple" can mean different things to different people, plan to preach a series on discipleship—something like, "What Is a Disciple and How Do You Become One?" (You can access an article I wrote with this title at www.pastoringmen.com. Focus on the biblical command to make disciples, texts that describe discipleship (see figure 1, chapter 5), examples of how Jesus' disciples responded, and examples of discipleship—calling, equipping, and sending—that are already taking place in your church. For example, tell them about Michael who never before did much of anything but became excited about serving Christ through Meals on Wheels and, as a result, recently signed up for a growth group.

THE CREATE-CAPTURE-SUSTAIN CYCLE

Let's say you have the vision to disciple every man in your church worked out. Here's an example of how the create-capture-sustain cycle "revolves" around the vision.

A. Create Momentum

Create momentum with men by inviting them to have breakfast, attend church, play softball, or be your guest at a special men's event. You create momentum by offering men something they want—"something of value." Any meeting of two or more men can create momentum.

Let's suppose your church hosts a men's dinner with an outside speaker on the topic, "Success That Matters." A team of five or six men invests one hundred hours or more to push the event over the top. The marketing resonates with your men. They perceive the event will be a "valuable" use of their limited time. It's the best event you've ever had. Fifty of your 125 men attend. You're jazzed. (Next time have your team go to disciplemen.com, find a church that did a similar event, adapt their graphics and materials, and save up to sixty hours.[2])

B. Capture Momentum

Now what? You've expended an enormous amount of energy to overcome the inertia in men. You turned them out. You created a lot of excitement—and momentum. But unless you "pre-planned" something to "capture" the momentum, you may as well heat your home to a comfortable 70 degrees in the dead of winter and then leave your windows and the front door open. You've expended a lot of energy but have not captured it. This is what makes for a roller coaster men's ministry.

Instead, offer what we call a "believable next right step" for the men who attend the dinner—a step to help "capture" the momentum. For example, what if you say, "Men, we've had a wonderful time tonight hearing about God's perspective on success. For the next six weeks we are going to have discussion groups meet for one hour a week to unpack more about success that matters."

You have already purchased follow-up booklets with six weeks of discussion questions. You put them in the middle of the table—enough for every man. Then you form the men into groups of five or six right there on the spot (do this at the event—strike while the iron is hot). Happily, thirty-four men sign up. You tell them to pick a leader, a mutually convenient meeting time, and have them write down everyone else's name and contact information.

Our experience after conducting over one thousand events is that on average two-thirds of the men will take the offer and join a short-term follow-up group. That's because it is a "second gear" task. In other words, instead of trying to shift them from "first gear" (the event) to "fourth gear" (a long-term Bible study), you give them a believable next step. The men hear your offer and think, "I can do that." They can visualize themselves succeeding at what you've suggested. This is huge.

C. Sustain Momentum

How do you sustain the momentum? What do you do with the men once the six-week groups are over? Well before the groups end—at weeks four and five—you begin to plant seeds for the "sustain" steps. From the pulpit, you mention the discussion groups. Have a man give a testimony about how God is using the group to change him. Then you give your men several options. The concept is to integrate them into the "existing" ministries of the church. You can also offer something "new." Remember, men do what they want—not what you want. So offer several options for both growth ("equipping") and service ("sending"):

- A book study that will discuss a chapter a week
- A "how to find your service niche in the church" meeting during the Sunday school hour
- Join an existing Bible study or home group
- Start a new round of Bible study groups

- A missions trip
- Join the prison ministry team on its next trip
- An opportunity to visit one of three local ministries to the poor and homeless
- A class to uncover your spiritual gifts
- Leader training for elders or deacons or men's ministry
- An ongoing weekly Bible study that you teach as pastor
- Any ministry of the church that needs volunteers

Also, keep in mind two special groups of men. Some of the men in your six-week groups may already be up to their eyebrows in growth and service, so they will go back to what they were doing. Give men like that a nod as you speak. It is discouraging to be all out for Christ and never get a word of appreciation and encouragement.

Another group of your men may need to rest, not hear about more to do. Give men in your church permission to "come unto me all who are weary and burdened" and take a season to rest. Let them be "takers" until they are filled to the overflow in their relationship with Jesus and *want* to become "givers." The key word here is "want." Yes, you can get men to do what they "need" to do for a while, but ultimately men will always end up doing what they "want." So let them worship, hear about Christ's love, abide in him and, at a point, they will naturally *want* to do something to better know and serve their Lord.

How many men can you expect to be involved after one cycle of create-capture-sustain?

RESISTANCE: THE PRINCIPLE OF THE PARABLE OF THE SOWER

The command to make disciples must always be juxtaposed against the principle of the parable of the sower. Jesus said, "Go and make disciples." He also said that when we do, some seed will fall on the path and be snatched, some on rocky soil will spring up but soon wither, some will be choked by life's worries and riches, but some will produce a crop.

Remember, resistance is one of the nine major themes of successful organizations. The resistance here is the inertia in men. Because of the principle of the parable of the sower, attrition is "expected" every time you ask for additional involvement.

So what is a reasonable set of expectations for a pastor of 125 men who has fifty of them attend an "over the top" event?

TAKING STOCK: SUCCESS OR FAILURE?

In our example, fifty men came to the "create momentum" event and 67 percent—thirty-four men—joined the six-week "capture momentum" follow-up groups. Let's suppose that once those groups run their course, out of the thirty-four men five take up your offer for more "equipping" and/or "sending." I know that sounds low, and you may get more. But let's stick with five men for our illustration.

Think about it. You have 125 men in your church. You turned 50 of them out for a great event that in and of itself accomplished quite a bit of discipleship. The speaker's message hit several key points about stewardship of money (equipping). The speaker's evangelistic close resulted in one man becoming a Christian, and six men rededicated their lives (calling). Then thirty-four of those men went through a six-week group. That's quite a bit more discipleship (equipping). And now you have five new men previously inactive who are involved in the life of the church at a whole new level. And their families become more involved too.

If you had not "captured" and "sustained" the momentum, the man who professed faith and the six men who rededicated would likely have slipped through the cracks. The lessons learned about money from the speaker would have been like seed scattered on rocky soil. Maybe one man might have on his own initiative figured out how to get more involved. Instead, you laid down "tracks" for the men to run on and

- one man received Christ,
- six men renewed their faith,
- thirty-four men dug deeper into success that matters, and
- five new men got involved in ongoing discipleship (equipping and sending).

Let's say that before your event, 40 percent of your 125 men were already disciples. That's fifty men. In only one cycle of create-capture-sustain you have experienced a 10 percent increase in the number of men committed to discipleship. That's impressive.

Here's what one cycle of the No Man Left Behind model looks like. Note how it accounts for men dropping away because of the principle of the parable of the sower:

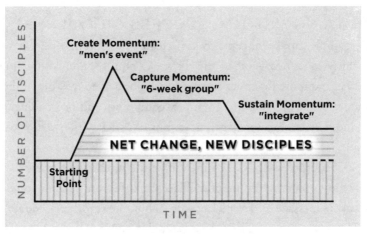

FIGURE 4
One Repetition of the Create-Capture-Sustain Cycle

What would have happened if you did not have a strategy to capture and sustain momentum from your event? After a few weeks you would be right back where you started—as though the event had never happened. So at first the "net change, new disciples" may not seem like much, but it's a lot compared to the alternative of doing nothing.

REPEAT THE CYCLE: THE CONVEYOR BELT

So you've completed one cycle. Now what? This is where it starts to get interesting. This is where sustainable long-term growth and change becomes a real possibility for your church.

Once a cycle has run its course, you repeat the cycle. I like to think of this as "steady plodding." It's like a people mover that steadily moves men forward.

Repetition builds on the momentum already in place—like the flywheel concept in Jim Collins's *Good to Great*. Every revolution of the Create-Capture-Sustain cycle allows for incremental progress by taking small steps forward. Without a repeating cycle it seems unlikely an effective ongoing program can be implemented. The conveyor belt would simply stop moving.

Here's what three cycles of Create-Capture-Sustain look like:

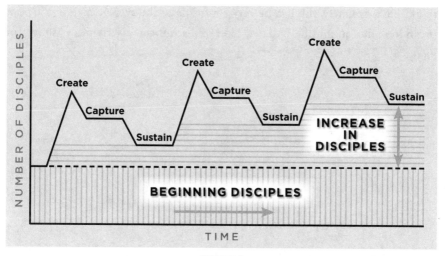

FIGURE 5
Three Repetitions of the Create-Capture-Sustain Cycle

This model is thrilling because it's believable, manageable, doable, and—best of all—it works. This approach pulsates to the rhythm of the gospels. Many repetitions help work the create-capture-sustain cycle into the "routines" of the church—in essence, a sustainable strategy.

THE FOUNDATION

And there you have it—a "system perfectly designed to disciple men into passionate followers of Jesus Christ." Now let's turn our attention to the foundations upon which it's built—the "portal priority" (your philosophy of ministry), a "man code" (the environment you create for men), and the "three strands of leadership."

The Portal Priority

Suppose a man has attended your church for four months. What will he think is the first priority—the organizing idea—of your church?

One week he hears that worship ought to be a top priority. The next week he hears that he needs to be a cheerful giver. The following week he hears that committed believers go on mission trips. The week after that he is asked to attend evangelism training. The next week he learns about the compelling needs at the crisis pregnancy center. A weekend seminar greatly emphasized the importance of private study and devotions. If you were a new man in Christ, what would you think? Unfortunately, this can be very confusing to the average man in the pew. It can look like an undifferentiated blob of disconnected activities as shown in Figure 6.

	Preaching	Teaching	Christian Literature		
Leadership Training	Godly Families	Service/ Missions	Worship		Bible Studies
	Fellowship	Discipleship	Evangelism		
Informal Discussions	Stewardship	Social Justice	Vocation		Private Study
	Seminars	Mentoring	Small Groups		

FIGURE 6
Undifferentiated Church Priorities and Activities
(as they appear to a relative newcomer)

With so many priorities, is it any wonder some men end up confused? The sheer number of priorities seems overwhelming! What's the starting point? Where does he focus? Where do *you* focus? Consider a few more questions:

- How can a man worship a God he does not know?
- How can a man have genuine fellowship unless he knows why he should love his neighbor as himself?
- How can a man be a good steward if he doesn't understand and believe that everything he has is a gift from God—his time, talent, and his treasures?
- How can a man serve effectively if he doesn't know his gifts and that God can use him—or even that God wants to use him?
- How can a man bring about social justice if he doesn't know what is just?
- Why would a man want to share his faith if he doesn't understand the Great Commission?

As you can see in Figure 7, one idea sits squarely in the center of all the other *desired outcomes*. The focusing priority of a thriving church is discipleship. Sheep cannot do right until they know right. Discipleship is the "portal" priority through which all the other priorities of your church can be achieved. It is the method of Jesus (Matthew 28:18–20) and the first of the three foundations in Figure 2. Organize your church by putting discipleship in the center, and then draw arrows out to each of your desired outcomes (yours may vary) like this:

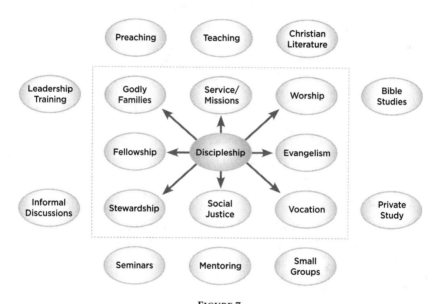

FIGURE 7
Desired Church Outcomes
Organized around Discipleship as the "Portal" Priority

Next, how can your church implement discipleship as the portal priority? The items around the outside of figures 6 and 7 represent the *methods* a church engages in to help build disciples. Draw arrows from each method to the portal priority (see figure 8).

Remember these methods are not ends in themselves, but rather focus on helping people learn or live out what it means to be a disciple. The figure illustrates this: All activities on the outside lead to discipleship in the middle. Now we have a clear picture of discipleship as the portal priority by which every other goal of the church can be accomplished. For example, we don't preach to make "worshipers" but to make "disciples" who see God in a way that men can't help

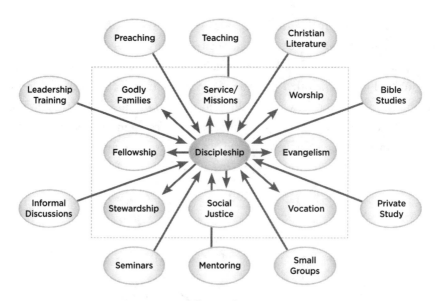

FIGURE 8
Methods of Making Disciples to Reach Other
Church Priorities and Goals

but worship. We don't preach to make "workers" but to make "disciples" who understand that bearing much fruit brings glory to God (John 15:8).

The focus is not, for example, "feed the poor." It's "make disciples," some of whom, as a result, catch a vision for feeding the poor.

Discipleship is the portal priority through which all the other priorities of a church can be achieved. This concept can give you and your leaders a way to filter your activities and programs for a tighter focus on the mission. You can download a PowerPoint presentation of figures 6–8 to use with leaders at www. pastoringmen.com.

A Man Code

How do men dress at your church—casual clothes, slacks and sports coat, business casual? When a new man starts attending, how does he figure out what to wear? You obviously don't publish a dress code, but every man still figures out the dress code in short order, right?

In the same way, you have an unwritten "man code" that defines what it means to be a man in your church. The man code is the second foundation shown in Figure 2. Like the dress code, your men observe what is expected of them to be a man in your church. And being performance-oriented, men will tend to give you back exactly what you ask for. If you want them to be strong disciples—spiritual leaders, men of integrity, and strong husbands and fathers, then they will work to those ends.

From the décor, to the announcements, to how men are involved in the worship service, you can create an atmosphere that says: "Men matter here. Men can make a difference. God is doing something in and through the men of this church." Would you need to modify your "man code" for men to feel like this?

The Three Strands of Leadership

Successful discipleship ministries for men need strong support from the senior pastor, a committed leader, and an effective leadership team—three strands of leadership (like the cord of three strands in Ecclesiastes 4:12). These form the third foundation in Figure 2.

We've already detailed your involvement as the pastor. You certainly don't have to attend every meeting, but you do need to regularly ask the question, "Are my men being discipled and how can I help?"

You also need a passionate leader who wakes up in the morning praying that God would use him to help disciple the men of your church and community. Don't let this leader self-select himself into the job—that may work, but more often fails. Instead, you pick the leader and go after him. He should be the kind of man that other men will follow.

Let your men's discipleship team leader select his own team. Together, have them implement the No Man Left Behind Model. Emphasize from the beginning that you're going after long-term, sustainable results.

On top of this foundation, you can think of the interactions your church has with men as a "conveyor belt"—the process of your ministry to men. Here are two key concepts to keep in mind: (1) the all-inclusive mind-set and (2) getting men to connect.

THE ALL-INCLUSIVE MIND-SET

The "all-inclusive mind-set" was mentioned in the chapter 7 under the theme of "vision." To reiterate, however many men you have in your church, that's the size of your men's ministry.

The era of "men's ministry" as an activity off to the side of the church is an "old wineskin." It created far more problems than it solved. The traditional definition of men's ministry was "activity that happens when men are by themselves"—like a Saturday morning breakfast or a weekend retreat. Those activities certainly are men's ministry, but don't exclude men who serve in other ways in your church—like worship or sports activities with kids. Using an "all-inclusive mind-set," include all your men when you say "men's ministry." Better yet, say "ministry to men."

Help your leaders see that everything your church does that touches men is "men's ministry," from the worship service to ushering to kitchen helper. An "all-inclusive ministry to men" disciples men right where they are. For example, you don't need your male Sunday school teachers to join a separate men's ministry. Instead, have them gather thirty minutes early once a month to discuss "the challenges of being a male Sunday school teacher."

GETTING MEN TO CONNECT

The business axiom is so true: "Your system is perfectly designed to produce the results you are getting." The No Man Left Behind Model is a system perfectly designed to help you produce men who are passionate disciples of Christ. For a fuller explanation, see our book *No Man Left Behind.*

I suggest you develop a one-year plan to complete one cycle of create-capture-sustain, and then reevaluate. You can start with any kind of event to create momentum. Then have a short follow-up to capture the momentum. Near the end of the follow-up, offer men multiple entry points into the existing ministries of your church to sustain momentum.

After the drop-off because of the principle of the parable of the sower, the residual of new committed disciples will add to your base. Next year, you can repeat the cycle. In this way, men not "ready" this year get another opportunity. This will give you a system that regularly invites men to connect with you when they are ready. The No Man Left Behind Model is a sustainable strategy that best addresses all the problems we have seen in working with men.

POINTS TO REMEMBER

- Your church has a "system" perfectly designed to produce the kind of men you have sitting in the pews.
- The key to sustainable strategy is "managing momentum."
- If you do not have a strategy to capture and sustain momentum from your event, after a few weeks you will be right back where you started.
- Here are the nine key concepts of the No Man Left Behind Model:

1. Clarify Your Vision: Describe every involvement that men have with your church in terms of this vision.
2. Create Momentum: You create momentum by offering men something they want—"something of value."
3. Capture Momentum: Strategically offer a "believable next right step" for the men who attend any event—something at which they can visualize themselves succeeding.
4. Sustain Momentum: The concept is to integrate them into the "existing" ministries of the church. You can also offer something "new." Offer several options for both growth ("equipping") and service ("sending").
5. Repeat the Cycle: Without a repeating cycle the conveyor belt would simply stop moving.
6. The Portal Priority: Discipleship is the "portal" priority through which all the other priorities of your church can be achieved.
7. A Man Code: In the same way you have an unwritten dress code, you have an unwritten "man code" that defines what it means to be a man in your church.
8. Three Strands of Leadership: Successful discipleship ministries for men have strong support from the senior pastor, a committed leader, and an effective leadership team.
9. All-Inclusive Mind-set: However many men you have in your church, that's the size of your men's ministry.

WHY THE MAN IN THE MIRROR MEN'S BIBLE STUDY WORKS —A CASE STUDY

Think of this chapter as a study in best practices. You may or may not have, or start, a Bible study exactly like this one. But I am confident you will pick up several useful ideas from the lessons we've learned. At the end, I will show you how you can reproduce a similar Bible study in your church.

In 1986, five of us decided to start a weekly men's Bible study here in Orlando, Florida. We went on a field trip to Atlanta and observed how a friend, Chris White, ran his group. When we came back we imitated his model—starting in a bar with fifteen men. That quickly grew, and we moved to a local civic center. We have held steady around 150 men since about 1990. I teach for about thirty-five minutes, then groups of six to ten men sit around tables and discuss the message under the supervision of a table leader.

THE ETHOS OF OUR BIBLE STUDY

From the start we designed the study to be like a warming hut at the bottom of the ski slope. It's a place where injured men can be brought until we can get them to the *real* hospital (church). For "well model" men, it's an oasis where they can come at the end of the week and get a drink.

If I were to put a banner over the front door it would say, "Come here all you who are weary and burdened and find rest." I figure that only one out of every five thousand men in the Orlando area drag themselves out of bed early on Friday to attend our study. I know they didn't come to be shamed, beat up, and told they are doing a lousy job with their lives. I know some may need a kick in the pants, but they all need a hug from God. They want to leave sensing that God has spoken to them, that they have been in His holy presence, and that He cares.

We are a disciple-making ministry. Our mission is to engage men in our community with a credible offer of Jesus Christ, help them grow in their knowledge and love for Christ, and equip them to serve God in the home, church, workplace, community, and world. The greatest contribution we can make to these men is to help them change the core affections of their hearts.

Our weekly gathering at the civic center is first, foremost, and always a spiritual enterprise. We meet every Friday morning except the Friday after Thanksgiving and the Friday between Christmas and New Year's Day. About eight times a year I'm out of town, but we still meet with a guest speaker—often a pastor.

A TYPICAL FRIDAY

We start at 6:50 a.m. with coffee, juice, and donuts. Some men come early to visit or sit quietly. The men pay $3.00 at the door, get their caffeine and carbs, then sit at round tables. Once seated, the men put on nametags that fit in plastic sleeves and are clipped onto lanyards. They sit at the same table each week. However, all the tables are open seating, so men can move if they need a change of scenery (e.g., bad chemistry).

At 7:00 a.m. sharp (guys love punctuality, even if they themselves are not) our emcee greets the men, puts everyone at ease, welcomes the visitors, and gets the men to open their Bibles to the day's text—an important signal about our purpose for assembling. Then I give a message that runs about thirty-five minutes.

I usually teach a series, but sometimes I'll do a single message—like a hot topic or something special God is doing in my own life. Sometimes I teach series on books of the Bible, but most seem to be topically organized. (The Web site for this book, www.pastoringmen.com, includes a copy of the "Grace-Based, Application-Oriented Bible Study Preparation Worksheet" that I use each week to keep my message preparation on track).

The men arrive at their tables, which have handouts for taking notes. Some use the handouts; some don't. After the message the men can get another cup of coffee, and then they spend twenty minutes discussing the topic of the day with the other men at their table. The handout also has three discussion questions— one *icebreaker*, one *knowledge*, and one *application* question. I used to prepare more questions, but three is plenty.

We break at 8:00 a.m. sharp. We want to give them a dependable ending time since a lot of men have appointments or have a set starting time.

Most of the men leave right away, but it's pretty common to see several groups of two, three, or four men in the parking lot talking with each other. Several groups go to different restaurants and eat breakfast together. Lots of men e-mail and phone each other during the week. They move from *acquaintances* to *friends* and eventually become *brothers*.

TABLE LEADERS

Each table has a leader. Each table leader has a written job description (go to the Web site www.pastoringmen.com to read it if you'd like). The table leader shows by his actions that he really *cares* about his men *personally*—that's his main responsibility. His table becomes an outlet for personal ministry. For example, some leaders want five men at their tables and some prefer a dozen. It's up to them.

After the message, he leads his men into a meaningful discussion about the topic of the day using the questions printed on the handout. We want to give men time to process, unpack, and apply the message to their lives. Our motto is, "Air time for every man every week." Table leaders should not speak more than 25 percent of the time.

Table leaders must call each man on Thursday evening every week to remind him about the meeting. Some e-mail instead, and that's okay if it works. I know the calls sound cheesy, but when I see attendance drop off at a table over a few weeks, I sometimes walk over to the leader before we start and whisper in his ear, "Have you been making your calls?" Invariably not.

TABLE LEADER QUALIFICATIONS

We have a mixture of seasoned veterans and newer leaders. Half of our twenty-plus leaders have been with me for fifteen or more years. Whether new or veteran, this is what I look for in leaders:

- Full throttle after their own discipleship
- Passionate about seeing other men become disciples
- Wanting to shepherd a group of guys
- Members of a local church
- Attractive to the kind of men we want to reach

Also, I'm specific about what I *don't* want in leaders—those who are:

- Looking for a group to teach. (We need shepherds and discussion facilitators—I've just taught a lesson, now let's discuss and apply it, not teach another lesson.)
- Short on social skills, who talk too much, and who miss important social cues.
- Not willing to make—or have someone make—the weekly calls (an evidence of caring and love).

Near the beginning of the year, each table leader agrees to the terms of his job description for one year. In essence, he gets a one-year "contract." At the end of each year every table leader is out of a job! This gives both of us a time to reevaluate his commitment and effectiveness. If either one of us has a question, we discuss it candidly.

I want everyone to have a graceful exit strategy. Without an exit strategy, men hang onto their positions long after their passions and callings have changed. They lose effectiveness, but inertia keeps them from giving up their post. I would much rather have a man leave at the top of his game than have him do a half-hearted job for two or three years and lose everyone's respect.

Assuming we both want to proceed, he signs a new one-year deal. By the way, I used to allow sabbaticals, but that has never worked out. Once the flame is gone, I have never seen it return in my experience.

MEETING WITH THE TABLE LEADERS

I have always thought of the table leaders as my main ministry—my "group." Since we began, I estimate that I've discipled about one hundred men through the table leader community. Considering the model of Jesus, I have always considered this my greatest accomplishment in ministry.

The leaders gather at my home office once a month. We also have an annual half-day planning retreat. So we do have some organization behind what we do—we just don't want the men to see it! We figure that most men are already so over-calendarized and over-organized that it's nice to have a place where all they have to do is "show up." Sometimes I call it "show up" Bible study.

My friend and mentor, Tom Skinner, told me repeatedly, "We must become the live demonstration of the kingdom of heaven so that anytime someone wants to know what's going on in heaven, all they have to do is check with us." So the leader meetings are not "business" meetings. We meet for our own growth, to pray for each other and our men, to discuss changed lives, and for fellowship. We do an awful lot of laughing.

TREATING OUR GUESTS RIGHT

Visitors

We put business cards on each of the tables every week to invite visitors. We encourage the "regulars" to pick one up and invite someone during the week. Each week we have three to eight visitors. "Like attracts like," so the visitors resemble the bringers.

We work hard to make the Man in the Mirror Bible Study a "safe place" for men to come and investigate the claims of Christianity. First timers do not pay the $3.00. When they arrive they are directed to a special table where a man welcomes them, orients them, and gives them a name tag to fill out. At the bottom of the name tag is a tear-off that includes their contact information. We send each visitor a follow-up letter or, if later in the morning they prayed to receive Christ, a special follow-up letter.

Once the meeting starts, the emcee welcomes the visitors in a low-key way. He asks them to raise their hands in unison, and the men clap to welcome them. No one gets singled out or embarrassed in any way.

After the message, I invite first-time visitors to join me at an empty table in one corner of the room. I give them the lay of the land. First, I explain the schedule—guys like to know the "agenda." Second, I explain the three kinds of men we typically see visit—*seekers, new Christians,* and *mature Christians.* Third, I ask them to share where they are on their spiritual pilgrimage.

When they share they usually identify with one or more of the three categories I have spelled out. By the time everyone has shared, I know where they stand with Christ.

I conclude by telling the visitors we have a threefold concept. First, through the message and table discussions we want to help men see a little larger glimpse of "the God who is." Second, we want to invite men to jettison a little piece of "the god (or gods) they have wanted." Third, because it is an application-oriented Bible study, we want to help men connect the dots—it's 9:00 a.m., the phones are ringing, and the customers are complaining. How do you make the transition? Then I invite them back and point out the second-timers' table.

If a man hasn't received Christ, I ask him if he can stay an extra ten minutes after we adjourn. They almost always do, and I share Campus Crusade's Four Spiritual Laws booklet with them. Most receive Christ. I believe that God sends them to us because he knows we will be faithful to share the gospel with them.

Second Timers

Many men come just once. They don't like the format, they don't like my teaching, it's too early in the morning, or they are just visiting Disney or in town on business. That's okay. Now they know a place where they can point men they meet.

If a man does come back, he sits at the second-timers table for one week. The main task of the second-timers table leader is to help men get situated at a table that's "right for you." We tend to always have a new table forming, and that becomes the default location when the other tables are full.

MEN FROM ALL BACKGROUNDS

We don't really have a "Saddleback Sam" profile. From the start—I think because of Tom Skinner's influence on my life—I have always wanted the Bible study to be egalitarian. So we have always emphasized diversity. We have a bell curve distribution of men from the poorest of the poor to the richest of the rich, and from every age bracket—and they sit together at the same tables! We have also achieved a healthy dose of ethnic diversity. We haven't fully arrived, but we are a lot closer because we've tried.

ATTRITION OF MEN

Every table experiences attrition—some more, some less. Reasons run the gamut from increased church involvement, job changes, moving, or loss of interest. The shepherding skill of the table leader is certainly a main factor.

We have a Bible study administrator, who regularly asks the table leaders,

"Who needs more men for their tables?" He then coordinates with the second-timers table leader to funnel new men to those existing tables.

HOW THE BIBLE STUDY HAS CHANGED

The ministry has morphed from the early days. I would describe our *ethos* originally as "Evangelism with Discipleship and Fellowship." Today, it has morphed to "Discipleship with Fellowship and Evangelism"—no small change. We used to have new men come to Christ almost weekly. Now it's less frequent.

This happened for many reasons. First, I don't think we put as much emphasis on inviting non-Christians as we once did. Second, the messaging probably suits a growing Christian better than a seeker. Third, the percentage of men who have been attending for a long time has increased, and a lot of these men have run through their non-Christian contacts.

Fourth, the makeup of the group has morphed. Today about one-third of our men lead their own ministries—pastors, parachurch workers, elders, deacons, and lay leaders. They lead businessmen's Bible studies, home groups, run churches, teach youth and teens, operate recovery programs—you name it. Many of these men started their service because they grew in faith at the Man in the Mirror Bible Study. Others, especially pastors, have found it a great place to come and "just be a guy." We put zero emphasis on "who you are" or "what you do."

CHALLENGES TO KEEP THE PROGRAM DYNAMIC
Challenge #1

Over the years the weekly Bible study has faced several challenges. Here's the first of seven challenges we've faced and how we adapted in response.

In the early 1990s I just about destroyed the whole deal. I got on this kick that we needed to discover all our problems and fix them. For month after tedious month, I led the table leaders into a death spiral. It was downright depressing to them. After awhile, I got depressed too.

Then one day I remembered that men were regularly coming to Christ and that the table leaders were deeply impacting many of the men at their tables. We changed the focus from "fixing our problems" to "discussing changed lives." We started spending our time talking about what God was doing in men's lives. I swore to never again surface a problem unless it really was a problem. Within days things started to look exciting again—and still do!

Challenge #2

With the busy "ten talent" men we have as leaders, I always considered two-thirds attendance at leader meetings to be great—roughly equal to the Rotary's perfect attendance. At about the fifteen-year mark, though, table leader attendance at the then twice-monthly meetings dropped from about two-thirds (or more) to about one-half (or less). I didn't know what to make of it—or whether to take it personally. On one hand, the Bible study was cooking right along, so why upset the apple cart? On the other hand, it says right in the job descriptions they sign that they will attend!

Eventually I realized that the "burnout clock" for table leader meetings must start ticking before the "burnout clock" for leading a table on Friday mornings. Some of those leaders had been with me for a dozen or more years! One day when I was praying about it, the Lord spoke to my heart and said, "Love them more." A strange answer, for sure, but that's what I did. Looking back on it, I'm quite sure I would have completely destroyed the Bible study if I had tried to force their attendance. Of course, if a table leader doesn't attend leader meetings and his table falls off, that's a whole different story.

At the twenty-year mark (after five years of "love them more"), nothing had changed. The leader meeting attendance was still down to 50 percent (and sometimes less). I figured, *Maybe it's just too much to ask.* So we dropped from twice monthly to once monthly. Do you think it helped? Frankly, I like it better, but it didn't make a twit of difference in attendance.

Then someone had the idea of requiring table leaders to attend *or send a man* from their tables. The meetings would be full, the visitors would catch a whole different vision for the Bible study, and potential leaders could be groomed. It worked for a while, but it was an idea that just didn't want to work long term.

It is easy to look at the data and come to the wrong conclusion. It's easy to go off half cocked and solve the wrong problem.

I knew that the devil would like nothing better than for me to "blow up" our very successful Friday morning Bible study over the table leader meeting attendance issue.

I knew I needed to wait on the Lord to clarify the problem, but now several years had gone by. Finally the issue did clarify. I could find no correlation between leader attendance at the meetings and success at leading a table on Friday mornings. Quite the contrary, the men who didn't attend leader meetings all had awesome tables on Friday morning. So they didn't *really* need to be at the leader meetings from that standpoint. At the same time, leaders who are not "plugged in" are ripe to get picked off.

Here's the solution: Together, the table leaders and I decided the Man in the Mirror Bible Study and the table leader meetings are "two separate ministries" (versus "one ministry with two parts"). We decided a table leader doesn't have to attend the monthly leader meetings *provided* he is part of some other group that provides a measure of accountability. But I love the monthly meetings—it's my "table"—so anyone who wants me to be their "table leader" can come to the monthly meetings.

And, best of all, God gave us the wisdom to not blow up a perfectly good ministry over an issue easily, if not quickly, solved in a different way.

Challenge #3

From time to time, the "burnout clock" runs out before the job description expires. When that happens—which is not very often—I have a special e-mail that I send. I call it my "Dear George" letter:

> Dear George,
>
> I've noticed (I think) that your table has dwindled. We need to decide what to do to rebuild it. Before that, however, I need to know how you are feeling about it.
>
> Over the years we've seen tables decline for two major reasons:
>
> 1. The normal attrition of men as they move on to other things.
> 2. The priorities of the table leader change.
>
> Before we rebuild the table, I would like to know if you still feel this is a calling and priority. The best way for you to assess that is to ask yourself three questions:
>
> 1. Have I been faithful to call my men? (This is probably the best "litmus test" for men to know "for sure" that you care about them personally.)
> 2. Have I led my men into meaningful discussions about the topics of the day with balanced participation? (This skill of drawing men out and

the leader not talking too much is a "make or break" issue.)

3. Have I been faithful to the table leader job description? (Best answered by looking it over in a spirit of prayer.)

My love for you, George, is unconditional and does not depend in any way on which way you want to go. You don't have to be a table leader to make me happy. I do have a responsibility, though, to make sure this is something you are truly committed to before we start rebuilding.

Why don't you think this over prayerfully and let me know.

Serving Christ together,

Pat

Sometimes a table leader's calling changes, and he doesn't even recognize it. I took one leader to breakfast to talk about his table. He had found a new passion that he was hard after. He was feeling guilty for not doing a better job as a table leader—and his table had dwindled. But he didn't want to leave the table! I proposed that we celebrate his past success and new calling, and let him return with dignity to non-leader status. He agreed, and a relationship was saved by dealing with it head on.

Challenge #4

Why have our numbers not grown since 1990? I really like our size. It's big, but not too big. In order to grow we would have to move to a bigger facility. But with our value of "working ourselves out of a job with every man," we would rather have men "flow through" into churches than accumulate.

After a man can stand on his own two feet spiritually, we want to pass him off so he can get his family vitally connected into the life of a local church. We have seen over three thousand men come through! Most have become better leaders in their families. Many have also become leaders for Christ's church—pastors, missionaries, parachurch workers, elders, deacons, teachers, and evangelists.

But God has outwitted us on size because, in 2001, one of our table leaders started webcasting the Bible study, and now we have thousands of downloads every week in every state and in thirty-eight countries. Each week small groups around the world watch the videos and print out the same discussion questions we use on Fridays.

Also, *The Man in the Mirror* book and Man in the Mirror Ministries grew out of the Bible study. Since its founding in 1991, Man in the Mirror has impacted over ten million men worldwide. Everything we do flows from The Man in the Mirror Bible Study. It's the incubator where new ideas get hatched—the laboratory where we experiment (and, usually, I am the laboratory rat upon whom God performs his experiments!).

Challenge #5

Around 2005 we started to find it difficult to recruit new table leaders who took 2 Timothy 2:2 seriously. Our solution was to start a "leadership development" table that runs for six weeks twice a year. Frankly, most of the graduates wanted the training for their "other" ministries, so we decided to encourage that too. We also have graduated some fine men as new table leaders, and now our leaders get up to speed much faster than before we did the training.

Challenge #6

Making the weekly reminder calls has always been a "sticking point" for some of our table leaders. It's ironic that the single greatest predictor of attendance—a reminder phone call—is the single greatest weakness for many leaders (sometimes it's hard not to admire the devil's cleverness).

I don't blame them. Calling leaders to remind them of our monthly leaders meeting is pure drudgery for me—it's too routine, structured, and another thing I "have" to do. So I have a man who loves to make the calls. The table leaders can also get a man at their tables to make the calls.

The reminder is a means, not an end, so I don't want the tail to wag the dog. Some table leaders can turn their men out with an e-mail reminder—so be it. A couple of leaders have men so faithful and disciplined that they don't need nor, in some cases, do they want a reminder call. That's fine. At the end of the day, what we really want is for each man to feel like somebody really cares about them personally.

Challenge #7

I know this will sound amazing, but for almost two decades we had thirty to fifty men each week not pay the $3.00 to cover the room rental at the civic center. On more than one occasion I have stood next to the "honor system" money basket and watch a man walk in, greet me warmly, look me straight in the eye, and then walk right by the basket! On the bright side, we must be attracting the kind of men who need to hear God's Word!

For most of those years, the coffee and donuts were donated by one of our men who owned the Dunkin' Donut franchise (effectively subsidizing the cheaters!). He sold his business, so in 2007 we had to start paying for coffee and donuts.

The problem was easily resolved. We manned the table with a cashier. I announced that if the money was a problem for anyone we would waive the $3.00, and two or three men took up that offer.

DISTINCTIVES AND VALUES

Together, the table leaders and I have forged a common set of beliefs about God's calling for our Bible study. What's important to us—the distinctives and values that make it work—include the following:

- Grace: an oasis where men can come at the end of the week and get a drink; men deserve grace just for showing up; show men Christ versus fix their behavior; unconditional acceptance
- Making disciples: grace-based, application-oriented teaching; change core affections of the heart; heart transformation, not behavior modification
- Changed lives: we measure our profits in changed lives
- Table groups: a place where men care about each other personally; the relationship is the task; a hub that extends beyond the Bible study; all tables are "open," but deep relationships develop
- Discussion time: at tables after the teaching to flesh out and apply the message; air time for every man every week
- Hurting men: a hospital for men with broken wings; a warming hut at the base of the ski slope; we want men to "feel the love"
- Egalitarian: a cross-section of our community; multi-denominational; multi-ethnic
- Low barriers; no preparation required, just show up
- Visitors encouraged: welcomed but not put on the spot; "multiple" personal invitations required; a process to assimilate
- We are a Bible study, not a church: we want to work ourselves out of a job, see men get involved in a church

- Leaders passionate about discipling men: full throttle after their own discipleship; make weekly reminder calls for Friday a.m.; shepherds not teachers
- Table leader community: table leaders meet monthly for study, prayer, and fellowship; annual half-day planning retreat

CAN THIS MODEL BE REPRODUCED IN A CHURCH?

While ours is a "community" Bible study, the largest Bibles studies in America take place in churches—typically mornings for churches in the suburbs and lunch for the downtown churches. But the location is secondary. What's primary is a passion to see men become disciples.

Take East Cooper Baptist Church, a church of 2,300 adults, in Mt. Pleasant, South Carolina, for example. After visiting the Man in the Mirror Bible Study as part of a No Man Left Behind Conference here in Orlando, their team went home and replicated the Bible study in their church. Here's how layman Randy Bates describes it:

> We came back and planned for a fall introduction of the Friday morning study, which we call Man2Man. We purchased 25 round tables to facilitate the discussions after the message.
>
> Within a short time 70 men were regularly attending each week. During our second year we averaged about 105 men and, in year three, we averaged around 145 men.
>
> We started with donuts like you do, but soon ramped up a full hot breakfast of eggs, bacon, sausage, biscuits, gravy, grits, hash browns, oatmeal, fruit, cereal, coffee, and juice. Food comes on at 6:20 a.m., I start the announcements at 6:40 a.m., and pray by 6:50 a.m. Our pastor, Conrad "Buster" Brown speaks until 7:10 a.m., and then we have table talk until 7:35 a.m. Most men can be at work by 8:00 a.m.
>
> The good news is not about the numbers—it's the fact that we are changing men's lives, and we're getting a lot of positive comments from the women at the church.

Frankly, growing the study beyond a dozen men is also secondary.

Here are the primary factors that need to be addressed if you want to start a similar Bible study:

- Vision: A vision to make disciples
- Environment: A welcoming, grace-oriented attitude and environment
- Love: Men respond when they feel like we care; especially keep an eye out for men who are hurting
- Messaging: A relevant, application-oriented message prepared especially for men presented by a decent speaker and followed by time to discuss it
- Barriers: Low barriers to attend (e.g., no homework—you can graduate men into deeper studies later)
- Visitors: A "visitors welcome" culture
- Systematic: Men love things that run smoothly

If you do grow, then you will need a table leaders level, but that can come later. When that happens, here are two more factors to address:

- Table groups: For men to connect "with a few" and do life together
- Table leaders: Form a community of leaders passionate about discipling men and who can build strong relationships at the tables

Of course, if you start a study you will develop your own vision, mission, distinctives, and values; but this gives you a proven baseline from which to begin. (You can download Chris White's "How to Build a Dynamic Men's Fellowship" at www.pastoringmen.com or in the "Find a Resource" section at www.disciplemen.com.)

PART 3

TEACH YOUR MEN

SEVENTY THINGS EVERY MAN NEEDS TO KNOW

1. Abiding in Christ
2. Accountability
3. Anger
4. Balance
5. The Bible
6. The Blessing
7. Calling
8. Change
9. Character of God
10. Church
11. Contentment
12. Counsel
13. Cultural Christianity
14. Cultural Mandate
15. Cycle Breaking
16. Decision Making
17. Discipleship
18. Disciplines, Spiritual
19. Evangelism
20. Faith
21. The Fall
22. Father Wound
23. Fathering

24. Fear
25. Friendships
26. Futility
27. God's Will
28. The Gospel
29. Grace and Performance
30. The Great Commission
31. Growth
32. The Heart
33. Holiness
34. Idols
35. Integrity
36. Jesus
37. Lies
38. Lordship
39. Loving God
40. Loving People
41. Man, Doctrine of
42. Manhood
43. Marriage
44. Money and Possessions
45. Mother Wound
46. Prayer
47. Pride

48. Priorities
49. Private Devotions
50. Purpose and Meaning
51. The Rat Race
52. Reading
53. Rest
54. Sabbath
55. Service
56. Sex
57. Small Groups
58. Spiritual Gifts
59. Spiritual Warfare
60. Stewardship
61. Success Sickness
62. Success That Matters
63. Suffering
64. Time Management
65. Unexamined Life
66. Witnessing
67. Work
68. The World
69. Worldview, Christian
70. Worship

11

SEVENTY THINGS EVERY MAN
NEEDS TO KNOW

In this chapter you will find seventy one-page (mostly) topical summaries in alphabetical order with a few talking points that I think uniquely apply to men. You will no doubt be able to think of others. (Note: In several cases I repeat points from earlier chapters.)

You can use these summaries to connect with your men. Four specific ways are suggested below. In addition to the topics, which include resources, I recommend you explore www.disciplemen.com for other men's resources. This Web site gathers the world's best men's discipleship leaders and resources together in a single online location.

Finally, you may want to only skim these now to get a feel for what's here. Then when you are preaching or teaching on a subject, come back and get a men's perspective that you can work in.

Here are four ways you can use this topical index with your men:

- Use this chapter as a reference tool when you're looking for some talking points to add a men's perspective to your sermons, worship services, counseling, leadership meetings, men's groups, breakfasts, luncheons, dinners, adult education classes, home groups, Bible studies, mission trips, service projects, or any other program, activity, or ministry.

- Emulate Pastor Pete Alwinson, who almost every Sunday will at some point in his sermon say, "Now men, let me tell you what this means for you," then offer a male-specific insight or application from this chapter or triggered by reading this chapter.
- Photocopy a page on a hot topic and use it as a discussion starter with your men.
- Let's say you will have a man and, if applicable, his family for three years. What lessons are so important to build into his life that if he left without them, you would feel like you failed him? Those lessons can become your discipleship curriculum—what you want to teach and impart to him. Use these seventy subjects to help you decide on a curriculum that best fits your men.

1. ABIDING IN CHRIST

Teach your men what it means to abide in Christ for a man. To abide in Christ means to "hold to my [Jesus'] teaching." Jesus said if you do that "you are really my disciples" (John 8:31). By abiding in him, Christ says we "bear much fruit, showing yourselves to be my disciples" (John 15:8).

Here's a manly story you can use to illustrate abiding in Christ: The bills had arrived faster than income for several months. For several weeks Tom had not slept well. The stress was excruciating. And now, an unpaid vendor was chewing him out as he quietly listened. His heart was heavy as he placed the phone back in its cradle. This was the first time in his career that Tom had creditors calling to ask when he could pay. Discouraged, he shut his door, slipped to his knees, and began to pray.

"Dear God, I owe you an apology. Somehow, I have taken over the ownership of this company. I know it really belongs to you, and I am sorry. I'm not doing too well. I'm stressed out, I'm not sleeping, I'm grouchy at home, and I'm neglecting my family. Right now, by faith, I am giving you back your company.

"Now, over there on my desk you have a pile of unpaid bills. I am going to trust that if you want this organization to continue that you will find a way to get them paid.

"In a moment, since I do trust you, I am going to get up, go home, have a nice meal, enjoy my children, and stop worrying about whether or not you want your company to succeed. Amen."

You wouldn't be surprised to learn that things turned around over the next few days, would you? They did.

For More: Go to www.pastoringmen.com and click on "1. Abiding In Christ" to read the article "How to Walk in the Spirit."

2. **ACCOUNTABILITY**

Teach your men how to have an accountable relationship. Most of our lives are lived at the cliché level. The accountable relationship is a tool to get past "news, sports, and weather."

Accountability means to be regularly answerable for each of the key areas of our lives to qualified people. A major purpose of the church is to provide a framework for accountability. Accountability helps men to persevere and abide in Christ. Accountability is crucial because we are a product of both the creation and the fall. Creation has made us a little like a god. The fall has made us a little like a devil.

Raging all around us is a titanic battle for the souls of your men. First Peter 5:8 says, "Your enemy the devil prowls around like a roaring lion looking for someone to devour." Every man, no matter how meek, is embroiled in a spiritual battle. Your men are being hunted.

On top of that, men are weak. As one leader said, "A lot of men are just one step away from stupid." Without the help of a few friends to keep us on track we, too, like sheep will go astray.

First Peter 5:9 says, "Resist him." Practically speaking, accountability is how we "resist him." No Christian ever led a vibrant, obedient life on his own. There are no successful Lone Ranger Christians.

To be "answerable" means to give someone permission to ask you how you are *really* doing (by phone is okay). Your men will lead shallow lives unless they let someone probe below the waterline. Visibility increases accountability.

"Regularly" means to meet at planned intervals. Weekly is good, but no less often than monthly is recommended. "Key areas" means relationships with God, wife, children; use of time and money; moral and ethical behavior; and any areas of personal struggle. "Qualified people" means those who are vested in your success in a given area. Wives make great accountability partners.

For More: Go to www.pastoringmen.com and click on "2. Accountability" to (1) download the article "How to Have an Accountable Relationship," (also in Spanish); (2) to order free wallet-sized accountability cards (shipping only) for your men; (3) stream or download the free online audio or video message "Accountability: The Missing Link" in The Man in the Mirror Remix series (also available in podcast at iTunes); and (4) read chapter 23, "Accountability: The Missing Link," in Patrick Morley, *The Man in the Mirror* (also in Spanish).

3. **ANGER**

Teach your men about anger. Anger is a gender issue. As many as three million women a year are physically abused by their husbands or boyfriends (2 percent per year). Depressed men commit suicide 300 percent more often than women. Significantly, depression has been described as "frozen rage."

Some anger is righteous and needed, but most is not. Challenge your men to figure out if they "get angry" or have "an angry spirit." Anger is "a strong feeling of displeasure and belligerence aroused by a real or perceived wrong." An angry spirit, on the other hand, is "the state of always feeling displeasure and belligerence aroused by real or perceived wrongs."

To have an angry spirit is to be easily provoked to anger. Ecclesiastes 7:9 says, "Do not be quickly provoked in your spirit, for anger resides in the lap of fools." Most men with an angry spirit have not been fathered (or mothered) well. Anger passed from fathers to sons is definitely an issue to bring up—it's part of repeating the cycle. Unresolved anger is like walking around with a volcano inside you—never knowing when it might erupt, or why.

Personally, when teaching on anger in 2007, I felt compelled to write a letter to my adult children. In that letter I confessed that I had "an angry spirit" when they were growing up and asked their forgiveness. By God's grace, he has healed me of an angry spirit, and my children readily extended forgiveness. I had to work this out with my wife too. Professional Christian counseling was a big help. Tell your men that their pride may make it hard to humble themselves and ask forgiveness. But the joy of reconciliation and wholeness is well worth it.

Help men (1) to overcome denial of an angry spirit, (2) to repent, (3) to grieve what could have been (e.g., with their fathers), and (4) to not succumb to a victim mentality. God is big enough to work it out. Help them be doers of the Word.

Be sure to give a nod to men who are getting it right—it will encourage them.

For More: (1) See chapter 18, "Anger," in *The Man in the Mirror*, and (2) go to www.pastoringmen.com and click on "3. Anger" to stream or download the free online audio or video message "Anger" (also available in podcast at iTunes).

4. **BALANCE** *(SEE ALSO PRIORITIES)*

Teach your men what it means to lead a balanced life. Personally, I like it best when I am "busy and balanced." It's a fine line. What can we tell men about the look of a balanced life, and how to achieve one?

Tell your men at least these few things (perhaps you can think of more):

1. No amount of success at work will ever be adequate to compensate for failure at home.
2. After God, but before all others, make your mate your top priority. Spend time together alone, touch her, listen to her, encourage her with words, take care of her financially, laugh together, and be her best friend.
3. Invest in your children with time, prayer, and encouraging words like, "I love you," and "I'm proud of you." There's no pain like child pain. If your children do well, all of your other problems will fit into a thimble.
4. Most men compartmentalize their family, but not their work. They think about their work when they're with their families, but not their families while they're at work. Tell men to put a time *and mental* boundary around their work. For example, "I will not work after 6:00 p.m." One man promised to take his wife out to dinner every time he broke the rule.
5. Let Jesus be your highest and best thought in every situation. Pray about everything. For example, you might say a silent prayer for five seconds as you pick up the receiver to make a call. Jesus will help you lead a balanced life if you're in constant communication.

For More: (1) Read chapter 3, "How Happy Do You Have to Be?," in Patrick Morley's *The Ten Secrets for the Man in the Mirror*; (2) read chapter 16, "Setting Priorities," in *the Man in the Mirror*; (3) go to www.pastoringmen.com and check "4. Balance" to stream or download "How Can I Lead a More Balanced Life?" (10 Questions That Trouble Every Thinking Man series).

5. **THE BIBLE**

Teach your men how to read, study, trust in, and use their Bibles.

Early in his ministry, the great evangelist Billy Graham attended a conference with some top seminary professors and intellectuals high up on a mountain in California. They told Mr. Graham their doubts about the Bible and showed him what they called the contradictions in the Bible. He was young. He had only been out of school for a short while and was having his first experiences in preaching. These men were persuasive, and he began to doubt.

Finally, he wandered out into the mountains, found a tree stump, and laid his open Bible on it.

"Oh, Lord," he said, "I do not understand everything in this book, but I accept it by faith as Your Word."

From that time his preaching was marked by a new and God-given authority. Teach your men:

1. The Bible is for now. "For everything that was written in the past was written to teach us, so that through endurance and the encouragement of the Scriptures we might have hope" (Romans 15:4).
2. The Bible is truth. "Sanctify them by the truth; your word is truth" (John 17:17).
3. The Bible is without error. "Every word of God is flawless; he is a shield to those who take refuge in him. Do not add to his words, or he will rebuke you and prove you a liar" (Proverbs 30:5–6).
4. The Bible is effectual. It produces the intended result. "My word that goes out from my mouth: It will not return to me empty, but will accomplish what I desire and achieve the purpose for which I sent it" (Isaiah 55:11).

Our job as teachers is to explain the Bible, not explain it away. A great Bible teacher is not a great teacher of the Bible, but the teacher of a great Bible. We use Scripture to explain our experience, not our experience to explain Scripture. Without the Bible to guide you, every path not obviously evil will seem obviously worthwhile.

6. THE BLESSING

Teach your men to bless their children. (For men who didn't receive a blessing, see "Father Wound.") In my book for high school boys, *The Young Man in the Mirror*, I recounted speaking to forty young men, ages fourteen to seventeen, in jail. These boys were major offenders incarcerated for serious crimes: rape, murder, robbery, weapons, and (mostly) drugs. Nearly 90 percent had no father figure.

I was able to keep their attention by telling how I quit high school, and how my brothers have struggled with alcohol, drugs, divorce, and bitterness. Also, I shared the tragic death of my younger brother to a drug and alcohol overdose.

At the beginning I handed each young man a nametag. Halfway through my talk, I asked each boy to write his name on the tag and stick it to his chest.

Then I went and knelt in front of each boy, one by one, read his nametag, looked him in the eye, and said, "Carlos Rivera (or whatever was on his tag), God knows your name. He loves you very much. He knit you together in your mother's womb. He knows every word you speak before it comes to your tongue. He knows when you sit and when you stand. [See Psalm 139:1–4, 13.] He knows everything you have ever done and will do, and He wants to forgive you. If you will reach out for Him, He is already reaching out for you. You can change your life. God wants to adopt you and be your father. Do you understand this?"

Like dry sponges, each soaked up what I was telling him about his identity.

Why did I do this? Sons need the *approval* of their fathers—sometimes called "the blessing." I certainly was not qualified to give those boys "the" blessing of a father, but I wanted to give them "a" blessing. I wanted them to know their identity—who they really were created to be. And I wanted them to know Jesus Christ was available to them even though they had done bad things.

Jacob cheated his older brother Esau out of his father's blessing. Their father, Isaac, had to tell Esau that he had already given Esau's blessing to Jacob. The Bible says, "When Esau heard his father's words, he burst out with a loud and bitter cry and said to his father, 'Bless me—me too, my father!'" (Genesis 27:34).

A lot of our identity comes from our *father's blessing*. In the Bible, to bless means "to endue with power for success, prosperity, fertility, longevity, etc." Help your men understand how crucial a father's blessing is to the well-being of his sons and daughters. It is his seal of approval.

7. CALLING

Teach your men that every vocation is holy to the Lord. The Bible makes no distinction between sacred and secular. For the Christian, all of life is "spiritual." Francis Schaeffer said: "A ministry such as teaching the Bible in a college is no higher calling intrinsically than being a businessman or something else."[1]

Many men who sense the desire to serve God welling up within them assume they must now do something else. That is rarely the case. For 99 percent of us, God probably wants us right where we are (see 1 Corinthians 7:17, 20, 24)—with a whole new orientation to pleasing Christ.

The call to service develops in three phases: calling, equipping, and sending. When God "calls," He rarely "sends" right away. Instead, we usually go through a season of "equipping" when we encounter delays, uncertainties, and hardships. God uses these times to work some things "into" and "out of" our lives.

Tell your men to employ the seven means of guidance: the Bible, prayer, the Holy Spirit, conscience, circumstances, counsel, and fasting (see "God's Will"). Help them understand their spiritual gifts (see "Spiritual Gifts").

Here are some teaching points:

- We are made to serve (Ephesians 2:10).
- God want us to bear much fruit (John 15:8).
- To help us He gives spiritual gifts (Romans 12:6).
- The ultimate purpose of our service is to bring glory to God (1 Peter 4:11).

Great Quote: "Jennie, Jennie. You've got to understand. I believe God has made me for a purpose—for China. But He also made me fast! And when I run I feel His pleasure! To give it up would be to hold Him in contempt. You were right. It's not just fun. To win is to honor Him," Eric Liddell, Gold Medalist, 1924 Olympics, from *Chariots of Fire*.

For More: Go to www.pastoringmen.com and click on "7. Calling" to (1) see or hear "How Can a Man Change?" from The Man in the Mirror Remix series and; (2) read the articles "12 Suggestions to Discover Your Calling" and "How to Discover Your Design," and; (3) read chapter 24, "How Can a Man Change?" in *The Man in the Mirror.*

8. **CHANGE**

Teach your men how to change. When we talk about "change," what are we talking about? Change means "to make something different from what it is, or would be if left alone."

Teach your men that *their part* is a conviction to change, to not conform to the world any longer (Romans 12:2), and a full surrender to the lordship of Jesus Christ. The great irony of surrender is that it leads not to defeat but victory.

God's part is to bring about transformation. Second Corinthians 3:18 says, "And we, who with unveiled faces all reflect the Lord's glory, are being transformed into his likeness with ever-increasing glory, which comes from the Lord, who is the Spirit."

Hebrews 12:1–4 tells us that God is the author and *perfecter* of our faith. Tell your men to fix their eyes on Jesus—that He is the perfect example of a man.

There's a great apocryphal story about an elementary school class that went to the studio of a famous sculptor. As the children entered they had to pass by the sculpture of a very ferocious, realistic looking lion. One of the students said, "Hey mister, how were you able to make such a realistic looking lion?"

He answered, "It was easy. I took a large block of marble, then simply chipped away everything that didn't look like a lion." In the same way, your men are like large blocks of marble. Encourage them to bring themselves into the "real presence" of God, and invite the Holy Spirit to chip away everything that doesn't look like Jesus.

How do men change? Men change their *behavior* when they change their *beliefs*. A man changes his beliefs one at a time, and slowly. He sits under your teaching, and one by one, the spiritual truths you teach and their practical applications undergo his review. Once he changes his mind he will not be satisfied until he also changes his behavior, and he has the Spirit to help.

Our role, then, in bringing about change is to create multiple opportunities for men to ponder truth and how it applies—sermons, small groups, any place where two or more gather to consider Christ.

For More: (1) See also "31. Growth"; (2) go to www.pastoringmen.com and click on "8. Change" to hear "How Can a Man Change?"; and (3) read chapter 24, "How Can a Man Change?" in *The Man in the Mirror*.

9. **CHARACTER OF GOD**

Teach your men about the character of God. Encourage them to meditate on the attributes of God. Over the years I have compiled a list of many of God's attributes and names to pull out when I need to experience His touch:

- Holy, sovereign, great, awesome, the Almighty, Creator, Sustainer, Redeemer
- Loving, gracious, merciful, faithful, patient, good
- Omnipotent, omniscient, omnipresent, omni-benevolent, self-existent
- All wise, eternal, infinite, immortal, invisible, immutable
- Transcendent, immanent
- Alpha, Omega
- King of kings, Lord of lords, President of presidents, CEO of CEOs
- God who was, is, and is to come, in whom there is no shadow of turning
- The Holy Spirit, the Comforter, the Counselor
- The Wonderful Counselor, the Everlasting Father, the Prince of Peace
- The Door, the Gate, the Good Shepherd
- The Bread of Life, the Living Water
- The Way, the Truth, the Life
- Savior, Lord, friend, the author and perfecter of our faith
- The soon and coming King
- The Lamb of God who takes away the sin of the world

Men like lists. Consider making your own list of God's attributes (or use this one). Print copies for your men. Suggest they put it somewhere handy. I keep mine in my Bible. Tell them to pull it out when, because of troubles, they need a reminder of God's greatness and goodness.

To dwell on the character of God will result in a very different life purpose than if you dwell on yourself. As someone has said, "A God spelled 'me' is not worthy of worship."

For More: Go to www.pastoringmen.com and click "9. Character of God" to see or hear the God and the Man in the Mirror series.

10. **CHURCH**

Jesus said, "I will build my church, and [all the powers of hell] will not overcome it" (Matthew 16:18). Teach your men the role and importance of *ecclesia*. Remind them (because they forget) how the church meets the needs of our families: weddings, baptisms, communion, confirmations, funerals, fellowship dinners, evangelistic outreaches, worship services, preaching, hymns, choir, spiritual education, ministry opportunities, accountability, softball leagues, small groups, Sunday school classes, conferences, retreats, nursery, and hospital visits. No institution supports marriage and family like the church.

Remind them what America would look like without the church. Where would be the great hospitals, schools, and universities? Where would be the food pantries, the coalitions for the homeless, the rescue missions? Would anyone be doing inner-city youth work or providing homes for unwed mothers? Where would be the voices calling out for abstinence from premarital sex or the right to life? Who would be the voice of justice and the hands of mercy? Who would be the feet of the gospel of salvation? Who would be the light in the darkness, the salt seeking to preserve society and culture? As someone said, "The church has many critics, but no rivals."

Jesus Christ is the head of the church. "And he is the head of the body, the church; he is the beginning and the firstborn from among the dead, so that in everything he might have the supremacy" (Colossians 1:18). We attend church because He wants us to attend. To attend church means to gather with other believers to worship the Lord. The *ecclesia* is the people, not the place, but we certainly need a place to meet.

Teach men to be actively involved in church (not merely attend) for the singular reason that the Bible tells us to: "Let us not give up meeting together, as some are in the habit of doing, but let us encourage one another—and all the more as you see the Day approaching" (Hebrews 10:25). Tell men that the church "assembled" is where they will experience a unique measure of worship, fellowship, growth, service, and accountability.

11. CONTENTMENT

The central idea in my book *Ten Secrets for the Man in the Mirror* is "The Christian life is a broad road of happiness, joy, peace, blessing, success, significance, and contentment, which is ironically gained by choosing the narrow road of surrender, obedience, self-denial, self-sacrifice, truth, worship, and service."

The world would say, "Want to be happy? Seek a better job. Live in this neighborhood. Take this vacation. Drive this car. Send your children to this school. Accumulate this much money. Join this club."

God says, "Want to be happy? Surrender your life to me. Obey me. Seek the truth. Live by faith. Give yourself away in service. Deny yourself." This is how contentment is found.

Often men cling to some selfish ambition that is at odds with leading a surrendered life. Ironically, when we yield our lives to Jesus, allow Him to be Lord, and walk in His way of obedience, service, and self-denial—things that sound like giving up happiness—He rewards us with every spiritual blessing.

Teach your men these things:

- If you are not content where you are, you will not be content where you want to go. Contentment is not about geography.
- God offers contentment in our circumstances, not escape from our circumstances (see James 1:9–11).
- The great secret of contentment is not getting what you want, but wanting what you get.

Ecclesiastes 7:14 instructs, "A man cannot discover anything about his future." Ironically, we often spend time stewing over that which we will never know. Doesn't that seem like a futile use of time? Would it not be more useful to once and for all accept that the future is the secret of God, then live by faith, trusting that because God is good, it will end "good"? What a comfort to trust and be content with our sovereign and good God.

12. **COUNSEL**

Most men are lone rangers. They need to be encouraged to seek wise spiritual advisers. Teach your men that it is both manly and wise to seek counsel. Give them permission to come to you for spiritual counsel. Remove all barriers between you and your men. If you run out of time, develop a cadre of elders, deacons, and others to whom you can "hand off" men.

When a man seeks counsel, tell him to let his counselor know whether he's looking for "a hug" or "a kick in the pants." Tell him to let his counselor know whether he is looking for "the voice of reason" (what to do) or "the voice of passion" (encouragement to take action).

There are two kinds of decisions for which men may want counsel: *moral decisions* or *priority decisions*. Teach men to know the difference.

Moral Counsel. If a man seeks counsel for a moral decision, he probably wants a "kick in the pants"—to be held accountable to do the right thing. Tell your men that if they need counsel on a moral issue, go to someone with (a) moral authority and (b) knowledge of the Scriptures. If facing a moral decision, they already know the right thing to do. They need someone to say, "You can do this. You can make it happen"—a kick in the pants.

Priority Counsel. Priority decisions are different. If you want to buy a good used car, you won't seek advice from a pastor or Bible study leader—unless, of course, they are really smart about cars.

There are two stances toward a decision. Either you think you know what you want to do, or you don't. Caution men against deciding what they want and then looking for counselors who will support the already made decision.

If a man honestly doesn't know what he wants, then he may already be muddled and easily confused. He needs a counselor who can help him see all the options. (See "Decision-Making" for more ideas.)

Teach your men to avoid counselors who give an overly quick reply. You know the type—they hear two or three sentences and then say, "Ooh, ooh, let me tell you what you need to do!"

Also, teach your men how to *offer* counsel. I have two rules for giving counsel:

• As a general rule, when your advice isn't sought, it isn't wanted.

• There is no greater loss than the right advice offered at the wrong moment.

13. **CULTURAL CHRISTIANITY**

In our work, we regularly meet men who have "prayed a prayer" for salvation, but for the last five, ten, or more years they have been living by their own ideas. They have built on the foundation of their own best thinking. They read the Bible for comfort, but the *Wall Street Journal* for direction. They are on the fringe—either barely inside or just outside the door of the church.

Men on the fringe are hurting. They are tired of running the rat race. Their energy has been depleted. Their marriages are rocky. Their children are preoccupied. Their finances are in disarray. They are thinking, "Is this all there is? There must to be more to life than this. There's gotta be!"

Biblically, these men have let the worries of this life and the deceitfulness of money choke the word and make it unfruitful (Matthew 13:22); they've let the yeast of culture work through the whole batch of dough (Galatians 5:9); they've done that which is permissible but not beneficial (1 Corinthians 6:12); they're high risk for a great crash because they built on sand and not the rock (Matthew 7:24-27).

Often men like this are what Os Guinness has called "the undiscipled disciple." They have not fully yielded their lives to the lordship of Jesus Christ. Their worldview tends to be a jumbled concoction of ideas cherry-picked from church, television, *Business Week*, positive thinking seminars, and the Harvard Business School. (The technical term for this is *syncretism*.)

They practice "spare tire" Christianity. They merely add Jesus to their calendars as another interest in an already busy schedule. They only know enough about God to be disappointed in Him. Their lives are shaped more by the herds of commerce than the footsteps of Christ.

When I hit the ten-year mark in my spiritual journey I realized something was desperately wrong with my life, but I couldn't put my finger on any one problem. I was sitting at the top of my career. Materially, I was taken care of wonderfully. I was an active Christian, reading my Bible and praying regularly, immersed in church life, a vocal witness, and pursuing a moral lifestyle.

Tired and feeling as though my life was coming unglued, I eventually realized I had become what we might call a *cultural* Christian, one of those men and women who want God "to be more of a gentle grandfather type who spoils us and lets us have our own way. . . . sensing a need for God, but on our own terms. [2] (A full discussion of cultural Christians appears on pages 67–69.)

As I wrote earlier (but repeat here for your convenience), men who are cultural Christians read their Bibles with an agenda, if they read them at all. They decide in advance what they want and then read their Bibles looking for evidence to support the decisions they have already made. In short, they follow the God they are underlining in their Bibles, which is like making a "fifth" gospel.

The solution for me and all cultural Christians? As someone said, "No matter how far you have gone down a wrong road, the only solution is to turn back." So periodically lead your men in prayers of renewal and recommitment.

For More: Go to www.pastoringmen.com and click "13. Cultural Christianity" to (1) see or hear "Becoming Lukewarm" in the A Man's Guide to Inevitable Events series and (2) "Biblical Christian or Cultural Christian?" in The Man in the Mirror Remix series; (3) read chapter 3, "Biblical Christian or Cultural Christian?," in *The Man in the Mirror*.

14. **CULTURAL MANDATE**

God calls us to *build* the kingdom and *tend* the culture. Teach your men about God's calling ("ordination") to tend the culture.

The Great Commission that concludes Matthew 28 is God's call to build the kingdom. The cultural mandate announced in Genesis 1:28 is God's call to tend the culture. This mandate is our calling to make the world a more livable place, raise families, and engage in productive work and service. Several other topics in part 3 touch on cultural mandate, including *calling, fathering, marriage, money and possessions, service, success that matters,* and *work.*

Teach your men that their work is not merely a platform to serve God—it is serving God. In other words, they don't simply endure work until a coffee break so they can witness to their coworkers; the work itself is important to God. Every vocation is holy to the Lord.

Great story: St. Francis of Assisi was out hoeing his garden one day. He was asked, "What would you do if you learned Jesus would return this afternoon?" He replied, "I would finish hoeing my garden."

What if a man can't figure out his calling, or if it seems to have faded on him? Teach your men to be patient and wait on God's timing. A man in his early thirties experienced frustration because he couldn't figure out where he was going. The man asked, "What should I do with my life?"

I counseled him, "You don't need to know where you are going. Relax. Let it come to you. Simply remain faithful to do what is already before you with excellence. Moses was forty years old when he was called, spent forty years in preparation, and another forty years living it out. Two-thirds of his life passed before God released him for his ultimate service."

Teach your men who have families to "tend the culture" as a family when possible. For example, the family might volunteer to help at a center for troubled youth. Give men a vision for family ministry.

15. **CYCLE BREAKING**

"I lavish unfailing love to a thousand generations. I forgive iniquity, rebellion, and sin. But I do not excuse the guilty. I lay the sins of the parents upon their children and grandchildren; the entire family is affected—even children in the third and fourth generations" (Exodus 34:7 NLT).

A lot of your men are affected by the "downstream" consequences of a parent's, grandparent's, or even a great grandparent's sins. For example, when a man abandons his family, he sets negative forces in motion that can impact his entire family lineage for several generations.

Christ is a Redeemer, and no amount of pain and dysfunction is beyond his reach or interest. Nevertheless, once a cycle of brokenness begins, it takes so much more emotional energy and so much more of society's resources to restore what should have never been broken to begin with.

Teach your men to consider the costs of starting a cycle. Teach your men how to break the cycle. Make it a badge of honor in your church to be a cycle breaker. Make it a point of honor for men to say, "By God's grace, it stops with me. I am going to set my family line on a whole new course for generations to come."

If you need a good illustration of starting and breaking a cycle, use my story that begins on page 22.

16. DECISION MAKING

Men are born to be decision makers. Your men face two kinds of decisions—
moral decisions and *priority* decisions. Moral decisions are decisions between
right and wrong. There is a morally correct answer and a morally wrong answer.
For example, whether or not to steal or commit adultery. As a pastor, you can
always advise your men on moral issues. Priority decisions—the vast majority
of them—are decisions between right and right. In other words, there are two
or more choices, any of which could be correct. For example, which job to take,
car to buy, woman to marry, or neighborhood to live in. As noted under counsel
(topic 12), a counselor may be able to offer perspective and suggestions for priority decisions.

During the course of a year, most of us only make two or three truly major
decisions. These might include whether or not to change jobs, which job to take,
whether to move to another city or across town, how many children to have,
which church to attend, what kind of personal ministry to undertake, what kind
of car to buy (and do I really need a new one?), how to adjust a lifestyle to a reduced income, and so on. Yet these comprise some of the most important and
difficult decisions we ever make.

Most of these major decisions are not dictated by Scripture. So what do we
do? Here are some considerations to help:

Know that many major decisions do turn out wrong. For example, a man became restless after twenty-one years with the same company. He could not isolate
the source of his feelings, but decided he needed a change. Since that time he has
bounced around from job to job, never keeping the same position more than
three years. So the seeker should pray and sense that God is leading him to the
decision, not his emotions or moods.

Count the cost of making the wrong decision. Perhaps the greatest lesson I've
learned about making major decisions is the cost of making the wrong decision.

Most decisions are obvious given enough information and time. When do we
make poor decisions? When we don't have our facts straight and when we are
hasty. Keep collecting data. Write the information down so you don't forget it.
The mind may blow one small fact out of proportion. Writing it down puts
things in perspective. Talk to wise counselors; get other perspectives.

It takes time to make a wise, major decision. The mind may know quickly
what to do, but it takes time for our emotions to catch up. We have vested posi-

tions that only time can change. There are very few decisions in life that can't wait two weeks.

Here is a useful, practical process for finding the will of God. Keep in mind this is not a process for getting our own way. We must be cautious that we truly want what God wants. Otherwise we will twist things. Each step builds on itself, and you may find the answer becomes obvious at any point along the way. If it doesn't make itself clear, keep moving through the steps until it does.

- *Write down the decision exactly.* Precisely what is the decision? What are the choices?
- *Next, write out a "purpose statement" which precisely explains why you are considering this decision.* It is helpful not only to know what you are trying to decide, but why. "Why" are you trying to decide "what" you are trying to decide? Do you have to make a decision? Is it a need or a want? Are you unhappy?
- *Submit your "purpose statement" to a series of questions.* Here are some suggestions:
    1. What is your objective, or desired end result?
    2. What are your expectations and why?
    3. What would Jesus do if He were you?
- *If your answer still hasn't become obvious, list each option on a separate sheet of paper.* On the left side list the advantages of that option; on the right side list the disadvantages.
- *At all times, employ the seven steps of guidance to discern God's will* (see topic "27. God's Will").
- *If the answer still hasn't come, wait.* You can never predict what God is doing in your life. Commit to let God set the agenda. Never push God. If the answer isn't obvious, trust Him to make it clear in His timing. Give Him the time He desires to work some things into—or out of—your character. And remember this: God is not the author of confusion. Satan, however, is. If you are still confused, wait. Peace is the umpire.

For More: Go to www.pastoringmen.com and click on "16. Decision Making" to (1) see or hear "Decisions: How to Make the Right Choice" in The Man in the Mirror Remix series; or (2) read "Decisions: How to Make the Right Choice," chapter 13 in *The Man in the Mirror*.

17. DISCIPLESHIP

There is one, and only one, way any of us can win the battle for our soul. It is simple and concrete. We need to become disciples of our Lord and Savior Jesus Christ. Discipleship is the process by which your men become civilized.

Teach your men what it means to be a disciple of Jesus and explain how to become one.

A disciple is someone *called* to live "in" Christ (evangelism), *equipped* to live "like" Christ (teaching), and *sent* to live "for" Christ (love, abide, serve). This is a highly practical and actionable definition. Everything you do with and for men can fall in one of these three categories. Help your men understand that spiritual transformation is always the goal in *everything* you, they, and the church are doing.

Explain to them how your church calls, equips, and sends men. Tell men how discipleship takes place: sermons, Bible studies, one-on-one meetings, adult education classes, as we serve, teaching a class, and any other way that connects men to Christ and His gospel. Invite men to participate. (See expanded coverage in chapter 5, "What Do Men Need?.")

There is a "compounding" nature to discipleship. The first time the disciples experienced Jesus calming the storm they said, *"What kind of man is this? Even the winds and waves obey him!"* (Matthew 8:27). By the second time they exclaimed, *"Truly you are the Son of God!"* and they worshiped Him (Matthew 14:33). Create an environment for the gospel to "creep up on" or "seep into" a man. Don't create any kind of "loyalty test" other than the gospel (e.g., such as controlled behavior or man-made rules).

Give men time to catch on. Most of the really "big ideas" about Christianity take years to sink in (e.g., the relationship between faith and works). Men need time to experience the reality of the gospel for themselves. They need to have their own God moments. Keep repeating and reminding men about the basics of faith; then trust God to apply it to their lives.

18. DISCIPLINES, SPIRITUAL

Teach your men about the spiritual disciplines. Spiritual disciplines are the regular practices men cultivate when they want a closer walk with Christ. Disciplines are the spiritual habits by which we cultivate a deeper relationship with the Lord of heaven and earth. We perform the disciplines because we want to please God, to lead peaceable lives, to be godly husbands, to raise godly children, and to be men of God.

Spiritual disciplines do nothing to improve your record with God. We don't perform the disciplines to make God happy (or avoid His wrath), or to earn favor or merit with God. All the merit we need, we already have in Christ. We place our trust in God—not in the disciplines.

Nevertheless, disciplines demonstrate to God how serious we are about following Him, and they also help us see how serious we are as well. When all is said and done, spiritual disciplines are the designated means for us to grow in this relationship that we have with Jesus. God is always speaking, so if we don't hear Him, it's not because He has suddenly gone silent. It is more likely that we aren't listening—or perhaps don't know how to listen.

Christian authors have been writing on spiritual disciplines since biblical times. Disciplines mentioned in contemporary books include: *celebration, chastity, confession, fatherhood, friendship, frugality, guidance, journaling, learning, marriage, meditation, perseverance, sacrifice, secrecy, silence, simplicity, solitude, study,* and *submission.*

In my book *A Man's Guide to the Spiritual Disciplines* (Chicago: Moody, 2007) I include: *creation, the Bible, prayer, worship, the Sabbath, fellowship, counsel, fasting, spiritual warfare, stewardship, service,* and *evangelism.*

Almost any Christian virtue or duty can be turned into a discipline.

For More: Go to www.pastoringmen.com and click on "18. Disciplines, Spiritual" to (1) see or hear the Spiritual Disciplines for the Man in the Mirror series; (2) read the article "A Man's Guide to the Spiritual Disciplines."

19. EVANGELISM

Figure out where the sting of the lack of the gospel is most keenly felt in the lives of your men as a whole and, to the extent possible, individually. No doubt you will find many men trapped by the futility of Ecclesiastes—"Meaningless! Meaningless!" (see related topics: "The Rat Race," the "Unexamined Life," "Success Sickness," and "Cultural Christianity"). Help your strong men understand the problem, and your weak men to want the solution.

Teach your men how to lead other men to Christ. First, teach them how to share a three-minute personal testimony. Get your men to do the hard work to pare their story to three minutes—one minute on their life before Christ, one minute on how they accepted Christ, and one minute on what difference He has made. Once they can give it in three minutes, they can easily expand it if they have more time.

Second, teach your men how to explain the gospel and lead someone in a sinner's prayer. You or your denomination may have resources for this already. If not, read "How to Lead a Man to Christ"(at www.pastoringmen.com). Personally, I teach men how to read Campus Crusade's Four Spiritual Laws booklet to a man and lead that man in the sinner's prayer.

Lower the hurdle by explaining that evangelism is simply taking someone as far as they want to go toward Jesus. We are not salesmen who have to close a sale to succeed. Success is being faithful to share and letting God do what He will do.

Teach your men to look for the signals that a man might be open to hearing about Jesus. Offer a Bible study to which men can bring their friends and associates, and offer the gospel there on a regular basis.

Use the Reach 3 Strategy explained at www.pastoringmen.com. Tell them, "Men who know Christ show men Christ." Exhort them to ask God for an unreasonable burden for at least one person's soul. Tell your men, "Since half the people in the world are not going to like you anyway, they may as well not like you for the right reason."

When someone is ready to receive Jesus, drop everything and help them do it. You need to do it right then.

20. **FAITH**

Teach your men the difference between saving faith and living faith. Explain that faith is also for a man's everyday life and that faith pleases God. "And without faith it is impossible to please Him, for he who comes to God must believe that He is, and that He is a rewarder of those who seek Him" (Hebrews 11:6 NASB). Here are elements of a vibrant faith:

- Faith believes God in the face of unbelievable circumstances.
- Faith believes the Bible when it makes no sense, humanly speaking.
- Faith relies upon the authority of Scripture instead of your own best thinking.
- Faith lets the reality of the unseen rule over the unreality of the seen.
- Faith is subordinating the tumult in your emotions to that previous decision you made in your will to trust Jesus.
- Faith believes God will do every single thing He has promised, in His perfect time.
- Faith is not trusting God where He has not promised, but where He has.
- Faith believes God will supply all your needs and that He has measured your needs on the scales of mercy.
- Faith continues to believe, trust, and wait when the hot, scorching breath of adversity blows unrelenting across the landscape of your circumstances.

There's a great story you can use to illustrate living "by faith, not by sight" (2 Corinthians 5:7) in topic 1, "Abiding in Christ."

Great Quote: "If one can believe in God there is no problem. If one cannot there is no solution"— Ingrid Bergman, playing a character in an early film.

21. THE FALL

The Bible doesn't describe a utopian world free of pain. That would make Christianity a wishful farce. Instead, the Bible describes the world exactly as we see it—a fallen world, but not without what Francis Schaeffer called "leftover beauty." The fall explains why we must look at the blazing beauty of a crimson sunrise through thick glasses that grace the bridge of a crooked, runny nose. Pascal said the fall is an offense to human reason but, once accepted, it makes perfect sense of the human condition.[3]

We must do our work while feeling the prick of thorns. To Adam God said, "Cursed is the ground because of you; through painful toil you will eat of it all the days of your life. It will produce thorns and thistles for you" (Genesis 3:17–18).

We must manage our lives against the fall. The fall is why we have the saying, "Perception is reality." We must work hard to "portray" what we really mean. People form "impressions" from tone of voice, eye movement, body language, and more. Because they, too, are managing against the fall, they are watching closely to see if they "think" you are lying. The fall explains why we have to choose our words carefully and why some things are better left unsaid. There are certain things I cannot say to you in public, and some things I cannot say at all.

I have to manage against the fall in you, and the fall in myself. And you must do the same. The fall into sin forces us to explain why we:

- Anxiously try to make a sale without appearing anxious
- Convince the lender we don't really need the loan
- Get a girl's attention while appearing to be disinterested
- Have "special" meetings before the meeting, then phone calls after
- Promote a book while appearing to not be promoting a book (like this one)

Teach men that because of the fall they need to be understanding with their wives, who, like men, are tainted by sin. In pronouncing the effect of the fall on women the Bible says, "Your desire will be for your husband, and he will rule over you" (Genesis 3:16). "Desire" meant *a desire that borders on disease*.[4] It is a desire subject to corruption (e.g., possessiveness, jealousy) and manipulation (e.g., controlling).

22. **FATHER WOUND**

A lot of a man's identity comes from his *father's blessing*—or lack thereof. It is his seal of approval. A high percentage of your men will feel as though they have never had their father's blessing. Few topics can bring men to tears more quickly. As one friend in his fifties told me, "No matter what I did, I could never please my father."

In the Bible, to bless means "to endue with power for success, prosperity, fertility, longevity, etc." Jacob cheated his older brother Esau out of his father's blessing. Their father, Isaac, according to the custom of that time had to tell Esau that he had already given Esau's blessing to Jacob.

The Bible says, "When Esau heard his father's words, he burst out with a loud and bitter cry and said to his father, 'Bless me—me too, my father!'" (Genesis 27:34). Whether you speak to men in their roles as dads or as sons, a father's blessing or approval is crucial to his well-being.

The spoken words are important. My dad never told me he was proud of me. I sensed he was, but he never said it. I worked for his approval. When I was forty-seven, I wrote on his birthday card, "Dad, I hope you're proud of me."

Without looking up from the card, he said, "Well, you know I am." That was it. That's all I ever got—before or after. But it was amazing. It was his approval—his blessing, and it has made all the difference in my life.

You can't just tell men to "get over it." Instead, help them grieve the loss. Show them how God, their adoptive Father, does approve and bless them. In some cases, you may be able to act as a "surrogate" father and give your men "a" blessing, even though it's not "the" blessing. I have done this with younger men who looked to me as a father figure (e.g., reread topic 6, "The Blessing"; see also *The Young Man in the Mirror,* "A Man's Identity," pp. 27–29).

On the other hand, tell your men "don't feel you're a victim"—but be gentle. To not receive a father's blessing by no means has to "define" a man—especially a follower of Jesus.

23. **FATHERING**

Jesus wasn't just born to a virgin woman, he was born to a virgin couple. Joseph planned to divorce Mary quietly. Jesus was going to grow up without a dad. God thought is was important enough for Jesus to have a father in the home that he intervened supernaturally to change Joseph's mind (and so Mary would not be disgraced as an unwed mother). Mary may have had the baby, but Joseph taught Him how to be a man. Jesus was a man's man, and He didn't learn that from His mommy. Fathers *are* important.

There are basically two fathering styles: *fathering for performance* and *fathering the heart*. Most dads father for performance. They try to get their children to "do the right things." They exasperate their children. The Scripture warns, "Fathers, do not exasperate your children; instead, bring them up in the training and instruction of the Lord" (Ephesians 6:4). Fathering the heart is the approach the Bible recommends. "Out of the overflow of the heart, the mouth speaks," Jesus said (Matthew 12:34).

When a man fathers for performance, his emphasis is on conformity, and the child grows in an atmosphere of fear. In contrast, when a man fathers for heart change, his emphasis is on transformation, and the atmosphere is one of safety.[5]

Fathering for performance is law; fathering the heart is grace. Teach your fathers that they can raise their children under grace or law, but grace is better. If they raise their children under law, they will leave home as soon as possible and come back as little as they can.

Teach your fathers not to have (a) too much structure or (b) not enough structure. Encourage dads to give their children a voice.

A man's true character is most revealed by how he treats his family. No amount of success at work will ever be adequate to compensate for failure at home.

Encourage your men to every day tell each of their children, "I love you," and "I'm proud of you." There is biblical precedent for these words: the baptism and transfiguration of Jesus.

I did not grow up in a home where we hugged or said, "I love you." One year in my early thirties I invited my dad to lunch on his birthday, and it became an annual custom. One day, a few years after we started this new tradition, we left the cash register and were walking to our vehicles. For some still unknown reason I said, "Here dad. Let me give you a hug."

Before I had time to think about what I had just said, we embraced. I put my arms around my father, and my father put his arms around me. He squeezed so tight it felt like a grizzly bear had grabbed hold of me! Then, he let out a long, deep, primordial sounding groan. "Mmmmmmmmm. . . ." It must have lasted thirty seconds.

All I could think of was the deeply buried pain of not having a father of his own to mimic, of never having had a father tussle his hair, of never hearing a father's instruction about the ways of life . . . and of the missed years we had not hugged.

At the end of those thirty infinite seconds, warm, salty tears rolled down both of our cheeks. He looked at me, and I looked at him.

I said, "I love you, Dad."

He said, "I love you, too," and then we left, souls cleansed.

Frankly, I'm not sure anyone can adequately explain what happened in those precious moments. A century of sorrows boiled to the surface in one brief instant. The intangible pain of what could have been melted away. A taste of the shimmering glory of paradise broke upon us. The gracious hand of God broke down a wall. A reconciliation took place. It was a spiritual healing of unspeakable joy.

That single moment became a turning point in our family. Ever since we have become a family of huggers and lovers. And not just dad and me—everyone!

Teach your men that their family is their primary ministry and accountability. Teach men how to disciple their families.

For More: Go to www.pastoringmen.com and click on "23. Fathering" to (1) see or hear the "Twelve Tasks of an Effective Father" series, also available on CD-Rom; (2) see or hear "Children: How to Avoid Regrets" in The Man in the Mirror Remix series; and (3) read the article "The Goal of a Father."

24. **FEAR**

Teach your men about fear. All men struggle with the emotion of fear, though it is customary to conceal such feelings. Fear is "the feeling that something bad will happen, whether real or imagined."

Does fear make a man a sissy? No, fear is a normal human emotion, and it can be healthy. Fear will trigger a healthy dose of adrenaline in the fight-or-flight syndrome. It's good to be afraid when a car abruptly swerves into your lane.

What is not normal is a "spirit" of fear. Vast is the difference between fear and a spirit of fear. Second Timothy 1:7 says, "For God has not given us a spirit of fear and timidity, but of power, love, and self-discipline" (NLT). What kind of spirit, then, did He give us? It is the spirit of adoption. "For you did not receive a spirit that makes you a slave again to fear, but you received the Spirit of sonship [adoption]" (Romans 8:15). Sons don't doubt the good intentions of the fathers— especially when their father is perfect.

Even in times of extraordinary courage, men still feel fear. Fear does not preclude courage, nor is courage the absence of fear. Teach your men that faith leads to courage, and courage conquers fear.

Upon seeing Jesus walk on water, the disciples were afraid. Jesus said, "Take courage! It is I. Don't be afraid. . . . You of little faith . . . Why did you doubt?" (Matthew 14:27, 31). The issue is not having more courage, but more faith. "Faith" is the confidence that everything will work out in the end—that God is sovereignly orchestrating our circumstances, and He is good. "Courage" is the state of mind created by faith that enables us to face bad things with confidence and resolution.

Who is afraid of what they already know? If you think about, all fear is oriented toward the future. Yet Ecclesiastes 7:14 says, "A man cannot discover anything about his future." Help your men put fear and worry in proper perspective.

Show your men how to find peace in troubles through prayer: "Do not be anxious about anything, but in everything, by prayer and petition, with thanksgiving, present your requests to God. And the peace of God, which transcends all understanding, will guard your hearts and your minds in Christ Jesus" (Philippians 4:6–7). In fact, this would be a good one for them to memorize if they are inclined to give Scripture memorization a try.

For More: Go to www.pastoringmen.com and click on "24. Fear" to (1) see or hear "Fear" in The Man in the Mirror Remix series or (2) read "Fear," chapter 17 in *The Man in the Mirror.*

25. **FRIENDSHIPS**

Male friendship leaves a unique heat signature, as most men organize times together around tasks, not relationships. Unlike women, men need a "reason" to get together. Most men find friendships hard to develop and difficult to maintain. Often a man's closest friendships are with coworkers. And many men have no friends—at least not beyond the cliché level of news, sports, and weather.

Friendship is a central theme of Jesus: "My command is this: Love each other as I have loved you. Greater love has no one than this, that he lay down his life for his friends" (John 15:12–13). "By this all men will know that you are my disciples, if you love one another" (John 13:35). God dispatches believers to encourage each other. Fellowship is encouragement from God.

We cannot love people unless we are connected to them in some way. Men confuse acquaintances, good-weather friends, and close friends. A close friend is someone you could comfortably call at 2:00 a.m.

Encourage your men to build lifelong friendships. If married, they can start with their wife. Next, they should develop friendships with their adult children; and then, extended family. Beyond family, any friendships of the sharing kind must be same gender only. Best bet: join a men's small group.

For a great friendship illustration, use the story about the pastor who invited one of his businessmen to lunch in chapter 2, page 42.

For More: (1) See also "Fellowship," "Loving People," and "Relationships" in this chapter; (2) read "Friends: Risks and Rewards," chapter 10 in *The Man in the Mirror*; (3) go to www.pastoringmen.com and click on "25. Friendships" to see or hear "Friends: Risks and Rewards," in The Man in the Mirror Remix series.

26. **FUTILITY**

A man's futility sharply contrasts with a woman's futility. Women feel the pain of the fall in their children and marriage (relationships); men in their work (tasks) (see Genesis 3:16–19). Men must do their work while feeling the prick of thorns.

Glucose is composed of three chemical elements: carbon, hydrogen, and oxygen. In a similar way, the world is composed of three forces: *good*, *evil*, and because of the fall, *futility.* For your average man, evil is a small problem compared to his futility. A lot of his life just doesn't seem like it really matters—probably for you too. Futility, however, is the grace of God that is saving men:

> For the creation was subjected to frustration[6] [futility], not by its own choice, but by the will of the one who subjected it [God], in hope that the creation itself will be liberated from its bondage to decay and brought into the glorious freedom of the children of God. (Romans 8:20–21)

Teach your men that futility is the chief tool by which God sovereignly draws us to Himself of our own free will. In other words, He sovereignly makes life so miserable that we turn to Him of our own free will. What an amazing God! (Incidentally, this perfectly explains the relationship between sovereignty and free will). God even bends the free will of unbelievers to His will through futility (e.g., consider Pharaoh, "let my people go," the plagues, and the eventual exodus).

Teach men that God not only uses futility to reach us, but for us to reach others. Paul said of his futility, "All this is for your benefit, so that the grace that is reaching more and more people may cause thanksgiving to overflow to the glory of God" (2 Corinthians 4:15). Teach men why their futilities, like those of Paul, are worth it.

Jesus taught his disciples to pray, "Deliver us from evil." He did not teach them to pray, "Deliver us from futility." That is worth pondering.

27. **GOD'S WILL**

To assist us in finding His will, God has given means of guidance. Let's briefly explore each of seven different means.

1. *The Bible.* The single most important question to ask is, "Has God already spoken on this matter?" The Bible is chock full of *commands* (which are duty) and *principles* (which are wise). We don't have to wonder if not reporting $1,800 of incidental income to the IRS is God's will. We know it is. Obedience is the trademark of a biblical Christian.

2. *Prayer.* Jesus said, "Until now you have not asked for anything in my name. Ask and you will receive, and your joy will be complete" (John 16:24). Over and over and over again we are invited to present our requests to God. Prayer is the currency of our personal relationship with Christ.

3. *The Holy Spirit.* God lives in us in the person of the Holy Spirit. He is our counselor, convicter, comforter, converter, and encourager. Consciously depend upon Him, and He will both guide you and intercede for you. "The Spirit intercedes for the saints in accordance with God's will" (Romans 8:27). The Holy Spirit will never lead in contradiction to His written Word.

4. *Conscience.* In seeking God's will we must live by the pledge of a good conscience toward God and other people. "If our hearts do not condemn us, we have confidence before God" (1 John 3:21). While a guilty conscience provides clear evidence you are not in God's will, a clear conscience may not guarantee you have correctly discerned God's will. Conscience is more effective as a red light than a green light. To go against conscience is neither wise nor safe.

5. *Circumstances.* Some people are born short, some tall. Some in America, some in Argentina. Some to poor parents, some to rich. God's will is often revealed clearly by the circumstances in which we live. "He determined the times set for them and the exact places where they should live" (Acts 17:26). If you want to purchase a house that will require a $200,000 mortgage and you can only qualify for $150,000, then circumstances have told you God's will.

6. *Counsel.* "Plans fail for lack of counsel, but with many advisers they succeed" (Proverbs 15:22). Often we need nothing more than a good listener

to help us crystallize our thoughts into coherent words. Other times, we need the advice of a trusted friend.

7. *Fasting.* Fasting is a lost spiritual discipline in this age. Fasting slows down the physical functions so that the mind can be more in tune with Christ. Fasting demonstrates a seriousness about your concern to the Lord.

Employ these constituted means for finding the will of God. Do them only occasionally and it will amount to nothing more than priming a rusty pump. Do them regularly and the will of God will gush forth like deep well springs.

28. **THE GOSPEL**

One of the most elegant expressions of "the gospel" is found in Romans: "For the wages of sin is death, but the gift of God is eternal life in Christ Jesus our Lord" (6:23). This text addresses the three main issues raised by the gospel: *the problem of man, the issue of Jesus,* and *the gift of eternal life.* Here is a manly way of presenting the gospel that addresses these three issues: (1) Adam failed. (2) Jesus nailed. (3) Grace prevailed.

First, *Adam failed.* The true tragedy of our existence is not what we have become, but what we could have been. We all sense by intuition that mankind has not reached its potential. We each have an instinct that tells us the human race was destined for better, that our dignity has been tarnished. Logic tells us that something catastrophic has happened to mankind.

Christianity teaches that this catastrophe took place in the garden of Eden. Evil entered the world, and people began to make sinful choices. A downward spiral of sin continues to the present day. All people are guilty of sin, which halts our progress toward an abundant life. Not only is progress halted, but we also have become alienated from our Creator.

Second, *Jesus nailed.* The Christian solution for sin is that God came into the world to be a Savior. The *history* of Jesus is the story of His *incarnation.* Jesus was a living person who existed in history, performed remarkable miracles, claimed deity, was put to death, and was resurrected from death. If the birth, life, death, and resurrection of Jesus had never happened in history, there would be no Christian religion. Christianity *is* Jesus Christ. The *doctrine* of Christ—"he died for our sins"[7]—is understanding that Jesus Christ claimed to make *atonement* for our sins, or to satisfy the "wages of sin is death" problem in Romans 6:23.

In his own words Jesus said, "I came to seek and to save the lost. For God so loved that world that he sent me into the world so that whoever believes in me will not perish but have everlasting life. I tell you the truth, whoever hears my words and believes him who sent me has eternal life and will not be condemned, he has crossed over from death to life. All that the Father gives me will come to me, and whoever comes to me I will never drive away. I shall lose none of them that he has given me, but raise them up at the last day."[8] About his identity Jesus said, "He who has seen me has seen the Father. The Father and I are one. I who speak to you am he [the Messiah]" (adapted from John 14:9; 10:30; 4:25–26).

Third, *Grace prevailed.* The core point of Christianity is that no matter how futile a man's life has become, Jesus Christ wants to restore him to his original dignity and give his soul rest, both now and forever. This is true Christianity: No matter what he has done, he can be forgiven. The biblical term for this is grace.

Christianity is unique among all religions because it is the only religion based on nonperformance. Becoming a Christian is not about "doing" something but about acknowledging one's inability to do *anything* to save oneself.

Rather, the work of salvation is a work of *grace.* The apostle Paul wrote, "But because of his great love for us, God, who is rich in mercy, made us alive with Christ even when we were dead in transgressions—it is by grace you have been saved" (Ephesians 2:4–5). Once this simple idea called *grace* is grasped, it begins a chain reaction in the soul. There is no "merit" to be earned. Rather than receiving justice, we have through God's mercy received grace, which leads to godly sorrow and to faith.

For More: (1) See the topics "Eternal Life," "Forgiveness," "Salvation"; go to www.pastoringmen.com and click on "28. The Gospel" to read "How to Lead a Man to Christ."

29. **GRACE AND PERFORMANCE**

My son airs radio and television ads for his residential real estate business. When women call on his ads, they generally ask for the free information packet. When men call, they're ready to do business. Men are by nature performance-oriented.

This performance orientation lures many men into thinking (1) they must do something to make God happy (or avoid His wrath) and then, (2) continue performing to keep God happy.

Such thinking is perfectly designed to produce despair, because no matter how much this man does, it is never enough. So tell your men that the principal requirement for becoming a Christian is to admit that you are not worthy to be one. Becoming a Christian is not about modifying your behavior to make God happy.

Your men are immersed in a performance-based culture for all but a few hours each week. To get the reward, they must produce. For this and other reasons, the full sense of the concept of "grace" often will take many years to sink in.

Many men who are Christians still feel like they are not "good enough," haven't done enough, still have "one more thing" they need to add, and so on.

Teach your men: No matter what you've done, you can be forgiven. Because of sin you will never be good enough to grasp salvation; because of grace you will never be bad enough to be outside of God's grasp.

There is also a "living" grace so men don't have to feel constantly weighed down by man-made rules and regulations. About once a week my computer gets so crossed up the only solution is to reboot, to push the restart button. Grace is like that restart button. Living grace is always available, so our daily sins can be forgiven. Teach men how to walk in the power of the Spirit day by day. Show them how grace is not only for salvation but also for sanctification and leading an abundant life by faith.

What a wonderful contribution to a man to help him understand and accept the grace of our Lord and Savior Jesus Christ—but it will take patience and repetition.

30. **THE GREAT COMMISSION**

Teach your men to embrace the Great Commission. More millions of people and more billions of dollars have been mobilized by Jesus' brief message found in Matthew's gospel than any other speech in recorded history.

> All authority in heaven and on earth has been given to me. Therefore go and make disciples of all nations, baptizing them in the name of the Father and of the Son and of the Holy Spirit, and teaching them to obey everything I have commanded you. And surely I am with you always, to the very end of the age. (Matthew 28:18–20)

This is the most compact distillation of the Christian mission ever uttered. Our final marching orders from Jesus are, "Go and make disciples." Those orders still stand. They have not been amended, altered, or rescinded. The central mission of the church—the overarching goal—is to "make disciples."

For men, it's all there. Authority. Challenge. Mission. Adventure. Power. Direction. Purpose. Comfort. Eternal Security. It is our task. It is our mission. And it is great.

Discipleship is the process by which we become civilized. There is one, and only one, way any of us can win the battle for our soul. It is simple and concrete. We need to become disciples of Jesus Christ.

So challenge your men not only to become disciples, but also to participate in the great work of making disciples themselves: "And the things you have heard me say in the presence of many witnesses entrust to reliable men who will also be qualified to teach others" (2 Timothy 2:2).

For More: Go to www.pastoringmen.com and click on "30. The Great Commission" to see or hear the Discipling Men's Hearts series or Personalizing the Great Commission series (also on DVD).

31. **GROWTH**

Paul wrote, "For physical training is of some value, but godliness has value for all things, holding promise for both the present life and the life to come" (1 Timothy 4:8).

Teach your men how to grow into kingdom men—men of faith. I've been meeting with men for over three decades. Many of those men exude a contagious joy and contentment. Their lives are peaceable, orderly, and recommend Christ. They're downright happy!

Most of these happy men exercise six spiritual habits (disciplines) that keep them "growing" and "abiding in Christ." The dictionary says a *habit* is "an acquired behavior pattern regularly followed until it has become almost involuntary."

These six habits are no litmus test to judge a man's walk with Christ. That would be extremely dangerous. These habits create no special merit with Christ.

They are, however, indicators or "clues" of a deeper commitment to live by faith and make a difference in the world.

- *They read the Bible regularly.* They love God's Word and want to regularly read and meditate on the Bible. Encourage your men to read their Bibles (see the topic "The Bible").
- *They pray with their wives.* This symbolizes a depth of relationship with God and with his wife.
- *They are in a small group.* They are personally vulnerable and seek to be held accountable with a few men, or only one other man. They can meet for Bible study, discussion, fellowship, prayer, or a combination.
- *They are active in a church.* Active involvement is the overflow of a deeper work that Christ is doing in a man's heart.
- *They tithe.* I've never known a man who tithed who was not happy.
- *They are serving the Lord.* They have a passion that their lives will make a difference in the world. They pursue a life of significance. They view everything as serving the Lord.

What about men who just won't stick with it? Teach your men: Sometimes you have to substitute discipline for a lack of natural interest.

For More: Go to www.pastoringmen.com and click on "31. Growth" to see or hear the Six Habits of Spiritually Happy Men series.

32. THE HEART

Since "the heart" sounds like a "girly" word to many guys, you will need to help them understand that tending the heart is also manly. Jesus said, "The good man brings good things out of the good stored up in his heart, and the evil man brings evil things out of the evil stored up in his heart. For out of the overflow of his heart his mouth speaks" (Luke 6:45).

The single greatest contribution you can make to your men is to help them change the core affections of their hearts. How? Here are a few suggestions:

- Teach them how to each day come humbly to the foot of the cross and surrender to the lordship of Jesus.
- Teach your men that Christianity is not *behavior modification*; it's *heart transformation*.
- It is a spiritual operation first and foremost. Tell your men that they can cooperate with God's sanctification by consecrating themselves to holiness.
- Teach your men that people do exactly what they want to do in their hearts. Their behavior reflects what's in their hearts.
- Since belief determines behavior, teach them this progression:
    Right reading→Right thinking→Right believing→Right behaving
- Therefore, one of the greatest tasks a man can undertake is to align his heart into a one-to-one correlation of his Bible, his belief, and his behavior.

For you? Attend to the core affections of your own heart. Minister out of the overflow of your own expanding relationship with our Lord and Savior Jesus. If you can't, you must go into a quiet wood and stay there until you hear His voice, see His face, feel the warmth of His embrace, and feel the salty taste of repentant tears running down your face.

33. **HOLINESS**

God is holy, and He makes us holy. Christians are a people whom God is making holy, conforming us to the image of His dear Son, Jesus. *Sanctification* is this process by which God "sets us apart" for Himself and makes us holy. If we belong to Him, God is sanctifying us—whether we know it or not, whether we cooperate or not.[9]

Imagine a father with two sons whom he desires to teach good manners. One son seems eager to learn. Every time his father advises or corrects him, he thanks his father for teaching him good manners. But the other son kicks, screams, fusses, and fumes against his father's counsel. He rebels and rejects his father's instruction. One resists while the other cooperates. Do you think the father will be any less committed to teaching both sons good manners simply because they respond differently? What loving father would so easily give up on his child? The difference: For one child the experience is entirely pleasant, but for the other it is pain and torture.

We, too, can cooperate with the Father's plan of sanctification—moving toward holiness—or we can resist. If we cooperate, the results come more quickly and with considerably less pain.

To cooperate with God is to consecrate ourselves to Him. *Consecration* is another word for sanctification. God sanctifies us and, in return, we are exhorted to sanctify ourselves to him. "But sanctify the Lord God in your hearts" (1 Peter 3:15 KJV). "Offer your bodies as living sacrifices, holy and pleasing to God" (Romans 12:1). Our part is to consecrate ourselves to cooperate with what God is going to accomplish anyway.

Here's a good illustration you can use with your men. The evangelist Dwight L. Moody took up the offer to consecration after hearing these challenging words: "The world has yet to see what God will do with, and for, and through, and in, and by the man who is fully and wholly consecrated to him."

Moody thought to himself, "He said a man. He did not say a great man, nor a learned man . . . but simply 'a man.' I am a man, and it lies with the man himself whether he will, or will not, make that entire and full consecration. I will try my utmost to be that man."[10]

34. **IDOLS**

I race a vintage Porsche and have used racing as a platform to build relationships with men and share my faith. One day a man who never misses a chance to race asked me quite seriously, "When does my passion for racing become an idol?" Good question.

All idolatry is rooted in *unbelief.* This unbelief can take many forms, but at its root is the powerful lie, "Jesus Christ alone is not enough to make me happy. I need something else."

An idol is something we worship. The issue is looking to anything except Jesus Christ for identity, meaning, and ultimate purpose. An idol is anything that becomes the object of inordinate affection. An idol is anything of which we say, "I *must* have this to be happy."

John Calvin said that men are "idol factories." Perhaps nothing interferes with a man's faith more than the root problem of making idols—it's the "next step" after believing a lie (for "lies," see topic 37).

The average American Christian male has made an idol of something that competes with his full surrender to Christ. Men are addicted to everything from money to secret thought lives to comfortable little secluded environments they spend all their waking hours to create. Men can make idols of almost anything, but common examples today include homes, cars, boats, motorcycles, titles and positions, their intelligence, and their bodies.

All these affections are horizontal and worldly. All such friendship with the world is spiritual adultery (James 4:4). C. S. Lewis lamented how men were so easily satisfied with lesser things. Idols make promises they cannot keep, which is why a man can be on a winning streak and still feel empty.

35. **INTEGRITY**

Former Wyoming Senator Alan Simpson said, "If you have integrity nothing else matters. If you don't have integrity nothing else matters." I'm sure women struggle with integrity too, but my experience leads me to conclude men have more temptations than women in an average day. For example, to lie to get a sale, not work a full day, "borrow" supplies, fudge on expenses, not report all the income, look at pornography, and cheat all are temptations for men.

Most observers agree we are in the middle of an integrity crisis. I personally know dishonesty is rampant among the clerks and cashiers where I get my Starbucks and movie tickets— because they often try to give me a price break as though, together, we are "sticking it to the man."

I get nervous when I hear a message or read a book that exhorts me to *behave* my way out of a situation I have *believed* my way into. For example, if a man doesn't think that it's necessary to tithe, that there's nothing wrong with "looking at the menu" when it comes to women other than his wife, or that there's nothing wrong with little white lies—it's doubtful that a "behavior modification" scheme is going to change him long term.

Belief determines behavior. To change behavior we need a "belief modification" plan. To say it even better, we need a "heart transformation" plan (review topic 32, "The Heart"). Easily the greatest contribution we can make to a man is to help him change the core affections of his heart. Any such plan, for the Christian, necessarily starts with the Bible. So here's a good believer's definition for integrity: "Integrity is a one-to-one correlation between my Bible, my belief, and my behavior."

For More: Go to www.pastoringmen.com and click on "35. Integrity" to see or hear "Integrity: What's the Price?" or "Leading a Secret Thought Life" in The Man in the Mirror Remix series.

36. **JESUS**

"As a Jew, I have had nothing but the greatest and most profound respect for Jesus Christ of Nazareth. He was, after all, Jewish—born Jewish, died Jewish. I think Jesus Christ was the greatest single individual of both millenniums and He had more profound effect on mankind than any individual ever born. If there's one person in history I would like to interview, it would be Jesus."

Larry King, who has interviewed three American presidents and scores of movers and shakers on his TV program, would like to interview Jesus of Nazareth. No wonder. Jesus is the single most fascinating subject of all. Jesus is the perfect example of a man. Teach your men about Jesus.

I did a series at my Friday a.m. Bible study that went over very well, "Hanging Out with Jesus: Stories about Jesus from the Gospels." The more your men hear you talk about Jesus, the better they will know Him.

Talk about His identity, purpose, vision, mission, humanity, deity, strategy, determination, holiness, and leadership. Explain what He did, why He did it, who He did it with, and how He did it. Discuss what He thought, believed, wanted, said, and did.

Encourage men to let Jesus become their highest and best thought in every situation. Teach them that, yes, we believe in Jesus, but it's His belief in us that really transforms us.

Allow for mystery. There are only fourteen verses in the Bible to describe the first thirty years of Jesus' life. God could easily have told us more, but He chose not to. We believe that if He didn't, He had good reasons for doing so, but we'll never know in this life.

Great Quote: Spurgeon said, "In forty years I have not spent fifteen minutes without thinking of Jesus."

For More: Go to www.pastoringmen.com and click on "36. Jesus" to watch the Hanging Out with Jesus series. For a book that helps men surrender to Christ, read *Devotions for the Man in the Mirror.*

37. **LIES**

There are two languages in the world: *lies* and *truth*. The first language—the native tongue—of every man is the language of lies. When the Father of Lies was our father, "lies" was the only language we knew.

Before I became a Christian, I—like a lot of men—would often lie even if the truth could have served me better. It was my native tongue—a language that flowed freely from my lower nature.

When we receive Christ we become *bilingual.* We learn a second language—the language of truth. But what happens to anyone who doesn't regularly practice speaking their second language? They revert to their native tongue.

If we do not abide in Christ day by day, if we do not regularly practice our second language, we will revert to our native tongue. You know this is true because you know self-deceived Christians who regularly lie to you—and not about little things.

How do men fall back into their native language? Every morning your men go into a world where all day long they are tempted to exchange "the truth of God for a lie" (Romans 1:25).

All men either live by the truth or by a good lie. No man, Christian or otherwise, will choose to live by an obvious lie. Which counterfeit dollar bill is most likely to make it into circulation? It's the one that looks like the real thing. In the same way, the only lies that make it into circulation are ones that appear to be true. A good lie is probably only one or two degrees off course. Otherwise it would be rejected. The prosperity gospel comes to mind.

What does a good lie look like? A good lie can take many forms. For example, good lies about happiness might tell men that to be happy they need to . . . make this much money . . . get that promotion . . . drive a certain car. (For more of these "good" lies, see page 60.)

With false messages blaring from a thousand cell towers, TV antennas, newspapers, and even friends, the "father of lies" wants men to believe that God isn't capable of giving men true joy and contentment. As a discipler of men, it's good to remember that for every truth you tell your men, they are hearing hundreds of lies—many of them good lies—throughout the week.

38. **LORDSHIP**

We've all heard a man say something like, "I accepted Jesus as my Savior when I was seventeen years old, but I didn't make Him Lord until I was thirty-two." Just saying something is so doesn't make it so! And nothing could be further from the truth.

Men need to grasp that Jesus is the Lord of all men at all times in all places, whether they acknowledge it or not. "Are not two sparrows sold for a penny? Yet not one of them will fall to the ground apart from the will of your Father" (Matthew 10:29).

As Lord, Jesus is the *creator* and *sustainer* of all men (even those who spurn His name) and, as Savior, the *redeemer* of those who believe. We belong to Jesus. He is our "owner." He is our "benefactor." In fact, he is our Lord whether he is our Savior or not.

Teach men that our greatest source of strength and joy is to each day come humbly to the foot of the cross and there make a full, total, complete surrender of our lives to the lordship of Jesus.

There is no greater joy, privilege, or responsibility than to lead men into the kind of relationship with Jesus that Jesus wants. Peter declared, "Let all Israel be assured of this: God has made this Jesus . . . both Lord and Christ (Acts 2:36). Consider these Bible verses from the apostle Paul: "For this very reason, Christ died and returned to life so that he might be the Lord of both the dead and the living. . . . And there is but one Lord, Jesus Christ, through whom all things came and through whom we live" (Romans 14:9; 1 Corinthians 8:6).

For More: See Patrick Morley, *Ten Secrets for the Man in the Mirror*, chapter 1, from which portions of this page are excerpted.

39. **LOVING GOD**

Teach your men how to love God—the Great Commandment is to love God with all of our heart, soul, mind, and strength (see Matthew 22:37–38). In other words, we are to love God with the totality of our being, every ounce of our energy, and the sum of our strength. We should bring an intensity to loving God.

In the story of Martha and Mary (Luke 10:38–41), Martha was the "good sister"—the responsible one. She is the one who took care of "all the preparations that had to be made." The Greek here for "preparations" ("serving" in KJV) is *diakonia,* part of the word family from which we get "deacon." Obviously, serving is a very important part of Christian life. Martha excelled at serving.

Mary, on the other hand, was content to sit at the feet of Jesus "listening to what he said" (Luke 10:39), or in the KJV, she "heard his word"—(that's *logos* for "word.")

Martha was in the kitchen making dinner. The text says that "Martha was *distracted* by all the [*diakonea*]" (Luke 10:40, italics added). Making dinner for Jesus seems like such an opportunity. What wouldn't you give, pay, trade, or barter for such a moment? But distractions often come disguised as opportunities.

Jesus answered, "Martha, Martha . . . you are worried and upset about many things, but only one thing is needed. Mary has chosen what is better, and it will not be taken away from her" (v. 40). For Jesus, the relationship is more important than the task. In fact, the relationship *is* the task.

Jesus did not say, "Come unto me *and I will give you more work to do.*" Tell your men that it is okay just to sit and listen. "All you have to do to receive love is show up. You don't have to do something to be good enough to receive acceptance." Mary first *(logos).* There will be plenty of time for Martha *(diakonia).*

Jesus has given this as a model for how we can fulfill the Great Commandment. The way of Mary will accomplish what the way of Martha will miss.

Do you need to say to a man who is putting a lot of pressure on himself, you, and/or everyone else, "Jim, Jim, you are worried and upset about many things, but only one thing is needed"? Would it improve the climate of your church to teach all your members, "Brothers, Brothers, you are worried and upset about many things, but only one thing is needed"?

For More: Read chapter 13, "The Most Important Thing," in *Discipleship for the Man in the Mirror.*

40. **LOVING PEOPLE**

Love is the glue that holds us together, and the oil that keeps us from rubbing each other the wrong way.

Teach your men how to "neighbor love"—the New Commandment (see Matthew 22:37–39). Jesus did not say, "By this all men will know you are my disciples, *if you perfect your theology.*" Right theology is important, and bad theology is deadly. Yet lost and lonely people are not attracted by excellent theology (though ours should be excellent).

What Jesus did say was, "By this all men will know you are my disciples, if you love one another" (John 13:35). People are attracted to us by the way we love one another.

In the second century church, Christians were accused of treason (not pledging allegiance to the Emperor), cannibalism (drinking Christ's blood and eating his body), and sexual immorality (the kiss of peace). Yet against this backdrop the early church expanded rapidly. God was at work in the way Christians loved each other and the unlovely. Julian the Apostate, a pagan, said, "Those impious Christians. They support not only their own poor, but ours too." It had quite an effect. It still does.

Teach your men to see people the way Jesus sees people. "When he saw the crowds, he had compassion on them, because they were harassed and helpless, like sheep without a shepherd" (Matthew 9:36). He is patient, wanting all to come to repentance. His patience means salvation (2 Peter 3:9, 15).

Biblically, reconciliation precedes worship (Matthew 5:23–24). Teach your men how to resolve conflict and heal broken relationships. A cut on your body cannot heal unless the two separated pieces are brought into contact with each other. Likewise, two people can't heal until they are brought together.

Many task-oriented men want to be more relationship-oriented, but it goes against their nature. Tell them, "Choose to make *the relationship* into your task. Say to yourself until you grasp and believe this: 'The relationship is the task.' Turn spending time with your wife into a task—calendarize it if that makes you feel better."

For More: Go to www.pastoring men.com and click on "40. Loving People" to (1) see or hear "Broken Relationships" in The Man in the Mirror Remix series; (2) read the article "How to Get Along with Difficult People."

41. **MAN, DOCTRINE OF**

People in our society tend to believe one of two great errors about human nature. The first error is not that we think too highly of man, but not highly enough. Man's dignity has been degraded unnecessarily.

The second error is not that we think man so sinful, but not nearly sinful enough. We are all much more depraved than we let on (e.g., if our wives knew our secret thoughts, we would all be in trouble).

The paradox of man is that he is a product of both the creation and the fall. Help your men understand we have a "dual identity." The creation made us like a god, and the fall made us like a devil. We are simultaneously images of God and products of the fall.

When we observe the animals, we notice that we are the highest order of creatures by a wide margin. Intuition tells us that human beings have dignity. Christianity teaches that mankind is God's crowning achievement, the full expression of God's creative genius, and that He has good plans for us.

Psalm 8:4–6 asks, "What is man that you are mindful of him, the son of man that you care for him?" It then answers, "You made him a little lower than the heavenly beings and crowned him with glory and honor. You made him ruler over the works of your hands; you put everything under his feet."

Don't let your men be fooled by the world's low view of man—it's so much worse than that. In the heart of every man is the ability to revile people made in the image of God while simultaneously worshiping a four-wheeled god made of steel and leather.

Neither let them be deceived by the world's high view of man—it's so much greater than that. Your men are God's most excellent creation, His highest achievement, and the full expression of His creative genius.

For More: Go to www.pastoringmen.com and click on "41. Man, Doctrine of" to see the Biblical Manhood series of twelve messages.

42. **MANHOOD**

All men want to lead successful lives. Of course, men often fail, but I don't think anyone would suggest they fail on purpose. This conflict between "the man I want to be" and "the man I am" is the central question of "What does it mean to be a man?"

So what do men want? As noted in chapter 3, the list can be reduced to three things: (1) A *cause* we can give our lives to that will make a difference—a mission, significance, meaning, purpose; (2) A *companion* to share it with—wife, relationships, love, family, acceptance; and (3) A *conviction* that gives a reasonable explanation for why 1 and 2 are so difficult—a belief system, worldview, philosophy, religion.

This is the essence of manhood—finding *something* we can give ourselves to, *someone* to share it with, and a *system* that explains how to make sense of our lives. These are God-given desires—what we were created to do. You will feel most alive, most significant, and most useful when you are doing what you were created to do.

What keeps us from getting what we want? We have created a culture that requires more energy than most of us have to give. A lot of us catch a disease we might call "success sickness"—the disease of always wanting more, but never being satisfied when we get it. As a result, we are prone to get caught up in the rat race, lead unexamined lives, and become cultural Christians.

For More: Go to www.pastoringmen.com and click on "42. Manhood" to see the Biblical Manhood series.

43. **MARRIAGE**

Of all the problems we watch men wrestle with at Man in the Mirror, the marriage issue alone is bigger than all of the other problems combined. For most men, their marriage is not working the way God intended. Most men simply have not fully grasped their role as the spiritual leader of their homes.

Ephesians 5:25 offers the principal instruction to married men, "Husbands, love your wives, just as Christ loved the church." Tell your men that if they want a biblical marriage, they need to understand how Christ loved the church.

Many men mistake "Christ" for Jesus' last name. Of course, *Christ* is not a name but a title for Jesus that means "Messiah" or "anointed one." In the Old Testament there were many types of anointed ones. In the New Testament, as we shall see, husbands became anointed ones.

Jesus loved the church as its "Christ, or anointed one." Since husbands are to love their wives *in the same way as* the "anointed one" loved the church, they need to know exactly what Jesus was anointed to do.

Christ occupies the classic, threefold office of *prophet*, *priest*, and *king*:

1. *The Role of a prophet.* A prophet represents God to people. In the Old Testament a prophet would face the people and speak. Jesus was a prophet who spoke the Word of God to the people and was, in fact, the Word incarnate. A prophet speaks for God.

   A husband is to be the family prophet. He represents God to his wife (and by extension to his family). When his wife reacts emotionally, he calms her with his wisdom. He proclaims the gospel of faith to his family. He provides biblical instruction and training to his wife and children without becoming legalistic. He prepares family devotions and encourages private devotions. He is the arbiter of family values. He insists on regular church attendance. He is a *messenger* from God to his family.

2. *The Role of a priest.* If a prophet represents God to people, then a priest represents people to God. In the Old Testament a priest would turn his back to the people and mediate for them before God. Jesus is the High Priest who mediated between people and the Father by the sacrifice of His life. A priest mediates before God.

   A husband is to be the family priest. He represents his wife and children to God. He spends time in prayer each day remembering the needs and concerns of his wife. He prays for the salvation of his children. Like Job, he asks the Lord to forgive the sins of his children. He sets the spiritual temperature in the home. He is a *mediator* to God for his family.

3. *The Role of a king.* A king takes responsibility for the welfare of his people. He provides both justice and mercy to his people. Jesus is a king from the line of David. A king provides for his people.

A husband is to be the family king. He provides for the needs of his family. He works diligently to earn enough for food and shelter. He administers discipline with fairness. He quickly forgives and overlooks offenses. He acts in a manner worthy of receiving honor. He treats his wife with consideration and respect. He is careful not to be harsh with her. He is a *provider* for his family.

Husbands are to be the anointed spiritual leaders of their wives. Tell your men: "God has anointed you to lead your wife as her prophet, priest, and king. Because of the fall, your wife has a desire for you that borders on disease (see the topic "The Fall" for more details). You must be gentle and wise because she is more fragile than you. It is God's will for your marriage to work. Give her a voice in the marriage. After God, but before all others, make your mate your priority."

For More: Go to www.pastoringmen.com and click on "43. Marriage" to (1) find *Devotions for Couples* from which this is excerpted, and *The Marriage Prayer* by Patrick Morley and David Delk; (2) watch or hear four messages: "Surviving a Marital Crisis" in the A Man's Guide to Inevitable Events series, "The Crucified Husband" in the Family and the Man in the Mirror series; "Restoring a Broken Marriage" in The Husband in the Mirror series; and "Wives: How to be Happily Married" in The Man in the Mirror Remix series. Also, see the Husband in the Mirror series with twelve messages.

Also, can you imagine what would happen if every married person in your church prayed for their spouse every day? **The Marriage Prayer Challenge** is a simple strategy to help make that happen. Find free tools and resources at www.themarriageprayer.org.

44. **MONEY AND POSSESSIONS**

Ironically, most men think money will do what it can't and that God can't do what He will. A man cannot love both God and money (Matthew 6:24). A man cannot love both God and the world (1 John 2:15). Teach your men that money is God's chief competitor, and they must choose between the two.

Teach your men that money is a hand of providence. Not the only hand, but by money God directs the affairs of men. By giving it to us or taking it away, God directs us into His best plan and purpose for our lives. Men must feed their families, so He uses their need for money to direct them into work that "tends the culture."

Beyond exhorting us to share with the church and the poor, and to not make money a god, the Bible gives us great freedom over money and possessions. While all things are permissible, however, not all things will leave us happy. Here are three ideas to help your men think through their own "theology of money and possessions."

First, don't own things you do not use on a regular basis. For seven years we owned a weekend lake house just outside of town. Virtually every Friday afternoon we would "kidnap" our children and spend the weekend doing country things. When our daughter turned eleven, though, her in-town friends became very important to her. We only went to the lake house once that year, so we decided to sell the property. There was nothing wrong with owning the property; there was no requirement to sell the property; there was no special virtue to own or not own the property. It did, however, keep us lean and responsive to God's leading in our lives.

This idea is not for everyone. Nor does it make one man more spiritual than another. However, it may free a man up tremendously. Why? Everything you and I own requires maintenance, worry, insurance, money, and represents an opportunity cost.

Second, don't own things just because you can. A neighbor about a mile down the shore owned a completely restored mahogany 1957 Chris Craft Sportsman inboard boat. I mentioned that I would be interested if he ever wanted to sell. Six months later he did, and we agreed upon what I considered a fair price. But a test drive revealed the boat needed several maintenance items.

It took nearly a month to have the repairs made. During that time I continued to pray about selling our boat to buy the antique Chris Craft. One day the question came to mind, "Why not deny yourself this boat?" Since I had been thinking about this boat for three years, that thought came as quite a jolt. However, I had also been wondering if I should buy it just because I could. Over several days I came to the conclusion that, for me, it would be a good lesson in self-restraint and personal discipline to forego the purchase. On the other hand, there were other financial purchases I was considering at the time with which I went ahead and felt just fine.

Third, the more you give away the happier you will be. Because Man in the Mirror is a 501(c3) charitable organization, we receive financial gifts from donors. Over the years I have developed beautiful friendships with many of these donors and have been able to observe their lives. Here is an iron law: The greater proportion of a man's income he gives, the happier he is. I believe this is well borne out by Scripture.

Ironically, for some men, it's almost as though the more money they have, the more afraid they are that it's going to run out. If that has been the concern of one or more of your men, teach them the Bible makes it clear that if they are generous toward others, God will be generous toward them. Tell your men, "You are not going to run out of money."

For More: (1) See topic 60, *Stewardship*; and (2) read chapter 6, "Do What You Don't Want to Do and Become What You Want to Be," in *Ten Secrets for the Man in the Mirror* (Zondervan) from which this page is excerpted. Also go to www.pastoringmen.com and click on "44. Money and Possessions" and (3) watch or hear "Money Trouble" in the A Man's Guide to Inevitable Events series; and (4) watch or hear "Money: A Biblical Point of View" and "The Four Pillars of Financial Strength" in The Man in the Mirror Remix series; (5) read the two articles "Money and Possessions" and "How to Get Out of Debt."

45. **MOTHER WOUND**

Not many of us want to talk badly about our mothers—I know I feel guilt even writing this first sentence. However, when my mother passed away I confess that I did not feel anything. That was odd, so I went to Christian counseling.

My counselor concluded that I was not a product of good parenting. Essentially, I was not mothered. There was a lack of touch, verbal affection, and time, which indicates a betrayal—even if not intended.

I was a little boy with a hole. Something was missing. I didn't feel precious and deeply cared for. A little boy cannot handle the thought, "My mother does not delight in me. I am not loved." When my parents didn't go to my baseball games, the little boy in me substituted, 'I really don't want them at my games.'"

Apparently I decided, "If they don't need me, then I don't need them either." My counselor thinks I pushed my parents away because I couldn't handle the thought that they really didn't want me (real or imagined). I know I wanted to be wanted. I wanted them at my games. I wanted them to rescue me from my downward slide.

What's confusing is that my mother was such a wonderful human being. Of course, today I realize that neither my mother nor my father were ever discipled or otherwise trained to parent me. They did the best they could.

Frankly, I never grieved what could have been until she was gone—I didn't know what had me in bondage. I was in full-fledged denial because who wants to admit, "I don't feel like my Mama cares"?

What is the effect of a mother wound? For many of your men (maybe you too) unsatisfied longing keeps them in bondage, keeps them taking abuse, keeps them feeling betrayed, and keeps them from coming to rest. In my case, the effect has been over-sensitivity. Early in my life I made a vow: "If you're not going to give me what I need, then I'm done with you." I am loyal to a fault. But once I feel betrayal, I tend to close off my spirit toward that person and write them off. Through counseling and by God's grace, this has virtually gone away.

It's up to me (and each of your men) whether to be a victim or a victor. By God's grace, I chose victor and so can your men. The Bible says so: "Even if my father and mother abandon me, the Lord will hold me close" (Psalm 27:10 NLT).

Men wounded this deeply probably need professional Christian counseling. Sharing these points with your men could help some of them identify a problem they might otherwise miss.

46. **PRAYER**

Teach your men how to pray. Here is the logical starting point for prayer: There is nothing for which we cannot pray, and there is nothing God cannot do. This opens up "everything" as subjects for prayer.

Prayer is the "language" God has made available for us to communicate with Him. It is the "voice" He hears. Prayer allows us to engage God in meaningful "conversation."

Prayer is God's designated means of pouring our hearts out to Him, of personal relationship, of communion, of praising and worshiping Him, of getting our needs met or interceding for others, of ushering the kingdom of God into human affairs. Prayer is our means to seek and receive forgiveness, pledge allegiance to Jesus, express gratitude for his "goodness and unfailing love that will pursue me all the days of my life" (Psalm 23:6 NLT). Prayer is the means of healing, of mercy, of grace, of wisdom and guidance, and of filling by the Holy Spirit.

Though God doesn't answer audibly, the Bible says He does answer when we pray according to His will: "This is the confidence we have in approaching God: that if we ask anything according to his will, he hears us. And if we know that he hears us—whatever we ask—we know that we have what we asked of him" (1 John 5:14–15). Suggest men ask themselves, "Who would know better if a prayer should be answered the way you want—you or God?" Teach your men to trust that God has their best interests in mind.

Teach men to pray regularly with their wife (if married) or an accountability partner. Tell your married men to try praying with their wife every day. Have your men take "The Marriage Prayer Challenge" at www.themarriageprayer.com.

Prayer is hard work, but it is the only work that releases the power of the kingdom of God into our human actions.

Great Quote: "Unless in the first waking moment of the day you learn to fling the door wide back and let God in, you will work on a wrong level all day; but swing the door wide open and pray to your Father in secret, and every public thing will be stamped with the presence of God"—Oswald Chambers.

47. **PRIDE**

Pride is a gender issue, and the deadliest sin. C. S. Lewis said in *Mere Christianity*:

> There is one vice of which no man in the world is free. Which everyone in the world loathes when he sees it in someone else, and of which hardly any people, except Christians ever imagine they themselves are guilty. I have heard people admit that they are bad tempered or that they cannot keep their heads about girls or drink. Or even that they are cowards. I do not think that I have ever heard anyone who was not a Christian accuse himself of this vice. . . . There is no fault that make a man more unpopular and no fault of which we are more unconscious of in ourselves. The more we have it ourselves the more we dislike it in others. The vice I am talking about is pride or self conceit. And the virtue opposite to it in Christian morals is called humility.

There is a right kind of pride and a wrong kind. Teach your men the difference between being proud of their son for getting a hit, what I call "Type I", and looking down on others because their sons didn't (Type II).

Pride Type I is "a healthy sense of self without comparison to others, because the heart is right."

Pride Type II is "an inordinate opinion of one's own dignity, importance, merit, or superiority, whether as cherished in the mind or as displayed in bearing or conduct." Humility is "a modest sense of one's important, rank, etc."

The apostle Paul has written, "Each one should test his own actions. Then he can take pride in himself, without comparing himself to somebody else" (Galatians 6:4).

For More: Go to www.pastoringmen.com and click on "47. Pride" to watch or hear "Pride" in The Man in the Mirror Remix series.

48. **PRIORITIES**

Teach your men how to set biblical priorities. A priority is "something to which we assign a degree of urgency or importance." Priorities become filters through which we sift decisions. Priorities are "pre-decisions" that act as tie-breakers between competing uses of time and money.

First, Jesus made decisions based on His priorities. "At daybreak Jesus went out to a solitary place. The people were looking for him and when they came to where he was, they tried to keep him from leaving them. But he said, 'I must preach the good news of the kingdom of God to the other towns also, because that is why I was sent'" (Luke 4:42–44).

Teach men how Jesus handled priorities. First, people tried to keep Jesus from leaving. Perhaps they appealed to His compassion. The better job you do, the more people will ask you to do. Without intending to, people will ask you to do things that meet their needs but don't necessarily match your priorities.

Second, Jesus knew His purpose. He said, "I must preach the good news . . . because that is why I was sent." His purpose determined His priorities. He did not let the emotion of the moment cloud His judgment. Since he decided in advance what he should do, he was not distracted.

Third, Jesus did what He was called to do. The pressure to do that which is good but not best has put many wagons in the ditch. There is one great rule for priority living we glean from the example of Jesus: Make decisions on the basis of your *priorities*, not your *pressures*.

No man can do everything. Choices must be made. Setting priorities helps us make choices about how we invest our limited time and money.

Teach that every man must take personal responsibility for his private life and set priorities in the following seven areas: (1) relationship with God; (2) relationship with wife (if married); (3) relationship with children (if a father); (4) vocation; (5) finances; (6) ministry; and (7) health, leisure, and rest. No one else will, or can, set a man's priorities. If he fails in any of these areas, people will feel sorry for him but they won't feel responsible.

For More: (1) see also the topics *Balance, Stewardship*, and *Time Management*; (2) read "Priorities: How to Decide What's Important," chapter 14 in *The Man in the Mirror*; and go to www.pastoringmen.com and click on "48. Priorities" to (3) see or hear "Priorities: How to Decide What's Important" in The Man in the Mirror Remix series.

49. **PRIVATE DEVOTIONS**

Whenever a man tells me that he doesn't feel very close to God, the first question I ask is, "Tell me about your devotional life." Often the problem is just there.

Teach your men how to have private devotions or a "quiet time." Tell them, "A quiet time is a routine period, usually at the beginning or end of the day, in which five, fifteen, thirty minutes, an hour or more are set aside to read and study God's Word, pray, and possibly perform other spiritual disciplines."

Actually, the Bible calls for continual prayer and Bible meditation. "Pray continually" (1 Thessalonians 5:17). "Pray in the Spirit on all occasions with all kinds of prayers and requests" (Ephesians 6:18). "His delight is in the law of the Lord, and on his law he meditates day and night" (Psalm 1:2). The quiet time, then, is an accommodation to an overly busy culture. Nevertheless, it can greatly enhance anyone's walk with God. In fact, without it, it is questionable if a man can really have an ongoing relationship with Christ.

How much time should you devote to daily quiet time? Tell men, "If you don't already have a quiet time, why not consider giving five minutes a day to read one chapter of the New Testament (read one chapter a day five days a week and you will complete the 260 chapters of the New Testament in one year). Then say a prayer like the Lord's Prayer, or you could use the ACTS acrostic (Adoration, Confession, Thanksgiving, Supplication). Consider setting a maximum time limit for devotional life, rather than a minimum. This will keep down the guilt. Later if you want to increase the time you spend, fine.

But they should start with a realistic goal. Explain: "The best length of time is the one you will actually do. Don't bite off more than you will chew."

How often should your men have a quiet time? Have them aim for five days a week (allowing for early-morning meetings, glitches, etc. Tell them: "You wouldn't expect to eat once or twice a week and be healthy. Neither can you feed your spirit only once or twice a week and expect spiritual health."

One benefit of daily devotions for your men is that they will develop the sense of an ongoing spiritual pilgrimage, not something that he accomplishes once for all. The impatience of wanting to "be there" is turned to a holy patience by coming daily to the table in search of a piece of bread.

For More: Go to www.pastoringmen.com and click on "49. Private Devotions" to read the article "How to Have a Consistent Quiet Time."

50. **PURPOSE AND MEANING**

A man's greatest felt need is his need to be significant—to make a difference and know that his life matters. Apart from God, life has no meaning and no purpose. Teach men that God has a purpose for their lives. Teach your men that God has eternal and earthly purposes. Teach your men that all men are alike in certain respects and, as such, God prescribes four universal earthly purposes for all men. Teach your men that God also has a personal earthly purpose for each man. That purpose is the unique way in which God blends the four universals together in time, place, relationships, work, and so forth. It looks like this:

I. Eternal Purpose

    God's eternal purpose for us is eternal life.

II. Earthly Purpose

    God's earthly purpose for us is to live as disciples of Jesus Christ.

    A. Universal Earthly Purpose

       There is a sense in which all men are alike, and God gives all men the same universal purposes. *The Bible reveals four universal purposes* (or, if you prefer, one purpose with four parts)—two that relate to relationships and two that relate to tasks:

       1. The Great Commandment (Matthew 22:37): To love God
       2. The Royal Commandment (John 13:3–35): To love one another
       3. The Great Commission (Matthew 28:18–20): To build the kingdom
       4. The Cultural Mandate (Genesis 1:28): To tend the culture

    B. Personal Life Purpose

       Each man is unique, and God gives each a different personal life purpose (Philippians 2:13; Acts 17:26; Ephesians 2:10; 1 Peter 4:10–11). Like a fingerprint, one's life purpose is a one-of-a-kind set of marching orders that combines the four universal purposes to which God calls all men. That unique combination draws from a man's spiritual gifts, natural abilities, acquired competencies, assigned times and places, roles, deeds, service, love, and the Spirit—all of which issue from Jesus Christ.

Teach men how to find meaning in life. God has created us to find meaning, but God's meaning only comes in God's way. Within these four purposes, every man will find meaning in the way God intends. To that end, suggest men develop a Written Life Purpose Statement. (A guide can be found at www.pastoringmen .com.) Your men will feel most useful, most significant, and most happy when they are doing what they were created to do.

For More: (1) Go to www.pastoringmen.com and click on "50. Purpose and Meaning" to see or hear "Significance: The Search for Meaning and Purpose" and "Purpose: Why Do I Exist?" in The Man in the Mirror Remix series; (2) read "How to Develop a Written Life Purpose Statement."

51. **THE RAT RACE**

Picture men, lots of men, men under pressure, zooming down the fast lanes of life, straining to keep pace. Some are oblivious to what they're doing. Some are starting to wonder about it. Others are weary. Still others have "hit the wall."

In the process of pursuing their career goals, many men neglect their wives emotionally; and slowly, the two of them grow apart. Taking a cue from dad, kids today often run in their own mini-rat races, and dads sometimes feel left out and unappreciated. Twenty years later it slowly dawns on these men that they gave their best years to careers that promised what they couldn't deliver.

As a result, many men have been knocked off balance. Some ask honest questions: "How can I be so successful and so unfulfilled at the same time? Is this all there is?" The rat race charges an expensive toll. It will take everything a man is willing to give.

What is the rat race? As noted in chapter 4, it is the conflict between who a man is *created* to be and who he is *tempted* to be. It is the endless pursuit of an ever increasing prosperity that ends in frustration rather than fulfillment. Tired, pressured, restless—many of your men have a pervasive lack of contentment. The price of pace is peace. We have created a culture which requires more energy than men have to give.

How do men get caught up in the rat race? In Galatians 5:7 Paul asks the question this way: "You were running a good race. Who cut in on you and kept you from obeying the truth?" He teaches the answer two verses later: "A little yeast works its way through the whole batch of dough" (Galatians 5:9). A big lie has entered his mind. (See topic 37, "Lies.")

Teach your men that there is another race. Teach them that perseverance comes from fixing our eyes on Jesus, "the author and perfecter of our faith" (see Hebrews 12:1–3). Teach them to locate their authority in God's Word. Teach them that Satan knows where they are vulnerable—what makes them discontent. Equip them for the battle.

For More: Go to www.pastoringmen.com and click on "51. The Rat Race" to see or hear "The Rat Race" in The Man in the Mirror Remix series; or read chapter 1 of *The Man in the Mirror*.

52. **READING**

True or false: *Men don't read.* If you answered false, look around the boarding area the next time you fly. Men read all the time. That said, reading habits for Christian books vary widely by gender.

When it comes to Christian books for men, there are two kinds of readers. Pastors and leaders are the "first readers." They hold influence over a second group we might call "relational readers." "Relational readers" either (1) take a recommendation from a respected pastor, layman, or spouse on a book that hits a felt need, (2) receive a book by a "first reader" or spouse, or (c) get in a small group led by a pastor or leader who picks the book.

"Relational readers" are often men who don't read well and/or don't like to read. As a result, they don't read much, can take or leave books in general, and wouldn't take an interest in reading except as a response to a pastor, leader, or spouse.

As to why many men do not read, I've been offered many wise opinions—here are three: (1) they come home from work mentally and emotionally exhausted; (2) many alternative activities to reading exist; and (3) they don't read well, which leads to frustration and loss of interest.

Yet reading is very important. One leader said it well: "The men who read the book chapter we study before they come to our small group are growing, and those who don't read it are stagnant. The stagnant ones just can't understand why their lives are not changing."

I have always been amazed at how a man will get hold of a book, and then God will use the book to get hold of the man.

53. **REST**

If I could only make one observation about how men are doing, I would say, "Men are tired." Physically tired, yes, but also emotionally, relationally, psychologically, and financially tired—exhausted by the pace of a culture that requires more energy than they have to give.

These men don't come to church, at least initially, looking for "work." They are tired. Jesus didn't say, "Come to me all you are weary and burdened, *and I will give you more work to do.*" He offers—make that *promises*—them rest. Make sure your church delivers what Jesus promised.

You will have to teach your men how to rest. Rest is a highly neglected priority. First, give your men permission to not work sixty hours a week. God will provide. Second, teach men to find their rest in Christ by spending time with Him—see the topics "Disciplines, Spiritual" "Growth," and "Private Devotions."

Third, I think every man needs a couple of hours a day to himself to recharge. This might include his private devotions, a visit to the gym, a hobby, a sport, reading a book, a date with his wife, a movie with his children, or watching television.

A lot of men never feel like they are doing enough to make money. They don't have enough faith to trust God and rest. Challenge these men to put God's Word to the test. Other men never feel like they are doing enough to serve God. They are riddled with guilt. Tell them, "It's okay just to come and sit when that's what you need to do."

54. **SABBATH**

Teach your men how to treat the Sabbath. God has made it "legal" for us to rest one day a week. For some of us twenty-first-century hard chargers, rest really requires an act of discipline. It's not our natural response. We're more comfortable working and involved in activity. Yet God thought it was important enough to make it one of His crucial mandates. I see at least four reasons to practice the discipline of the Sabbath:

- *The Sabbath is integral to orthodox Christianity.* It is included in the Ten Commandments—arguably the most important piece of legislation ever recorded. They helped form the foundation for Western culture.

- *The Sabbath expresses our trust in God's provision.* Our obedience communicates that our faith is in God—not in ourselves. By resting we say, "I believe God will take care of me. I don't always have to be scrambling. I can trust Him."

- *The Sabbath protects us from ourselves.* Many years ago it was said that when Frenchmen in Paris stopped observing the Sabbath, suicide rates increased. During that time, the suicide rate in Paris reportedly became the highest of any city in the christianized world. Constant work will wear us down, put us on edge, and make us unbalanced.

- *The Sabbath is badly misunderstood, often abused, and frequently neglected.* Whether it's mowing, shopping, or just doing lots of chores, many men don't relax on the weekends. Many men who do relax leave God out of this day of recreation. They often ignore their families.

If you feel you can't get by without working on the Sabbath, you may want to ask yourself, "Am I trusting God? If not, what am I afraid of?"

For More: Read Patrick Morley's, chapter 5, "A Man and the Sabbath," in *A Man's Guide to the Spiritual Disciplines* .

55. **SERVICE**

Most Christian men have it in their hearts to serve God, but find it difficult to develop a personal ministry. They need someone to show them "how."

God wants every believer to have a personal ministry. "For we are God's workmanship, created in Christ Jesus to do good works, which God prepared in advance for us to do" (Ephesians 2:10). God has a particular task, good work, or personal ministry for each of us.

A personal ministry is based upon a man's spiritual gifts (see the topic "Spiritual Gifts").

Our two principal tasks are *redemptive* tasks "to build the kingdom" (the Great Commission, Matthew 28:18–20) and *cultural* tasks "to tend the culture" (the cultural mandate, Genesis 1:28). For most men, more than 80 percent of their time will be spent "tending the culture" through their families, work, civic duties, and community life. Some will have more opportunity than others to share their faith at work, but all can demonstrate the reality and relevance of Jesus through the way they work. As Francis of Assisi said in his familiar saying, "Go ye into all the world, preach the gospel and, if necessary, use words."

Here are six areas where a man can develop a personal ministry:

1. *In the family.* This must be a man's first and top priority in ministry. Here are activities you can recommend: Pray before all meals. Have a fifteen-minute daily devotion three or four days a week during the school year. Pray for children daily (you may be the only person in the whole world willing to pray for your children on a regular basis). Consider paying your kids to do private devotions. Use the honor system and make them keep track over a period of months. After God, but before all others, make your wife your top priority. If you want a powerful ministry, disciple your own family.

2. *In the church.* The next place to have a ministry, if he can, is in the church. Most men will find an outlet for their spiritual gifts in the church.

3. *At work.* Men don't have to wear their faith like an outer garment (but you can). Be sensitive for opportunities to care for people. Be excellent. People will decide if Christianity is true or not based upon how you work when you think no one is looking. Francis Schaeffer said, "If you do your work

well you will have a chance to speak." You can take a more active role, such as teaching or organizing a Bible study at your office before work or during lunch.

4. *In the community.* Use your imagination. Start a community-wide annual prayer breakfast. Consider becoming foster parents. Dedicate your home to Christ and open it up for a Bible study group. Organize a neighborhood Christmas party at which you give your personal testimony. Serve dinners to homeless people at your local shelter on Thanksgiving or Christmas.

5. *Across culture.* Get to know a person of different racial/ethnic/cultural background. Take "The Three Week Reconciliation Challenge": Invite someone racially different to have breakfast, lunch, or coffee once a week for three weeks. Share where each of you are on your spiritual pilgrimage. Learn about each other's families, work, interests. If you are making progress, you can keep meeting. Take away each other's apathy and anger. Dispel myths. Quell fears.

6. *To the world.* Have a missionary family stay at your home during the church's missions conference. Pray for missionaries using a globe. Write missionaries and support them financially. Send care packages for their children's birthdays. Take a mission trip if you can. It's a real eye-opener. It is good to walk among the poor, to see their hunger for God, to feel the weight of their conditions and become sensitive to them personally.

For More: See chapter 18, "Developing a Personal Ministry," in *Discipleship for the Man in the Mirror* (Zondervan), from which this article is excerpted.

56. SEX

You can reasonably assume that most of your men are biblically naïve about their sexuality. Teach your men about sex as a gift, about sexual temptation, and sexual immorality (adultery, premarital relations, lust, and pornography). Research reveals that at least 50 percent of churched men have a major struggle with pornography. Teach your teenaged men about the purpose and meaning of sex.

The best teaching on the sexual duty is 1 Corinthians 7:1–7, and 1 Corinthians 6:12–20 presents a clear teaching on sexual immorality.

Remind your men that sexual pleasure is a beautiful gift of God for married couples. Biblically speaking, sex is good! We men have a sexual drive altogether different from our wives. We want sex right now, and then on to the next project. Our wives, however, want to enjoy sexual intimacy as a by-product of a deeper love relationship built on the foundation of regular conversation, meaningful time together, and small kindnesses done throughout the week, like holding the door, clearing the dinner table, and mutual help.

Also, our wives love to be touched—quick hugs, long embraces, pats on the arms or shoulders, squeezing her knee or hand, putting your arm around her shoulder, walking through the mall holding hands, kisses, and sitting on the sofa close enough to touch when you watch TV.

A major problem develops when a husband makes physical demands on his wife without making emotional investments in return, like nonsexual touches and conversations. Here are a few suggestions to offer your men:

1. Touch (nonsexual) and kiss your wife every day.
2. Talk to her about her day; tell her about yours. Be intentional about it.
3. Set a time to talk with your wife about your sexual relationship. (The more awkward this seems to you, the longer you have probably put off what should be done regularly.) Just do it.

For your single men, assure them that the Bible teaches that sex is an altogether good thing. Sex is one of God's greatest gifts to the human race when it is used according to His plan. God created sex for two purposes: to make babies and for a married couple to enjoy physical intimacy with each other.

St. Augustine wrote that everything bad is a corruption of something that was originally meant to be good. When sex is used outside of God's plan, a lot of things can and do go wrong. This includes developing sexually transmitted diseases (some of which are incurable—approximately one of every three adults has an incurable STD), infertility, cervical cancer, and AIDS. Add to that a loss of reputation, depression, discipline from God, and pregnancy out of marriage, and we can understand why we should guard our sexuality for marriage.

Actually God does not put limits on sex. He puts limits on sexual immorality.

Here are some special suggestions for teenage boys in the church. Since sex is for propagating the human race, women get pregnant—and they don't have to be married or over twenty-one. Many families know the pain caused by teen pregnancy. God can redeem it, but I'm old enough to have seen it create a lot of sadness. Often an unplanned pregnancy defines who people become—even in my own extended family. Either you, the youth pastor, or a staff counselor need to make sure teenaged boys understand the consequences of unexpected teenage pregnancy—consequences that affect the guy and the girl as well as their parents. Remind your young men and women that the number one reason God has guidelines for human sexuality is that sex works very well for its principal purpose—making babies. (For a list of the overwhelming decisions that must be addressed by an unexpected teen pregnancy, read chapters 8 and 9 "Sex" and "Dating" in *The Young Man in the Mirror*, a portion of which is excerpted here.)

Great Quote: "Keeping to one woman is a small price for so much as seeing one woman," G. K. Chesterton in *Orthodoxy*.

For More: Go to www.pastoringmen.com and click on "56. Sex" to (1) read Patrick Morley's, *What Husbands Wish Their Wives Knew About Men,* a free downloadable book; (2) watch or listen to the Sex and the Man in the Mirror series.

57. **SMALL GROUPS**

In my experience, a lot of the real transformation in men's lives takes place in small groups. I think several factors are involved. First, men get "air time" to flesh out the concepts for themselves—concepts that can take ten or twenty years to fully grasp. Second, they get to "observe" how other men react to the same concepts (e.g., are they solemn, joyful, convicted, encouraged?). Third, they see "changed life" in other men. Fourth, a small group provides "visibility" and "accountability" a man doesn't get any other way. Finally, if it's a men-only group, he can talk about male-specific issues in a male-specific way.

If I could have men do only two things in addition to the worship service, it would be to read the Bible for themselves and be in a small group with other men. Over the years, these are the two most effective disciplines or habits for men's discipleship and spiritual transformation.

Encourage your men to form or join small groups. In the best cases, you might build to 80 percent of your men in small groups. A solid effort might be 50 percent of your men.

Group size can vary, but I suggest not less than four. Also, once you get more than eight, air time starts to become scarce.

Don't let men self-select themselves as small group leaders. Do have a training process so they know how to handle different situations (e.g., a man who wants to fix everyone or a man who talks too much). Don't recruit teachers to be leaders. Instead, recruit shepherds who want to take care of a flock.

Don't micromanage your small groups. Men don't like to be micromanaged.

For More: Go to www.pastoringmen.com and click on "57. Small Groups" to find numerous free, downloadable articles.

58. **SPIRITUAL GIFTS**

It would be foolish to try to become a lawyer if you prefer to work with numbers. In the same way we pursue vocational employment based upon our aptitudes and abilities, we pursue our spiritual service based on an understanding of how God has gifted us.

Every believer receives at least one spiritual gift. "Now to each one the manifestation of the Spirit is given for the common good" (1 Corinthians 12:7). The Holy Spirit determines our spiritual gifts. "Each man has his own gift from God . . . he gives them to each one, just as he determines" (1 Corinthians 7:7; 12:11).

The purpose of our spiritual gifts is to serve Christ by serving others, helping to fulfill the Great Commission. "Each one should use whatever gift he has received to serve others, faithfully administering God's grace in its various forms" (1 Peter 4:10).

While theologians and teachers often differ on how to precisely classify and name spiritual gifts, the following generally captures the gist of the different gifts:

1. *Service gifts*. Service gifts are often low-profile, behind-the-scene gifts. They include showing mercy, service (or helps), hospitality, giving, administration, leadership, faith, and discernment.
2. *Speaking gifts*. Speaking gifts include knowledge, wisdom, preaching, teaching, evangelism, apostleship, shepherding, and encouragement.
3. *Signifying gifts*. The signifying gifts are miracles, healing, speaking in tongues, and the interpretation of tongues.

To better understand their gifts, have men study the four passages of Scripture that deal with spiritual gifts: Romans 12:3–8; 1 Corinthians 12:1–31; Ephesians 4:11–13; and 1 Peter 4:9–11. Prayerfully have them write down the gifts to which they are drawn.

For More. Go to www.pastoringmen.com and click "58. Spiritual Gifts" to read "How to Determine Your Spiritual Gifts," including one-sentence explanations of each spiritual gift (or read chapter 18, "Developing a Personal Ministry" in *Discipleship for the Man in the Mirror*).

59. **SPIRITUAL WARFARE**

There is raging in the cosmos and all around us a titanic battle between the forces of good and evil for men's souls. This battle is raging out of control in neighborhoods across America—your neighborhood. The apostle Peter put it this way: "Your enemy the devil prowls around like a roaring lion looking for someone to devour." (1 Peter 5:8). Your men are being hunted.

Equip men to fight a spiritual battle. Spiritual warfare, of course, includes the conspicuous, overt battle between good and evil *behavior.* But most Christian men have their outward morality under control. The deeper battle is for the mind—or *belief.* The Devil's strategy is confusion and disinformation—to make good seem evil and evil seem good.

Help your men grasp the difference between "tempting" and "sinful" thoughts. We have no more control over our thoughts than over the vulgar words of the man at the next table in a restaurant. We do control what we do next. Temptations are not sins, but every sin begins with a temptation. (James gives the progression in James 1: 14–15.) And, of course, a man will tend to "hear" fewer tempting thoughts at a Bible study than a bar.

Galatians 5:16–17 says that if you live your lives according to the Holy Spirit, "then you won't be doing what your sinful nature craves. The sinful nature wants to do evil, which is just the opposite of what the Spirit wants" (NLT). You can tell which is winning by the fruit your life bears.

People who are winning the battle exhibit the "fruit of the Spirit," which Paul describes as "love, joy, peace, patience, kindness, goodness, faithfulness, gentleness and self-control." People who demonstrate these qualities are "in step with the Spirit" (Galatians 5:22–25). They are winning the spiritual battle, and they enjoy the favor and peace of our great God.

Throughout this passage, Paul challenges us to cooperate with God in this process. Most of us realize our participation is required, but in our efforts to achieve superiority over ourselves, we face two potential errors:

1. We publicly pretend we have conquered the flesh. No one can win this war on his own strength. We win only through the Holy Spirit.

2. We privately deny the possibility of conquering the flesh. We all face a temptation to look at Scripture with disbelieving eyes. But the Scripture

declares as truth that if we "live by the Spirit . . . [we] will not gratify the desires of the sinful nature" (Galatians 5:16).

Teach your men that the enemy army is the world, the flesh, and the Devil. Show your men how to keep "short accounts" with God and cleanse themselves daily from sin and temptation. For temptation, have them meditate on 1 Corinthians 10:13; for sin, 1 John 1:9. Challenge your men to work all this out in a small group.

For More: See (1) chapter 9, "Spiritual Warfare," in *A Man's Guide to the Spiritual Disciplines* (portion excerpted here); (2) chapter 22, "Leading a Secret Thought Life," in *The Man in the Mirror*; and (3) chapter 14, "Your Secret Thought Life," in *The Young Man in the Mirror*. Also, go to www.pastoringmen .com and click "59. Spiritual Warfare" to (4) watch or hear "A Man Winning His Spiritual Struggle" in the Biblical Manhood series or "Leading a Secret Thought Life" in The Man in the Mirror Remix series.

60. **STEWARDSHIP**

Teach men that stewardship means to honor God with 100 percent of their time, talent, and treasure. Challenge your men to consider and choose among four lifestyle/spending approaches.

First, to live "above" their means. The spendthrift lives up to limits of his income and beyond. He teeters perpetually on the brink of financial disaster. He is constantly refinancing and borrowing more. Teach men that debt is dumb. The problem is you have to pay it back. It has not occurred to most men that it takes more energy to earn a living and service a debt, than just to earn a living. The Bible doesn't prohibit debt, but it is never recommended. The Bible is full of cautions against debt and offers much counsel about how to overcome the negative consequences.

Second, to live "at" their means. A lot of men want more of the good life. However, they are not so foolish that they borrow for "experiences" or depreciating assets, but neither are they so wise that they think about a rainy day. They are like the man who hears God's Word, but the worries of this life and the deceitfulness of wealth choke it and make it unfruitful.

Third, to live "within" their means. Men who live within their means recognize that everything they have belongs to God, and the Bible calls all men to be stewards of what God has entrusted to them. Not only do such men save for a rainy day, but they have a well thought out retirement plan as well. They tithe joyfully.

Concerning tithing, teach your men to tithe. Many men think the concept of tithing is an Old Testament idea that no longer applies. Yet tithing is fully ratified by Jesus himself. "What sorrow awaits you teachers of religious law and you Pharisees. Hypocrites! For you are careful to tithe even the tiniest income from your herb gardens, but you ignore the more important aspects of the law—justice, mercy, and faith. You should tithe, yes, but do not neglect the more important things" (Matthew 23:23 NLT). Jesus said, in essence, "Look! You scrupulously give ten percent of every nickel you earn, but you're careless about your behavior! You need to add ethical behavior, without neglecting the tithing you already do." Remember, belief determines behavior. Let God's Word do its work.

Fourth, to live "below" their means. This unusually disciplined man has decided to live a lifestyle lower than he could easily afford. He wants to model the right values to his family. He does not want to be distracted by the worries, riches, and pleasures of this world. Though he uses the things of this world, he has not become engrossed in them. He has the gift of giving, and would rather make eternal investments than spend up to the limits of his income.

Only men in the third and fourth categories can reasonably expect to become financially independent in retirement. Ask your men, "Which category do you live in? Which category do you think God wants you to live in?" Then give them these practical suggestions:

1. Don't get engrossed with your possessions.
2. Take care of the possessions you do have.
3. Give 10 percent of your income to the work of the church.
4. Give above a tithe as God blesses and as you feel led.
5. Save 10 percent of your income.
6. Get out of debt. Debt is dumb.

For More: (1) Read the related topics *Priorities* and *Money and Possessions*. Also (2) see part three, "Solving Our Money Problems," in *The Man in the Mirror*, and (3) chapter 6 in *Ten Secrets for the Man in the Mirror*.

61. **SUCCESS SICKNESS**

All men want to be successful in what they do. That's normal and healthy. However, many men get carried away and end up catching "success sickness." Success sickness is the disease of always wanting more, but never being happy when you get it. It is that intangible pain that comes from not achieving goals that should never have been set or achieving them only to find out it didn't matter. Regrettably, many men don't learn this lesson until they've given it twenty or more years—often the best years of their lives. What a strategic opportunity to pastor men about success sickness and success that matters.

Biblically speaking, three things keep men from getting what they want: the world, the flesh, and the Devil. In practice, lies and idols infect many men with "success sickness." The unhappy result of believing that "success will make you happy" lie is that many men today are struggling with problems that success can't solve. No wonder so many men feel what Søren Kierkegaard called "the sickness unto death."

The passion that fuels can also consume. In the chase to "be somebody" a lot of men end up struggling with problems that success can't solve. Problems like a wife who feels emotionally neglected or kids who have to guess at normal behavior because their dads are not around enough to mentor them. In short, these men are off balance.

You should assume that most Christian men want to do the right thing. Christian guys don't get up in the morning planning to fail. No man wakes up and says to himself, "I wonder what I can do today to irritate my wife and neglect my kids." But it happens.

62. **SUCCESS THAT MATTERS**

The greatest problem we see in our work at Man in the Mirror is not that men are failing to achieve their goals. In most cases, they are achieving them. The problem is they are the wrong goals. Many men get what they want only to find it doesn't matter.

Failure means to not get what you want. Another way of defining failure, though, is to say that failure means to succeed in a way that doesn't really matter. What, then, is success that matters—true success?

Success that matters means a full-orbed, well-balanced, priority-based, thought-through success. It begins with the solid foundation of Christ as Lord. No man will sense he has been truly successful unless he can honestly answer "yes" to all of the following ten questions:

1. Am I growing in faith and love for the Lord Jesus every day?
2. Am I actively helping my family grow in their faith in Christ?
3. Am I making a significant contribution in my church?
4. Am I doing everything possible to help my children become responsible adults?
5. Am I building a strong, loving marriage?
6. Am I investing in other people's lives as a friend, counselor, accountability partner, and mentor?
7. Am I a good provider?
8. Am I living a life of integrity and good deeds?
9. Am I performing fulfilling work?
10. Will I go to heaven when I die?

Reprint these questions and give them to your men. Have men discuss these questions in small groups.

For More: (1) See part 7, "The Season of Success," in *Seven Seasons of the Man in the Mirror* from which the ten questions are excerpted; also (2) go to www.pastoringmen.com and click on "62. Success That Matters" to see or hear the Success and the Man in the Mirror series.

63. **SUFFERING**

C. S. Lewis wrote in *The Problem of Pain,* "If God were good, He would wish to make His creatures perfectly happy, and if God were almighty, He would be able to do what He wished. But the creatures are not happy. Therefore, God lacks either goodness, or power, or both. This is the problem of pain in its simplest form."

Of the many questions raised by suffering and evil, these four capture most of the heart issues:

1. Does God know? *(the issue of His omniscience)*
2. Does God care? *(the issue of His benevolence and love)*
3. Can He do anything about it? *(the issue of His omnipotence)*
4. If He knows, cares, and can do something about it, why doesn't He? *(the issue of His purposes and will)*

So much about suffering and evil remains opaque and impenetrable. On the other hand, a lot is knowable. Here's the elevator speech:

• *In this world we all will suffer.* Faithful Christians suffer (see 1 Peter 4:12; John 16:33). The perfection of creation was corrupted by the fall and, with it, human nature. So, because of the fall, we must do our work while feeling the prick of thorns. Humans are not capable of not sinning in their own strength. As it is, suffering plays a large part in the Christian faith on the road to redemption.

• *We are called to suffer.* We all must go through hardships (see Philippians 1:29; 1 Peter 2:21; Acts 14:22; 1 John 3:13). Not only have we been given the privilege of trusting Christ, but also of suffering for Him. He said, "In this world you will have trouble. But take heart! I have overcome the world" (John 16:33).

• *There is purpose to suffering.* We can handle anything if we think it is for a purpose (Romans 8:20–21; 2 Corinthians 1:9; 1 Peter 1:6–7; Romans 5:3–5). "Our light and momentary problems are achieving for us a glory that far outweighs them all" (2 Corinthians 4:17).

- *There is comfort in suffering*—because there is purpose to it (Psalm 119: 67, 71, 75, 92; Hebrews 12:7–11). Like David we all can say, "It was good for me to be afflicted. Now I obey your law." God uses suffering to redirect us back to him.

I love suffering. Not while it is happening, of course. But as I look back, most of the progress in my life took place after God "refined" (by fire) something that I could/would never have dealt with on my own. Some of our greatest heroes discovered and declared this truth: Daniel (Daniel 11:35), Paul (2 Corinthians 12:8–10), Peter (1 Peter 5:10), and James (James 1:2-4)

I love suffering because it produces in me the life of Christ, and I know of no other way to get it. I haven't been able to get it by self-will. I didn't get it through prosperity. It hasn't come to me through learning.

Great Quote: "He whom God loveth he beateth the hell out of."—Jamie Buckingham.

For More: Go to www.pastoringmen.com and click "63. Suffering" to (1) see part 6, "The Season of Suffering," in *Seven Seasons of The Man in the Mirror*; and (2) see or hear "Avoiding Suffering" in The Man in the Mirror Remix series.

64. **TIME MANAGEMENT**

The greatest time waster is the time we have to spend undoing that which we ought not to have done in the first place. There are very few things in life that can't wait two weeks. Here are four points to teach your men.

First, *Don't give yourself to those who don't absolutely need you at the expense of those who do.* Triage is the military technique of deciding how to prioritize treatment of wounded soldiers when a wave of new casualties swamps the capacity of the medic unit. For our personal decision-making we should conduct a little civilian triage by asking the following:

- Who can't live without you, or you without them?
- Who would you help if you don't have to neglect anyone in the first group?
- Who are those who will be fine with or without you?

Let's prioritize everything on the basis of who will cry at our funeral.

Second, *never do anything someone else can do.* Many years ago I decided I would only do things I do well. That served a good purpose, because it kept me in my areas of competence. However, I have also realized that simply because I do something well doesn't mean it's the best use of my time. Since then I've added a "part two." I also don't do anything if someone else can also do it. This principle frees up an unusually large amount of time.

Third, *distinguish opportunity from distraction.* Many times distractions come disguised as opportunities. Unless we have thought through who we are, what our lives are all about, and what's important to us, we will not have the focus to choose the best. Author Al Ries says that focus is the art of exclusion.

Fourth, *recognize the difference between a good idea and a God idea.* We are naturally inclined to act on the impulse of a good idea. But sometimes good ideas get in the way of God ideas. Prayer removes the impulse of the good idea born of human ingenuity but not of God. Pray, then plan. It is the habit of a man who would distinguish between good and God.

For More: (1) Read the related topics of "Balance," "Priorities," "Stewardship;" (2) go to www.pastoringmen.com and click on "64. Time Management" to watch or listen to "Time Management: Doing God's Will" in The Man in the Mirror Remix.

65. **UNEXAMINED LIFE**

To lead an unexamined life means to rush from task to busy task but not call enough time-outs to reflect on life's larger meaning and purpose. Plato wrote, "The unexamined life is not worth living." Most men have not carefully chiseled their worldview by a personal search for truth and obedience to God and His Word. They are not thinking deeply about their lives.

Scripture exhorts, "Let us examine our ways and test them, and let us return to the Lord" (Lamentations 3:40). Pastoring men is all about holding up a mirror in front of men so they can examine their lives.

Here's a great story to illustrate leading an unexamined life (also in chapter 4). Many people had prayed for Evan's salvation over many years. He traveled to Texas to spend a day making calls with one of his salesmen. At the end of the day his salesman, Steve, walked Evan into the airport to catch his plane back to the Midwest.

As they parted, Steve said, "Evan, you're amazing the way you sell our product. You're brilliant. But as smart as you are, you baffle me. You don't have a clue about where you came from, you don't have a clue where you're going, and you don't have a clue about your purpose in life."

Evan flew home, but for months he kept hearing Steve's searing comments over and over. In February of the following year, Evan was invited to an evangelistic event where he gave his life to Jesus Christ. Two months later he had a heart attack and needed bypass surgery.

The night before the surgery, he took his wife out to dinner. Evan, only forty-four years old, described his feelings of incredible peace and calm. His wife, Tracie, on the other hand, was a basket case. Evan took her hand and echoed the words he had heard only months earlier. "Tracie, you're amazing when it comes to education. You're brilliant. But as smart as you are, you baffle me. You don't have a clue about where you came from, you don't have a clue where you are going, and you don't have a clue about your purpose in life."

Tracie stared out the window.

For More: (1) See chapter 2, "Leading an Unexamined Life," in *The Man in the Mirror*; go to www.pastoringmen.com and click on "65. Unexamined Life" to (2) watch or listen to "Leading an Unexamined Life" in The Man in the Mirror Remix series; and to read (3) the article "How to Conquer a Secret Thought Life."

66. **WITNESSING**

Teach your men how to talk about Jesus without sounding like a nut. Have them try three steps.

First, *develop rapport.* When a Samaritan woman, a complete stranger, came to Jacob's well to draw water. Jesus talked to her about water—living water. People are trying to solve their problems, not ours. So give people what they need, but do it in the context of what they want. A man and his girlfriend moved next door to us. A month later he was despondent over his lack of work. I tried to help him get a job that he didn't get, and because I was interested we built a friendship, and he did eventually give his life to Jesus Christ. (He also married his friend!)

To talk about Jesus without sounding like a nut, be sure to establish *rapport.*

Second, *be relevant.* In Acts, Peter boldly addressed his fellow Jews—the "religious" people—with a strong warning, a stern rebuke, and a straightforward challenge, "Repent and be baptized, every one of you, in the name of Jesus Christ for the forgiveness of your sins"(Acts 2:38, 40).

In other words, he spoke in a language they could understand. He was relevant. On the other hand, when Paul was in Athens, where the thinkers and philosophers gathered, he took a different approach after seeing an altar with an inscription: "To an unknown god." He said, "Now what you worship as something unknown I am going to proclaim to you" (Acts 17:23).

To not sound like a nut you must be *relevant.* As someone said, theology is best done with a Bible in one hand and a newspaper in the other.

Third, *recommend Jesus.* Paul told the Corinthians, "For I resolved to know nothing while I was with you except Jesus Christ and him crucified" (1 Corinthians 2:2). That's bold! Why would he park on that thought? Because Jesus had said, "But I, when I am lifted up from the earth [indicating the form of His death], will draw all men to myself" (John 12:32). Paul understood that if he would stick to recommending Christ, that God would do the rest.

Don't argue religion, but do *recommend* Jesus Christ. If Jesus, once understood, doesn't draw them, nothing you add will draw them either.

For More. Go to www.pastoringmen.com and click on "66. Witnessing" to read the following free articles: (1) "How to Lead a Man to Christ," (2) "How to Lead an Executive to Christ," (3) "How to Talk about Jesus without Sounding Like a Nut," and (4) "Reach 3 Strategy: An Engaging Offer of Christ for Every Man."

67. **WORK**

Each week a man will spend roughly half of his 112 waking hours working. Yet most men do not have a good "theology of work." Teach your men a theology of work. Here are a few points.

First, *every vocation is holy to the Lord*. God makes no distinction between *sacred* and *secular*. (Have men look up the word "secular" in their concordances.)

Second, *every man is ordained for ministry in the workplace*. Help your men understand what they have been "ordained" to do and they will forever be grateful to you. Some of your men are ordained truck drivers. Some are ordained computer programmers. Others are ordained farmers.

Third, *work is not just a platform to do ministry; it is ministry*. For example, if you are a waiter, every customer is an occasion to demonstrate the character of Jesus Christ. If you are a manager, every conflict between two employees presents an opportunity to model the love of Christ. If you are a salesman, every appointment is divine and every sale is sacred.

All men want to be happy. A man will feel most happy, most alive, and most useful when he is doing the kind of work he was created to do—even while feeling the prick of thorns.

Fourth, *to succeed at work but fail at home is to fail completely*. Caution men that we have a tendency to compartmentalize our families while we're at work, but not our work while we're with our families. Our bodies are at home but our minds are still at work. Striking a right balance between work and family is a cornerstone of achieving a true happiness.

For More. See (1) chapter 4, "Not Happy Here, Not Happy Anywhere," in *Ten Secrets for the Man in the Mirror*; and (2) chapter 6, "The Secret of Job Contentment," in *The Man in the Mirror*; go to www.pastoringmen.com and click on "67. Work" to read the free articles (3) "How to Build a Ministry through Your Work" and (4) "Interview for a Job"; and to (5) watch or listen to a twelve-part series on Doing Business God's Way.

68. THE WORLD

A lot of men don't understand their relationship with the secular world. There are four stances men can take toward the world:

- *Withdraw* (like the Essenes, they err toward *legalism*)
- *Embrace* (like the Sadducees, they err toward *licentiousness*)
- *Overthrow* (like the Zealots, they err toward *lawlessness*)
- *Engage* (like Jesus and Paul, they have a correct stance on *liberty*)

Jesus said we are "in" the world but not "of" the world (John 17:11, 14). So tell your men not to get engrossed with using the things of this world (1 Corinthians 7:31). Tell them not to love the world (1 John 2:15–17).

Jesus does not want to take your men out of the world; He wants to take the world out of your men. In John 17:15 He prayed, "My prayer is not that you take them out of the world but that you protect them from the evil one."

But Jesus also sends us "into" the world (John 17:18). Jesus did not come to abolish culture. Many men are convinced they are going to heaven, but are content to let the world go to hell. Christianity is lived "inside" cultures. Paul was more than willing to accommodate—make that *engage*—the culture:

To the Jews I became like a Jew, to win the Jews. To those under the law I became like one under the law (though I myself am not under the law), so as to win those under the law. To those not having the law I became like one not having the law (though I am not free from God's law but am under Christ's law), so as to win those not having the law. To the weak I became weak, to win the weak. I have become all things to all men so that by all possible means I might save some. (1 Corinthians 9:20–22)

Why was Paul such a chameleon? Because he understood that Christianity is not a culture of its own. Christianity is lived "inside" cultures. It is not our assignment to create a Christian culture. Our assignment is to represent God within the culture. To do that, we have to go "into" the culture. On matters not specifically commanded or prohibited by Scripture, we are free to adapt to the culture. We don't require the culture to adapt to us.

69. **WORLDVIEW, CHRISTIAN**

Teach your men a biblical perspective and Christian worldview. We are each part of the bigger story of what God is doing in the world. A Christian worldview— a kingdom perspective—is a framework or grid through which to perceive and interpret what is happening.

A Christian worldview means that a man looks at the world through biblically-colored glasses. His first impulse is to see what God sees. He asks, "What is God trying to say or do?" Without such a worldview, your men will be Christian in spirit but secular in practice.

While the Bible is a reliable guide for all matters of both faith and life, the most important spiritual themes are repeated over and over again in many different ways for emphasis. That's because most of the really big ideas about Christianity take ten or twenty years to sink in. Major themes include, for example, the Trinity, creation, the fall and sin, death and suffering, grace, repentance, faith, redemption, forgiveness, eternal life, the fruit of the Spirit, spiritual gifts, good works, relationships, the Great Commandment, and the Great Commission.

Christianity is the only system that is all true all the time. Fortunately, the Bible doesn't describe a utopian world free of pain. That would make Christianity a wishful farce. Instead, the Bible describes the world exactly as we see it: a fallen world, a world groaning in pain that needs a Redeemer, Sanctifier, and Sustainer.

More importantly, the Bible describes how a man can rise above futility, sin, and despair to find peace, hope, and victory by surrendering His life to the lordship of Jesus Christ. The irony of surrender is that it leads not to defeat but victory.

A man's ability to embrace and enjoy his place in the world depends largely on his ability to "think Christianly" about things. While this chapter 11 certainly doesn't cover every possible Christian worldview topic, it's getting close. Here's a goal to consider: Why not equip your men with each of the seventy topics in this alphabetized reference section?

For More: Go to www.pastoringmen.com and click on "69. Worldview, Christian" to watch or listen to "A Man and His Worldview" in the Biblical Manhood series.

70. **WORSHIP**

Teach your men why worship is manly. The Greek word for *worship* literally means "to kiss, like a dog licking its master's hand." Worship is an opportunity for proud, peevish, sinful men to come humbly before God, acknowledge His greatness and goodness, and give praise, thanks, and glory to God. Church gives us a special place to stoop down and render religious homage, respect, awe, and reverence to the God Who is.

Teach men they can worship anywhere: walking in God's creation, reading the Bible on the train, listening to music in the car, reading books, journaling at night, praying throughout the day, and adoring God during public and family worship and even during work. Anything that causes them to exalt and glorify God is worship.

Teach your men to not only worship with the *ecclesia,* but as a family. Teach them, if married, to not neglect leading their wives and children, if applicable, into a deeper holiness and experience of worship. Suggest they gather their families in the morning to pray for the day. Take five minutes and share how each saw God work the day before. Ask everyone for prayer requests. Dedicate the day to His glory and praise. When they gather for meals, ask God's blessing and offer thanks.

Gordon MacDonald has identified six "leading instincts of the soul" which lead people to prefer worshiping God along six different lines. You will likely be most inclined toward two or three of these. None of these styles is more right than another. Help men understand how they best worship: (1) worship in majesty (the aesthetic instinct that seeks to be overwhelmed by the majesty of God); (2) worship in joy (the experiential instinct to "feel" the presence of God); (3) worship in achievement (the activist instinct for service); (4) worship by listening (the contemplative instinct that cherishes the inner life); (5) worship with truth (the student instinct to learn truth about God); and (6) and worship by love (the relational instinct that finds God most present when people are bonded together in fellowship, worship, or mutual support.) For more information on these six styles, see MacDonald's book *Christ Followers in the Real World.*[10]

For More: Go to www.pastoringmen.com and click on "70. Worship" to watch or listen to "A Man Created to Worship" in the Biblical Manhood series and numerous free resources that pertain to worship.

AFTERWORD

As you return now to your pastoring duties, may the Spirit empower you to more effectively pastor *every* man in your church.

I have only one additional suggestion. Whatever your ministry to men will look like ten years from now will be pretty much decided at the moment you stop reading this book. So I suggest you set an appointment for yourself within the next week—for at least one hour—to start planning out the next steps of your vision, and to begin implementing any changes you want to make.

Finally, I really don't want our "relationship" to end. My mission, and the mission of Man in the Mirror, is to serve you. So please check out the "Bonus Material and Resources" on pages 250–51 and visit www.pastoringmen.com for tons of additional resources and ways to stay connected.

And now, a prayer . . .

Our dearest Father, because of his obvious desire to love and serve you, I pray you will bless this pastor with a great abundance in every area of life—relationship with you, relationships with loved ones, work, health, finances, education, and in every other way. In the wonderful name of our Lord and Savior Jesus. Amen.

For the glory of Christ and no other reason,

Patrick Morley

NOTES

CHAPTER 1: IS PASTORING MEN WORTH THE EFFORT?

1. Retrieved at www.usatoday.com/news/health/2007-09-19-divorce-census_N.htm.
2. Living Arrangements of Children [electronic version], U. S. Census Bureau, U. S. Department of Commerce. April, 1996.
3. American Academy of Pediatrics, "Family Pediatrics Report of The Task Force on the Family," *Pediatrics,* 111(2003): 1541–71.

CHAPTER 2: HOW ARE MEN DOING?

1. The Greek word Paul uses translated "frustration" is the same word the Septuagint selected to translate Solomon's "meaningless" from Hebrew to Greek. Hence, Paul and Solomon meant the same thing. *Meaningless, frustration,* and *futility* are synonyms.

CHAPTER 3: WHAT DO MEN WANT?

1. Michael Novak, *Business As a Calling* (New York: The Free Press, 1996), 29.
2. Viktor E. Frankl, *Man's Search for Meaning* (New York: Simon and Schuster: 1984), 107.
3. Ibid., 105.
4. W. R. Moody, *The Life of Dwight L. Moody* (Westwood, Ohio: Barbour,), 122.
5. C. S. Lewis, *God in the Dock* (Grand Rapids: Eerdmans, 1970), 280.

CHAPTER 4: WHAT KEEPS MEN FROM GETTING WHAT THEY WANT?

1. C. S. Lewis, *The Weight of Glory* (New York: Simon and Schuster, 1962), 15–16.
2. Michael Novak, *Business As a Calling* (New York: The Free Press, 1996), 29.
3. Francis A. Schaeffer, *How Should We Then Live?* (Westchester, Ill: Crossway, 1976), 205.
4. For the story of Walt O. and the Meloon family business, see James Vincent, *Parting the Waters* (Chicago: Moody, 1997).
5. Patrick Morley, *The Man in the Mirror* (Grand Rapids: Zondervan, 1989), 33.

CHAPTER 5: WHAT DO MEN NEED?

1. Population Statistics: Table 7, "Resident Population Projections by Age and Sex, 1980 to 2006, U.S. Census Bureau," retrieved from www.census.org/compendia/statab/tables/08s0007.pdf. We use fifteen for manhood because this is the age when young men tend to get a job and the car keys. Earning money and driving a 3,000 pound vehicle is as good a way as any to determine adulthood.
2. An estimate based on 39 percent indicating they are "born again"; retrieved from Barna Group at www.barna.org/cgi-bin/Pagecategory.asp?CategoryID+19.
3. Pastor Rogers told me this story during a telephone conversation a few years ago.
4. *Brother Lawrence of the Resurrection,* trans. John J. Delaney, "The Practice of the Presence of God" (New York: Doubleday,1977), 108.

CHAPTER 7: SUCCESS FACTORS IN DISCIPLING MEN

1. Arthur D. Little and McKinsey & Co. studies cited in Peter M. Senge, Art Kleiner, Charlotte Roberts, and George Roth, *The Dance of Change* (New York: Doubleday, 1999), 5; Business Intelligence study cited in D. Miller, "Successful Change Leaders," *Journal of Change Management* 2, no. 4 (2002): 360; Gartner Group study cited in Miller, 2002; A. Raps, "Implementing Startegy," *Strategic Finance* 85(12):49–53 (2004). This appears to be the case without regard to sector; whether public, private, for profit, nonprofit, business, government, education, or health care (e.g., P. Strebel, "Why Do Employees

Resist Change?", *Harvard Business Review* 74, no. 3 (2000) 86–92; P. Pluye, L. Potvin, and J. Denis, "Making Public Health Programs Last: Conceptualizing Sustainability," *Evaluation & Program Planning* 27, no. 2 (2004): 121–33.

2. Booz Allen Hamilton, *New Products Management for the 1980s*. (This consulting firm published their findings in 1982; obtained from secondary sources.)

3. S. Ogawa and F. Piller, *MIT Sloan Management Review*, "Reducing the risks of new product development" 47, no. 2 (Winter 2006): 65.

4. F. Okumus, "A Framework to Implement Strategies in Organizations," *Management Decision,* 41 no. 9 (2003): 871–82.

5. Jim Collins, *Good to Great* (New York: Harper Business, 2001).

6. Philip Thurston, "Should Smaller Companies Make Formal Plans?" *Harvard Business Review*, September–October 1983.

7. Collins, *Good to Great*, 21–22.

CHAPTER 8: MORE SUCCESS FACTORS IN DISCIPLING MEN

1. Billy Graham, "My Answer: Jesus' Methods Would Be Up-To-Date Today," *Christian Post*, February 11, 2008, retrieved from Internet February 11, 2008.

2. Robert Lewis with Rob Wilkins, *The Church of Irresistible Influence* (Grand Rapids: Zondervan, 2001).

CHAPTER 9: A STRATEGY TO REACH EVERY MAN

1. Note: While this chapter focuses on learning this model for men's discipleship, please consider applying the "perspective" of managing momentum to every area of your ministry.

2. Disciplemen.com is hosted by Man in the Mirror Ministries on behalf of the Christian Men's Movement and the National Coalition of Men's Ministries and includes a "Best Practices and Resources" section spotlighting programs from across the country. You can join the leadership directory and network with other pastors and leaders.

CHAPTER 11: SEVENTY THINGS EVERY MAN NEEDS TO KNOW

1. Francis A. Schaeffer, *Letters of Francis A. Schaeffer* (Westchester, Ill.: Crossway, 1985), 144.

2. Patrick Morley, *The Man in the Mirror* (Nashville: Nelson, 1989), 33.

3. Blaise Pascal, *Pensées*, #133.

4. C. F. Keil and F. Delitzsch, *Commentary on the Old Testament*, vol. 1 (Peabody, Mass.: Hendrickson, 1989), 103.

5. For other contrasts in these two approaches, see chart in Patrick Morley and David Delk, *The Dad in the Mirror* (Grand Rapids: Zondervan, 2003), 31.

6. "Frustration" here is the same word used to translate Solomon's "meaningless" in the Septuagint. It's translated "vanity" in the King James Version and "God's curse" in the New Living Translation. *Frustration, meaninglessness, vanity*, and *futility* are synonyms.

7. J. Gresham Machen, *Christianity and Liberalism* (Grand Rapids: Eerdmans, 1923), 27.

8. Adapted from Luke 19:10; John 3:16; 5:24; 6:37, 39–40.

9. Portions of "33. Holiness" are excerpted from Patrick Morley, *Discipleship for the Man in the Mirror* (Grand Rapids: Zondervan, 2002), 237–38.

10. W. R. Moody, *The Life of Dwight L. Moody* (Westwood, Ohio: Barbour), 122.

11. Gordon MacDonald, *Christ Followers in the Real World* (Nashville: Nelson, 1990).

BONUS MATERIAL AND RESOURCES

All of the additional resources mentioned in the "one pagers" in chapter 11 ("For More:") are one click away at www.pastoringmen.com.

Also, I've left a lot unsaid that just wouldn't fit! But I want to make some fantastic bonus material and resources available to you at www.pastoringmen.com. There you will find the following powerful resources:

For You

- "A Bulletin Insert Survey to Count Your Disciples." (Use this amazingly simple-to-administer survey to figure out exactly what percentage of your men are disciples—called, equipped, and sent.)
- "What Is a Disciple, and How Do You Make One?" (a quick synopsis of the definition for "disciple" used in this book and the many ways we can make disciples)
- "The 'Portal' Priority" PowerPoint presentation (downloadable—show this to your leadership teams and get them excited about focusing on the Great Commission)
- "Grace-Based, Application-Oriented Bible Study Preparation Worksheet" (to prepare a dynamic men's message or regular sermon—adapt or adopt this to save lots of time and keep your heart and mind on track)
- Sample "Table Leader Job Description" (the same one we use at Man in the Mirror Bible Study—a great way to keep everything on track and adaptable for leaders in all types of positions)
- Chris White's "How to Build a Dynamic Men's Fellowship" (the guide I used to start the Man in the Mirror Bible Study in chapter 10)

Additional Resources for You

- How to Run an Effective Meeting (unbelievably valuable, a must for every pastor)
- How to Sense the Presence of God Part 1, Part 2 (a fresh pastor is a powerful instrument in God's hands)
- A dynamic sample chapter from *No Man Left Behind* (our first book that fleshes out chapter 9)
- A two-minute civil prayer you can use

- Men's Statistics (great stats to pepper your messages)
- "19 Biblical Ways to Grow Your Church: A Study of Acts" (a quick review of all situations when "many disciples were added to their number")
- "40 of 'The Most Important Things to Know' about Ministering to Men" (some things already mentioned and a few new thoughts too!)
- "What Can Happen When Leaders Work Together in Community?" (a fantastic account of the Reformers and their impact)
- "Visionary, Strategic, and Operational Leadership" (to revolutionize the way you, your staff, and your leadership team work together)
- "24 Leadership Ideas for Your Men's Ministry" (what I say as "closing thoughts" to pastors and leaders who go through our No Man Left Behind training)
- "Let's Stop Beating Up on Men" (just a fantastic reminder about extending grace)
- "The Fellowship of the Red Bandanna" (a highly inspirational way to get your men involved)

For Your Men
- A Man's Guide to Mother's Day
- A Man's Guide to Father's Day
- A Man's Guide to Valentine's Day
- How to Parent Adult Children
- How to Lead a Family Devotion
- A Few Thoughts as You Head Off to College
- Pat's Transition from Business to Ministry (1984–1991)

NO MAN LEFT BEHIND

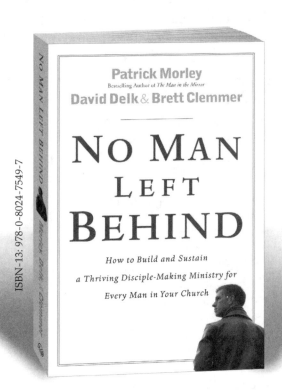

David Murrow's book *Why Men Hate Going to Church* has heightened awareness of an epidemic—Patrick Morley offers the solution. *No Man Left Behind* is the blueprint for growing a thriving men's ministry that has the power to rebuild the church as we know it, pulling men off the couch and into active involvement as part of the body of Christ.

MOODY PUBLISHERS.

1-800-678-8812 • MOODYPUBLISHERS.COM

THE MARRIAGE PRAYER

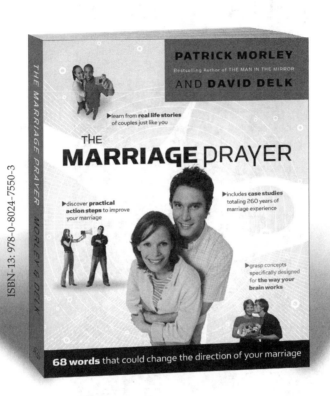

Marriage is the most significant human relationship we ever experience. Yet many people do not think about how a great marriage happens, and why. Designed to enhance learning and promote communication, *The Marriage Prayer* covers key topics ranging from worship and security to money and sex. Filled with case studies, application questions, and real-life stories, this book will keep you moving down the road toward a godly marriage.

1-800-678-8812 • MOODYPUBLISHERS.COM

A MAN'S GUIDE TO THE SPIRITUAL DISCIPLINES

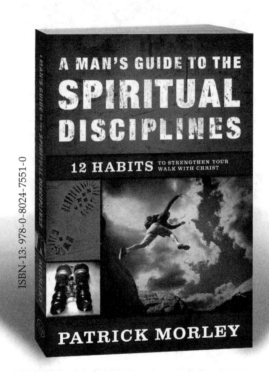

ISBN-13: 978-0-8024-7551-0

Strength isn't something you wish for; it's something you work toward. We need more than an annual men's gathering and regular church attendance to keep our faith strong. Here are the tools men need to reflect Christ in the context of marriage, family, and the daily grind.

1-800-678-8812 • MOODYPUBLISHERS.COM